Feet in the Fire

A Young German Girl's
Life in Nazi Germany
by
Margot Füsser Blewett

Fusion Press

Published by Fusion Press
A publishing service of Authorlink
(http://www.authorlink.com)
3720 Millswood Dr.
Irving, Texas 75062, USA

First published by Fusion Press
A publishing service of Authorlink
First Printing, August 2001

Printed in the United States of America

ISBN 1-928704-88-3

Dedication
In loving memory to my brother Josef
With love to my sisters Hilde and Erika

Acknowledgements
A Thank You to all the wonderful people who read
and critiqued my story.

A very special thanks goes to my friends
of the Friday Writers group for their untiring help
and encouragement: Charlotte Burns, Elaine Bucheri,
David Dennis, Dolores Donner, Nan Foley,
Carolee Jacobson, Elaine Lanmon, Karley Martin,
Margaret Schultz.

My two daughters, Jutta and Petra, are the reason
for the existence of this book. Over and over they asked me
as they grew up, "Mom, tell us more about the war,"
and later they encouraged me to write all these memories
down. "You have to tell them to our children. They need
to know." Without their prodding this book
would not have been written.

Last but not least a thank you to my husband
for his patience and endurance.

"The best man cannot live in peace
if his evil neighbor does not like it".
Friederich Schiller

TABLE OF CONTENTS

FALL, 1939

CHAPTER 1

The speedometer of our BMW climbed steadily. 120, 140, 160 kilometers. The ribbon of the Autobahn uncurled as we sped south past fields of ripening wheat, past villages clumped around white churches with steeples that poked the sky. Veils of thin, white clouds shrouded the sun. Two carnations, one white and one red, in a crystal bud vase at the dashboard swayed in the breeze from the slightly opened windows. Papa held the steering wheel steady in his big hands.

Mama beside him shot nervous glances at the needle hovering around 180. "Josef, do you have to drive that fast?" Her voice was edged with anger. "You don't have to pass every car in front of you."

Without answer he continued. He was used to Mama's complaints. So were we. We were returning from our vacation in Cuxhaven at the North Sea in August of 1939, and Papa wanted to be back in Düsseldorf by evening.

I was nine years old and sat in the center of the back seat. Erika beside me was eleven, Josef fifteen, and Hilde, at the window, seventeen.

Further south in the *Ruhr* district the traffic slowed. Military convoys as far as we could see lined the right side of the highway. Young soldiers in gray, stiff uniforms filled brand new, gray trucks, all marked with a black cross in a white circle. With radiant, expectant faces the soldiers smiled and waved at us.

On the car radio we heard that England's Prime Minister Chamberlain met with the *Führer*. Papa was silent for a long time, his eyes scanning the military trucks. He shook his head and cleared his throat. "Wonder what's going on? I think we're going to have a war."

A war? What would it mean to have a war? Would we still be able to go on vacation? Would Papa become a soldier? Not likely. He was severely wounded in 1917 in France when a grenade tore open his abdomen. He still wore every day a padded iron plate tightly pulled against the ugly, deep scar.

No, they would not draft him and, of course, Josef was just a boy. Now he listened carefully to Papa. "Why do you think we're going to have a war, Papa?"

Papa explained that Hitler had done a lot for our country, that most people had work. But so much else was wrong.

"What do you mean 'wrong'?" Hilde asked.

"Look what Hitler has done in the last few years. He had no right to annex Austria. Austria is not German. He took Bohemia and Moravia. He took *Sudetenland* from the Czechs. What's he trying to do? Does he think he can justify his actions with all this talk about 'people without space'?" After a moment he muttered, "And his henchmen, those black and brown shirts and the things they are doing to decent German people."

I knew, we all did, that Papa did not trust Hitler and his tactics, that he did not agree with the Nazi's. That was enough reason for him to refuse to join the Nazi Partei.

Mama shifted restlessly in her seat. "Josef, please, not in front of the children."

Hitler! How well I remembered him. I could still see his face, feel the cold touch of his hand.

Sitting between Hilde and Erika, I leaned deep into the

tan leather seat that still smelled new. My thoughts flew back to another vacation. 1935. I was five years old.

We were enroute to Bischofswiesen, a small farming community nestled deep in the Bavarian Alps close to Berchtesgaden. In our faithful Opel Olympia, with the top down, I snuggled in the warm July sun next to Hilde. We all wore linen travel caps, similar to those worn by pilots in an open cockpit. Especially Papa needed his to keep his shiny bald head from burning.

The winding road climbed up and down the rolling countryside past lush, blooming meadows. I could hear the melodic ringing of the cowbells above the hum of the motor. Whitewashed houses, their dark wooden balconies stretching along the upper floor and their window boxes spilling over with crimson geraniums, clustered around the white church with the red onion-shaped steeple.

Then, one community looked different. Red swastika flags lined the streets. Even the flower boxes were stuffed with little flags, flapping in the breeze.

Hilde sat up. "Good heavens, not another partei rally!"

People with flags lined the street and the upper balconies, waiting. Papa slowed. A few children waved. Somebody cheered. The crowd picked up the cheering.

Hilde looked from one side of the street to the other. "Are they cheering us? That can't be true!"

Papa was bewildered. "What's going on?" I turned around. Behind us the road was empty.

Josef grinned. "Imagine! They think we're somebody big from the partei." The cheering grew louder, then stopped abruptly.

Two officers, arms outstretched, stood in front of our car. One wore the black uniform of the *SS* [*Schutz Staffel*—"elite guard"], silver insignias on collar and cap glinted in the sun; the other one wore the brown *SA* [*Sturm Abteilung*

—"storm detachment"] uniform with a red swastika band on his sleeve, brown leather belt across chest, back and waist.

"Halt!"

I had stood up to see better, but at their sharp command and stern faces I sank back until I could just see them over the top of the seat in front of me.

"Halt! Where are you going?"

Vater stopped the car. "We're on vacation towards Berchtesgaden."

"You cannot continue. Turn into that side street."

"Why? What's going on?" Mama asked.

The *SA* man answered curtly, "We are expecting the *Führer.*"

We followed the outstretched arm into a small street, parked and walked back to the main road. In front of "*Gasthof Sonnenhof*" a large stage was set up. A spread-winged eagle adorned the podium in the center. Technicians unrolled long cords, hooked up microphones. We moved closer to have a better look.

To the side of the podium, the town musicians still organized their sheet music and adjusted the straps of their shiny instruments.

Erika and I, wearing white taffeta bows in our hair, held onto Hilde's hands. We three were dressed in matching dirndls with aprons Mama had sewn. Josef wore a pair of Bavarian *Lederhosen* ["leather pants"]. Several people look-ed and smiled at us, but I gave it no further thought.

Just then an *SS* officer walked up to Vater. "I would like your children to come with me to greet the *Führer.*"

Papa's left eyebrow shot up and instantly alarmed me. That meant danger. He stared at us, then turned to Mama, who looked away. Would he dare to refuse the request? For a moment time seemed suspended, but he finally nodded. We followed the officer through the staring crowd. I held tightly onto Hilde's hand, my heart beating fast. Where were we going? Why us? I glanced at my tall, blond sister whom I adored. Hilde looked straight ahead, her face betrayed no emotion.

Then, like the swelling of an incoming surf, we heard, "*Heil Hitler! Heil Hitler! Sieg Heil! Sieg Heil!*" Slowly a caravan of open touring cars with shiny, elongated hoods pulled up to the stage. Officers jumped out, ran to the lead car, opened the doors and snapped to attention.

Adolf Hitler! Without a trace of a smile he raised his right hand in the Nazi salute. The crowd roared, "*Sieg Heil! Sieg Heil!*" In brown *SA* uniform, he stepped out of the car and mounted the stage with a brisk stride. His left hand, clenched in a fist, was tucked behind his back. Uniformed men in black and brown swarmed around him. I held my breath. So that was Hitler. He stood not more than ten feet from us.

The officer shepherded us toward the podium. We waited. He walked up to the *Führer*, saluted sharply, clicking his heels. "*Mein Führer*, I thought you might like to have a look at these four youngsters here, fine examples of our German youth."

The Führer glanced at us, nodded and detached himself from the group. He crossed the stage towards us. His high boots, without a speck of dirt, pounded the hollow stage. Only dimly was I aware of the clicking cameras and of people cheering and clapping.

Hilde looked straight at him as he shook her hand, his face still motionless. Then he shook Josef's hand and Erika's. I wondered why Erika did not curtsy.

To shake my hand he had to bend down. I let go of Hilde. My heart pounded. His straight, dark hair fell into his pale face. The black mustache stuck under his nose as if it were pasted on. His dark eyes looked like burned-out coal with no warmth but great intensity.

He took my hand. Automatically I curtsied. "*Guten Tag.*"

He mumbled something I couldn't understand. His hand felt cold and clammy. The crowd still applauded. He straightened, nodded again at us and returned to the podium. The *SS* officer beside me clicked his heels. *"Danke, mein Führer"* ["thank you, my Führer"]. He took us along the partitioned off road back to our parents. Mama had pushed herself to the front row, craning her neck to follow every move. Her eyes sparkled with pride.

"Well, here you are! And you were asked to shake the *Führer's* hand! Imagine!" she announced so loud nobody in our vicinity could miss it. I cringed.

Erika murmured under her breath, "Why did we have to shake his hand?"

"Shhh!" Mama silenced her. "Not a word!"

Vater turned around. "Come on, come on. Let's get to the car. We are losing a whole morning." We threaded our way through the crowd. Behind us the brass band boomed the National Anthem.

In the car Erika asked again, "Why did we have to shake his hand? It was cold." She thought for a moment and added, "I didn't like him at all." She tossed back her heavy black braids for emphasis.

Hilde mumbled, "What a publicity stunt."

Vater studied the map for a different route out of the village. "Forget it. Let's get out of here and get on with our vacation."

Josef teased Erika. "Make sure you don't wash your hand."

She showed her strong white teeth in a grin. "That's the first thing I'll do."

As we left the village the echo of Hitler's voice drowned out the melodic sound of the cowbells.

My thoughts returned to the present. From my seat I watched Papa drive. He was an impressive man, tall and serious, not given to unnecessary words or easy smiles. His fierce temper flared mostly with Hilde, sometimes with Josef, seldom with me and even less with Erika. When he said something we listened. I felt awkward in his presence, never knew what to say. And yet, I was sure he loved us.

In the fading light of the summer evening, we pulled in front of our building. Neighborhood children still roller-skated and played tag. Oma, Papa's mother, sat at her open bedroom window on the ground floor, waiting for us. As soon as she spotted us she hurried in to open her door.

I ran ahead and up the white marble steps of our cool and quiet building to Oma's apartment. We crowded into her door and greeted her with hugs and kisses. Her cheek felt like warm parchment. At seventy-one she was alert and always ready to help whenever we needed her.

"How was your vacation? Did you have a good time?" Her gentle eyes moved from face to face. She patted Papa's cheek. "You look good, Josef. And Margot, your hair has gotten lighter." She brushed my wispy, blond hair off my forehead.

"Anything happen here while we were gone?" Papa asked.

"Herr Mevissen and his wife stopped by Sunday after-noon. They wanted to know when you would be back." The Mevissen's were our parents' best friends and the owners of our apartment building.

It grew dark while the adults talked, and we kids listened. Oma pulled down the gas lamp which hung above the kitchen table. She raised the glass cylinder, lit the finely meshed gas socket, adjusted the intensity of the light and tugged on the handle. Slowly the pulley carried the lamp back to its usual height.

This lamp fascinated me. The vibration of the double row of glass beads scattered specks of colored light through-out the room.

Mama took me by the shoulders. "We've got to get the

children to bed." Against my loud protest she marched me from the room.

I wriggled from her grip, ran back and gave Oma another kiss. "See you tomorrow, Oma." Upstairs in our apartment I fell into my bed, glad to be home again.

Over the next days Papa's fears came true. On September 1, 1939, the German army invaded Poland. During the following days every few hours another Polish city fell. People talked about a "*Blitzkrieg*". The soldiers took Poland with practically no resistance. The "war" would be over within days, even though no war had been officially declared.

In bed that night I asked Erika, who shared the room with me, "Erika, what's going on? I don't understand any of this. Why do our soldiers invade another country? People here didn't like when the French occupied the *Rheinland* after the last war. Remember how often Mama told us about that? How they all hated it? Now we are doing the same to others. Why?"

After a long silence Erika said quietly, "I don't know, Margot, I just feel this will take a long, long time." Papa was correct, something was terribly wrong.

I stared into the fading light of the open window. I could still hear Mama's voice, talking to Papa in the kitchen earlier that day. "Don't you care what happens to us? What if they pick you up because you don't want to join? What if they pick up all of us? All because of your..." she made a scoffing sound, "...your damn principles."

There was a long pause. I had held my breath and moved back into the shadow of the basement steps. "Trude, of course I care. You know I do. But I cannot do anything different." After a moment his anguished voice continued, "I cannot. I have to be true to what I believe."

Mama's voice was hard and bitter. "Oh sure. And never mind the consequences."

Their disagreements usually were not that quiet. They also were not that ominous. My heart was beating fast. How could Papa's not joining be dangerous to us all? What could the consequences be? I shivered with the feeling of danger surrounding our family. But what was I afraid of?

Every day we heard *Sondermeldungen* ["Special News Bulletins"]. A powerful, loud music,—a section of the tone poem *"Les Preludes"* by Franz Liszt—accompanied these *Sondermeldungen*. It quickly became a pattern: the victorious music interrupted the regular broadcast, the *Sondermeldung* announced that this or that town capitulated under the pressure of the heroic German army, more of the triumphant fanfares followed. Then the program resumed. Wherever we were, whatever we did, when we heard that music we stopped and listened.

One evening, I was in the kitchen helping Mama prepare dinner when Papa came home. His face was pale, the height of his arched eyebrow showed he was furious. What was wrong? Had I done something?

"What's the matter?" Mama asked as she poured him a cup of coffee.

He struggled to keep his voice calm. "Somebody... somebody from the *SA* came to the shop today."

Mama looked alarmed. "Why? What did they want?"

"What did they want? Our BMW. They took our BMW away. Confiscated it." He laughed angrily. "Simply took it."

The porcelain coffeepot crashed on the table. "What? Our brand new car? Josef, how can they? That's stealing!"

I was shocked. Who could take a family's car away? It was ours. We had paid for it.

Papa's fist hit the table. The coffee cup jingled. I moved back to the wall. "They obviously can do anything they damn well please. Some big Nazi wants the car. Oh sure, we may get paid something for it, but I had no intention of selling it. Besides, no new cars are being built. I cannot get a new one."

Mama stared at him. "Josef, what's going on? Why our car?" Papa's swearing, our car gone, the fear I heard in Mama's voice—my stomach tightened into a knot.

The next day brought more bad news: France and England declared war on Germany. We were at war with France, a country just a few hundred kilometers away? Why? We had visited that country often. Papa's grandfather came from France. His name, like Oma's, was LaMontagne. They were now our enemies?

That evening at the dinner table, Papa talked about a pact between Poland, England and France. Because Germany invaded Poland, France and England came, according to the pact, to the aid of the Polish people. But our radio and newspapers branded England and France as the aggressors. It was all very confusing and difficult to understand.

A dark cloud settled over our lives. Nothing was bright, shiny, and beautiful anymore.

The following day Mama reminded me that school would start soon. I would enter fourth grade, Erika sixth. I knew that at the end of the fourth grade I had to decide on the general direction of my education. Students wanting voca-tional training stayed in elementary school until fourteen and then learned a trade while continuing for two more years in a vocational school. Students wanting higher education changed after fourth grade to high school for an additional eight years to age eighteen.

Hilde and Erika both had decided on elementary school. Hilde had started her training as a seamstress. Her dream had been to become a kindergarten teacher, but *Vater* (as we called Papa often) said, "Absolutely not!" He did not want his daughter to have to bring up other people's children. So for the last two years she apprenticed with a seamstress.

Josef, being groomed to take over Vater's business, had no choice. After elementary school, three years as an apprentice and three years as journeyman, he would be, like Papa, master in his metal-working trade and ready to take over the business some day. A business that Papa had established with a partner, over the last fifteen years, in reconstructing and building radiators for cars and trucks. Through hard, reliable and honest work he had gained a solid reputation way beyond our city.

What Erika planned I didn't know, but I still had to make that decision. Hilde encouraged me to make the change to high school to have more options. So far my parents had not talked with me about this.

To prepare for the first school day in fourth grade I laid out my new clothes I wanted to wear: a black cotton jumper with a yellow and black checkered long-sleeved blouse; my favorite white, starched pinafore; a pair of white socks and my heavy black leather shoes. I surveyed my choices. *Ja*, I liked them.

When Mama checked my selection she agreed—until she saw the white pinafore. "You can't wear this. It's for Sunday only." She handed me a printed cotton apron. I didn't care for it, but I knew I had no choice.

From the bottom of the wardrobe, I was dragging out my leather book bag when the doorbell rang.

Mama opened the door. "*Guten Abend, Herr Schulte*, please do come in."

"*Heil Hitler*." A click of heels accompanied the sharply spoken greeting. "I am the air defense warden of this building. All windows have to be covered with black paper. Absolutely no light is permitted to shine out." He pulled from his pocket a handful of large metal buttons and counted six into Mutter's hand. "Here is a phosphorescent button for every member of your family. Wear them outside in the dark so others can see you. One more thing. Tomorrow night is an air raid drill. When you hear the siren, proceed immediately to the closest shelter. I shall be back tomorrow to check your apartment. *Heil Hitler.*"

As announced Herr Schulte came back the next evening. *"Heil Hitler."* His words clicked like his heels. Why did he continue to use this greeting in our own home? "Are your shades in order?"

"Good evening, Herr Schulte. My husband has covered most of the windows." Mama sounded apologetic. "We ran out of black paper."

Herr Schulte frowned. "By Saturday you will be fined if they are not in order. I shall be back. *Heil Hitler.*"

The next day we got enough paper. Papa and Josef came home early to finish the job.

Getting back to school was fun. I looked forward to see Inge, my girlfriend. I ran up to her when I saw her coming with Annemarie, a classmate. "Inge, I've missed you. How are you?"

She hardly stopped. "I've been around, just busy." They continued into the classroom, talking and laughing. Dumbfounded, I looked after her.

Fraulein Olligschläger's kind smile reassured me. She asked us to share something special from our vacation. I was glad I could talk about our vacation at the North Sea and our boat ride to Helgoland.

When at ten o'clock the bell rang, Inge and Annemarie left quickly. I walked home alone. What happened? Did Inge not like me anymore? I had to find out. I decided to stop at her apartment later to ask her to play.

Inge's mother opened the door. When she saw me, her smile disappeared. "Inge's very busy. I don't know if she can come out." When Inge did appear at the door, she hardly looked at me.

"I can't play, I don't have time."

"Maybe later?" I had to know.

"No! I don't want to play with you anymore." She closed the door on me. Slowly I walked down the stairs, wiping my streaming tears with my sleeve. Had I done something wrong? The hurt inside, the empty feeling spread. I knew her father was a high official in the partei that Papa refused to join. Was that the reason?

If a friendship could break that easily, for no obvious reason, it wasn't worth it. By the time I reached home I had vowed never to have a girlfriend again. I buried the pain and the tears deep, deep down.

The sudden wailing of the sirens startled me. We stopped everything. Papa took charge. "Trude, do you have your purse with your papers? Everybody, pick up your coats and get to the basement."

We filed out of the apartment and joined neighbors coming down the steps. Herr Schulte took his position beside the basement door. "Keep going, keep going." I looked back. Papa with Hilde and Oma followed at the end of the procession.

In the basement we settled down in our storage area. Herr Schulte, full of importance in his brown *SA* uniform and his new status, gave us instructions, distributed the gas masks and demonstrated their usage.

The feeling of something covering my mouth and nose filled me with panic. I couldn't breathe. It reminded me when in our vacation at the North Sea I almost drowned and could not breathe. The awful smell of the rubber nauseated me. Everybody looked like prehistoric monsters with those ugly green things over their faces. I hoped I would never have to wear one.

With the monotonous tone of the end-of-the-alarm siren we filed from the basement to pick up life where we left off.

In the beginning of October, the headlines of the

Düsseldorfer Nachrichten ["Düsseldorfer News"] triumph-
antly shouted, "The *Blitzkrieg* is over! German troops
occupy Poland! The war is won!"
Only then did we learn that Russian troops had entered
Poland from the east, the same time the Germans came from
the west, but nobody seemed to notice.

During the fall and winter of 1939-40, we had only
sporadic air raids. The sirens were mounted so close together
that even the deepest sleeper could not miss their wailing. At
first their piercing sound scared me out of my sleep and hurt
my ears so that I stuck my head under the pillow to shut it
off. After a while they became a nuisance to be endured.
Warned by the warden to be fully dressed in case of
emergency, we hastily put on street clothes to get to the
basement.
In the dim light of our storage area, between rows of
glasses with carrots and peaches, I could make out the faces
of our neighbors. So that's what Frau Zimmermann looks
like at night. Our neighbor, usually an attractive woman, sat
in an old wicker chair, her hair a mess, her disgruntled face
without makeup, heavy with sleep. Close by Papa snored
softly. I could hear Hilde and Josef's quiet conversation on
the other side of the potato bin, on which I perched. Mama
sat opposite me in an old kitchen chair, wide-awake, keeping
an eye on me.
The smell of apples on the shelves along the wall made
my stomach ache with emptiness. Hmmm, even a tart
Boskopf, Papa's favorite, would taste good. Carefully I
eased myself off the wooden bin and caught Mama's eye. I
knew she could read my thoughts. She shook her head.
"No."
At that moment the end-of-the-alarm sounded. The
planes had turned off to the east.

Our neighbors shuffled up the steps, some were mumbling, most were half-asleep. What a strange procession. Hilde, who slept in Oma's bedroom, went back with her. We climbed to the second floor and sat in the kitchen. I was wide awake and hoped to get something to eat. This was fun. Seeing neighbors in the middle of the night, sitting in the kitchen, eating and drinking tea—when else would I ever do this at this hour?

Holding a loaf of dark bread in front of her, Mama expertly sliced for each one a wafer-thin piece. We sat around the table, munched bread with homemade jam, sipped peppermint tea.

"Wonder where they dumped their bombs?" Papa asked between bites. He added quietly, "Poor people." I couldn't imagine what it would be like to be bombed.

This became our pattern. After an air raid we ended up in the kitchen to eat. It eased the tension, calmed our stomachs. Soon we were ready to sleep.

One afternoon I heard Hilde ask Mama, "You remember Willi's coming tonight?"

"*Ja,* you told me. Ask him to stay for dinner."

Willi and Hilde were not officially engaged, but I was sure they would marry some day. As a leader in the Roman Catholic Youth Movement he was often in our area and visited Hilde each time. She also attended many meetings with him.

An occurrence from his previous visit came to my mind, one I could not forget. We stood in our entrance hall to say good-bye to Willi when he told Vater in a low voice about a friend of his, the National Leader of the Catholic Youth. He and his bride had gone to Rome to be married in the Vatican. As they got off the train on their way home, three men in *SA* uniform stopped them. In front of his bride, the *SA* beat him up so terribly he spent months in the hospital. Papa was horrified. "Are you sure?" he asked Willi several times.

"Of course. I visited him in the hospital."

I didn't understand it but the thought made me shudder. Willi was one of my favorite people. He arrived in uniform. We all clustered around him. During the meal the grown-ups talked about the new Pope Pius XII. He had been the former representative of the Vatican to Germany and was well liked. They talked about an agreement Hitler made with the Vatican in 1933, promising independence, even in education, to the Catholic Church in Germany.

Willi shook his head. "Hitler won't stick to it. So far he has broken all other agreements."

I watched Willi. His startling blue eyes were serious, yet his round, tanned face broke easily into a smile. His blond, wavy hair had been butchered into a military style. I decided again if Hilde would not marry him, I would.

After the late dinner Mama ordered Erika and me to bed. I appealed to Papa. "Can we sing a few songs?" Papa always liked us to sing together.

"All right, but only a few."

Hilde tuned her guitar, Willi accompanied her on Josef's. Soon Hilde's clear soprano led us in one song after another. Songs about faraway lands, about wild geese flying north never to return, about mysterious flowers to be found only by those willing to search for them. I wished the evening would never end.

But Mama got up, gripped my hand. "To bed."

I kissed Papa good night, knowing what would follow. "Let's first pray together." As usual before Erika and I went to bed, we all knelt down. Willi prayed especially for our country and for our soldiers. By now I had exhausted all my delaying tactics. Reluctantly I kissed everybody good night.

The next morning Erika and I finished breakfast and

were ready for school when we heard strange noises from the street. I ran to Mama's bedroom window. Across from us somebody cried, obviously in great pain.

"Mama, something's wrong out there. I can't see who it is. I'll go downstairs."

"You stay here. I'll have a look." Mama went to her window. We both followed her. "Oh, it's Fraü Ackermann, Anna's mother. I hope Anna's not sick."

Frau Ackermann, a widow, lived with her retarded daughter Anna in a small apartment across from us. All day Anna sat by her open window. When it was cold she pressed her face against the glass from the inside. Whenever I left our building, I first glanced up to answer her wave and her smile. If I forgot, she demanded attention with loud noises.

Outside, Frau Ackermann hit her head and her fists against the front door, wailing and crying. The window above her was empty. No Anna. Mama hurried across the street. I hung back, feeling helpless. Other neighbors rushed up.

Frau Ackermann was difficult to understand. "Anna gone, my Anna, they took her," was all I could make out.

Mama tried to understand her. "Who took Anna, where did she go?" Mama held her hand, stroking it. "Frau Ackermann, calm down. Who took her?"

"They came. They banged on the door."

"Who's they? Who came, Frau Ackermann?"

"The *SS* officers. Three of them."

An icy silence settled over our little group.

"They banged on the door. They demanded Anna. They had come to pick her up. When I asked why, they shoved me aside. 'Stop asking questions! Get her! Now!' I was so scared. Anna heard us. She came out of her room. 'Get her dressed,' they shouted. They took her away. They took my Anna away." In her pain she rocked from side to side, holding herself.

She grabbed Mama's hand. "Frau Füsser, please, can your husband find out where they took her? What's going to happen to her?" Tears started to flow again. "What am I going to do?"

Mama assured her that Papa would do his best to find out, but she did not sound hopeful. I stared at the empty window. The *SS* took her away. To where? Why?

That morning Erika and I walked to school in silence. I held tightly onto her hand. What was happening? Dark clouds engulfed me. For the first time in my life, fear pervaded every ounce of my body.

When Papa heard about Anna that evening, he was silent for a long time. When he spoke, his voice sounded raspy. "*Ja,* the same thing is happening in other places. And it's not just retarded people they pick up. It's also those unwanted like the Jews; those that don't agree with them, mostly Germans, mostly men,—and," he added bitterly, "they're usually our best."

"Can you find out where they took her?" Mama urged him.

Slowly he shook his head. "Go to the *SS* headquarters and ask? I wouldn't come back. I'm on their black list. One wrong move and I'm gone." With both hands he wiped his face and rubbed his bald head. He stared at the floor. "How long do I have before they'll pick me up? How long? I just don't know."

The last few words were said in a hoarse whisper. In the dead silence only the kitchen clock ticked. Mama leaned against the gas stove, every bit of blood drained from her face. I didn't dare to breathe. He would know I heard something not meant for my ears.

For a long time he sat rooted to the floor. Then, without looking up, he slowly walked out, bent like under a heavy burden.

SPRING 1940

CHAPTER 2

The sooty train hall of the main railroad station in Düsseldorf looked even darker in the gloom of the nasty March morning. On the windy platform Mama gave Hilde an endless stream of last minute orders. Josef made fun of our Sunday dresses and coats. Papa was quiet, his face closed. In March of 1940, our parents had decided reluctantly, to my great and secret delight, to send us three girls to the small village of Winkl by Bischofswiesen, close to Berchtesgaden in Bavaria. Hilde, my favorite person in the whole wide world, at eighteen was in charge of us. We were to stay with the Schmidt family in their farmhouse where we had spent several vacations and where we would be safe from air raids. Papa promised, "When Paris capitulates, I want you to come home immediately. The war will be over."

With screaming brakes and a violent surge of air, the Rome Express raced into the station. We quickly found the section Destination Rosenheim.

I felt awkward saying good-bye to Mama. She shook my hand, gave me a peck on the cheek. "Remember to behave, Margot. Listen to Hilde."

"*Ja*, Mama. *Auf Wiedersehen*. ["Good bye"]"

We followed Hilde through the narrow hallway until we found an empty compartment. Josef and Papa stacked our three big suitcases into the overhead racks.

Papa turned to us. "Write so we know what you're doing.

Auf Wiedersehen." On tiptoes I kissed his smoothly shaven cheek. It smelled of shaving soap. Josef got a handshake and a peck too.

The loudspeaker boomed, "Close the doors. Rome Express is ready to depart."

The two hurried out. Doors slammed. Just as Hilde opened the upper part of the heavy window, the station-master held up the red signal and blew his whistle twice.

Mama waved. "Make sure you don't go too close to the train doors."

"*Ja*, Mama."

With a swift, silken motion our train slid out of the hall. We waved as long as we could see the little group on the platform. With a relieved sigh I sat back.

Hilde grinned. "Well, here we are. How're you two doing?"

I laughed. "Fantastic! Imagine! We're going by ourselves! No parents! And into the mountains! I still can't believe it." I let the wonderful feeling of freedom sink in. "I was so afraid something might come up in the last moment." It was like the fulfillment of all my dreams, to be with my two sisters and to be for months, if not years, in the mountains, my favorite place.

Our compartment was neat. Two wooden benches, comfortably shaped and rounded, flanked the walkway between door and window. Hilde propped up the little round table, giving the compartment a homey look and us a place to play. I claimed the forward seat beside the window to announce what was coming.

"How long until we get to Rosenheim?" My innocent question made Hilde laugh.

"Margot, don't start that. It will take all day. You have plenty of time to do all the things you planned for: read, sleep, play cards, look out the window, not to forget the eating. But don't get restless already."

Mama always said I couldn't sit still a minute, that I was easily bored. But this was different. After all, we traveled by ourselves and in the Rome Express. How often had I admired the streamlined Express when it passed our car along the *Rhein* where it raced faster than even Papa could drive on that curvy road. No, I had no reason to be bored or restless.

The two tall spires of the Gothic Cathedral of *Köln* ["Cologne"] appeared on the horizon. We crossed the *Rhein* and slowed for the approach to the station in the shadow of the towering Cathedral.

The station was packed with soldiers, saying good-bye to teary families and friends.

After a few minutes we were again in motion. Faces and waving hands went by faster and faster. The city disappeared. Gray clouds hung low and still over a bleak and wintry countryside.

I settled deep into my corner to check the treasures I had carefully collected for weeks: a checkerboard game, a card game, two small books, paper and pencils. And, most importantly, a chocolate bar, a Marzipan bar, a handful of chocolate candies and one apple.

The rolling hills along the *Rhein* looked beautiful in spite of the dripping grayness. The vineyards, row after long, waving row, all neat and trimmed, soaked in the gentle rain. As I watched it fly by I was proud of my country, proud to be a German. And I was especially glad I lived along the *Rhein* River. We sang many songs about the stately *"Vater Rhein"*. Yes, this was my country and I loved it.

The *Rhein* valley flattened out. The vineyards, instead of perching on steep terraces, curved around gentle slopes. Papa and the Mevissens were ardent admirers of German wines. Many Saturday or Sunday afternoons during the grape harvest were dedicated to the serious study and sampling of the newest wine in romantic small wineries along the *Rhein*.

We passed Wiesbaden and left the *Rhein* valley for München. A fine mist hung in the darkening afternoon air as we approached München. The train filled up with more soldiers. Through the open window from a passing cart we bought wrapped sandwiches to eat later. Right now I was too busy watching the crowd. Most of the soldiers were cheerful, smiling. But one group, off to the side, in brown uniforms, looked stern and different.

I pointed to them. "Hilde, do you think they ever smile?"

"Margot, for God's sake, take your fingers away! Don't point!" Hilde spoke sharply. "You know they are *SA* officers. Don't ask such silly questions."

Surprised, I looked at her. What had I done wrong? She really sounded like Mama sometimes. My interest in watching people was gone. I was hungry and sat down to eat my ham sandwich.

We left München. Hilde got up. "We'll soon be in Rosenheim. Get ready."

"What will we be doing in Rosenheim?" I wanted to know.

"Waiting for the next train, dummy," Erika answered.

"I didn't ask you." I stuck out my tongue.

Hilde sighed. "That's enough, you two. We have to wait for our connection to Berchtesgaden. Let's hope it won't be too long. At any rate, stay close to me, don't go running off. Also go now to the toilet, before we get there."

Erika grinned at me. "See, I told you."

Soldiers hefted our heavy luggage from the racks and carried it into the hallway. As soon as the train doors opened, cold, clear air surged in, smelling of mountains and wood fires. Butterflies stirred in my stomach. Mountains! I couldn't wait to see them. Hilde gladly accepted the help of two soldiers to carry our luggage to the waiting room. The stale air in the hall was so dense with cigarette smoke I could hardly see or breathe. The place was jammed with soldiers. Hilde opened her mouth and said something that I could not understand.

"Wait here with the luggage, I'll look for an empty table," she shouted into my ear. She pulled three chairs to a table where an older man and a woman were already seated and motioned for us to come. She ignored some soldiers' invitation to sit with them.

After we settled down she got us lemonade and a cup of *Ersatzkaffee* ["coffee substitute"], a brew made from roasted rye, for herself.

The heavy-set woman at our table had a friendly, round face. She asked Hilde, "Where do you come from?"

"From Düsseldorf."

The woman shook her head. "From Düsseldorf? And you three travel alone? With these soldiers around? That's not good. How long do you have to wait?"

Hilde was not sure and asked if she would stay with us while she checked our connection. She came back with an unhappy face. "We may have to sit here for a long time. They expect the *Führer*, but don't know when. All tracks have to be kept open. The stationmaster will let us know."

We had to wait in this smelly, ugly hall? The darkened windows were tightly shut. The few bare bulbs dangling from the ceiling did not even shed enough light to read.

The heavy woman moved her chair closer. She leaned forward, eager to share something with us. "Yesterday a terrible thing happened in this place," she whispered. I strained and listened intently. She glanced right and left over her shoulders. "A soldier sat at that table over there." With her fat thumb she motioned behind her. "His face must have been torn apart by a grenade. It was healed but it was terribly disfigured. Across the room an *SS* officer stared at him for a long time, then called a young soldier and ordered the wounded man to leave, that he could not look at him. When the injured soldier was told, he wanted to know, with a hoarse voice, who it was who didn't like his face. For a moment he just sat there, staring at the table. And then, would you believe, he jumped up, toppled his chair over, pulled his revolver and shot and killed the *SS* officer."

I gasped. "Served the officer right," I mumbled. A sharp kick from Hilde reminded me. I bit my lip and told myself, "Keep your mouth shut."

Hilde looked horror-stricken at the woman. "What happened to the disfigured man?"

She snorted scornfully. "You can imagine what happens to somebody who kills an *SS* officer."

"And you saw all that?" I asked.

"Sure did, with my very own eyes. Sat where you are sitting. Saw and heard the whole thing." She took a deep breath. "They marched him off between mounted bayonets."

We had been so intent on listening, we did not realize the room had quieted. I was tired but much to stirred up to sleep. I looked around: Luggage and sprawled bodies everywhere. In one corner a rowdy group of uniformed men played cards in the dismal light.

"I have to go to the bathroom." My loud announcement startled Hilde.

"Don't worry, I'll stay here," the friendly woman offered. "I'll watch your luggage."

"Thank you. Erika, come on, let's all go."

"I don't have to. I'm tired."

"I know. We're all tired. Come on, let's go." We trudged off with Hilde holding our hands.

We passed the table with the card players. One of them grabbed Hilde's arm and said something to her. Angrily she shook off his hand and pulled us past them. As we rushed into the rest room, I heard them laugh.

"Darn jerks!" Hilde muttered under her breath, washing her flushed face.

The woman shook her head when we returned. "You have to watch those guys." Finally the stationmaster announced our train. We could leave that dreadful place.

The local train was not as shiny as the Express, but it had plenty of space for us to lie on the wooden benches. "Erika, Margot, wake up! We are in Winkl!" Hilde shook us. The clanking train came to a grinding halt.

Through steamed windows, I vaguely saw the conductor swinging a reddish glowing lamp. With my sleeve I wiped off the steam, cupped my hands to the glass and pressed my face against the window to screen out the reflections.

Nothing. Utter blackness.

"Margot, hurry up." The massive train door opened, ice cold air rushed in. I was wide awake. So were the butterflies in my stomach. *Ja*, I could smell the mountains. We had reached our destination.

Dry snow crunched under my feet. Slowly my eyes got used to the darkness. The single light bulb, blackened with paint, shed an eerie light on the little station. We three stood alone on the platform, out in nowhere. The cold started to penetrate my light shoes. I shivered in my city clothing.

Hilde stomped up and down. "Come on, move with me to keep warm. Let's hope the Schmidts heard the train go by."

Muffled rumbling cut through the still night, running feet in heavy boots and fast words came closer. A bundle of dark clothes rushed down the snowy path, followed by a boy pulling a cart. From underneath a large woolen scarf hastily thrown over her head, Frau Schmidt's quick eyes darted over us and our luggage. Her smile was friendly and apologetic.

"*Grüss Gott, Grüss Gott*," ["greet God"] was all I could

make out from the stream of words while she pumped our hands. Without a word Hansl, who was my age, tipped his cap and loaded the flat cart. Frau Schmidt had an unlimited supply of air and words. Did Hilde really understand the strange sounds rushing past us? From our vacations I remembered it would take me a while to get used to the heavy Bavarian accent.

Walking along I caught a familiar sound, the murmur of water. Of course, the Ache, a small meandering brook in the summer, delightful to play in, a dangerously wild water at snow melt. The cart rumbled across the uneven bridge. The silhouette of the farmhouse appeared to our right. The low roof, huddled under deep snow, sheltered the house and the stables. The door opened. A shaft of warm light cut into the night.

Schmidt's oldest daughter Gaby, a year younger than Hilde, rushed down the glistening path. *"Grüss Gott, grüss Gott."*

I followed Hilde and Erika into the house. Its coziness and warmth smelled of wood fire, hay and spices. A feeling of happiness and comfort washed over me.

Herr Schmidt and Seppl came out of the *Stube* ["family room"]. Herr Schmidt removed the inevitable small pipe, clenched between his teeth, for a mumbled greeting. His craggy face with deep, hooded eyes almost smiled. His hand felt like a piece of wood, callused and rough.

Following our hostess, we climbed the steep and creaky steps. Hansl and Seppl brought our luggage. She opened two doors along the small hallway. "This is yours, Hilde, and Erika and Margot sleep opposite you."

I ducked under her arm to claim the bed closest to the window and sank into the downy featherbed to look at the room. With the two beds pushed against the wall, a handmade wooden wardrobe, dresser and night table—all hand decorated—the spacious room looked homey. Beside the window with billowy, white curtains and the ever-present black shades stood the washstand with a porcelain bowl and pitcher. Oh, we would have to wash again in a bowl and— with water from the spring? Hilde saw my expression of horror. She grinned. "Don't worry. You'll get used to it."

The steps creaked. Gaby stood in the doorway, a shy smile on her open, freckled face. "Mother would like you to come down and eat something."

I ran down, two steps at a time. At the blocky wooden table Herr and Frau Schmidt welcomed us with a steaming cup of chocolate milk and a plate of freshly baked bread.

Seppl, age thirteen, freckle faced and blond, sat on the bench in front of the ceramic tiled oven, warming his back. Soon the warmth and long day took their toll. Hilde took my hand, "Up to bed."

After tucking us under the enormous featherbeds, she took from the lower part of the night table a porcelain chamber pot. It was painted with the same glowing rose as the furniture. "Remember to use this if you have to. You can't go to the outhouse at night."

Sunlight streamed into the room. The gentle mooing and shuffling of feet was interrupted by Frau Schmidt's deft voice, scolding and prodding the cows as she milked them. Gaby clicked her tongue to call the chickens.

I sat up and stared out the windows. The mountains were etched in glittering white against a brilliantly blue sky. Happiness and a sense of fulfillment permeated me. This is what I had been waiting for. I shivered and crawled deep under the cozy featherbed. The room was so cold, I could see my breath. Barely peeking out, I engraved the picture into my mind. In the whole world nothing could be more beautiful, more peaceful than snow covered mountains.

Hilde opened the door. "*Guten Morgen, ihr Faulpelze.*
["Good morning, you lazybones"]. Time to get up."
    "In this icy room? How'm I supposed to get washed and
dressed without freezing to death?"
    Hilde laughed. "Easy! Get moving and keep moving.
However...." She waited to make an important
announcement.
    "Hmmm?"
    "However, just for this morning, to give you two a nice
and easy start, I'll bring you hot water. And only because
early this morning, Frau Schmidt set a large kettle for you on
the stove. But don't expect me to pamper you. You are both
old enough to take care of yourselves."
    Of course, I had known this all along. I smiled at her. "I
agree, and you are the nicest sister." She grinned and picked
up the empty pitcher. Content and at peace I pulled the
featherbed higher.
    Hilde came back with a steaming pitcher. I wriggled out
of bed. My long flannel gown still kept me warm.
    Hilde handed me my slippers. "Here, don't stand around
with bare feet." She poured hot water into the bowl, mixed it
to the right temperature. "Now get washed. Face first, teeth
last. Erika, I'll get some for you when Margot is finished."
    "No hurry," Erika mumbled from underneath her fluffy
mountain. Propelled by the numbing cold I washed and
dressed in no time, putting on layer upon layer as Hilde had
spread them out.
    Passing the front door I saw the latch was open. I slipped
out. Clean, cold mountain air filled my lungs. The meadow
in front of me stretched out like a soft, white blanket,
blinding me with its whiteness. The tall spruce trees at the
end of the wooden fence looked like giant Christmas trees.
The splashing of the mountain water into the hand-hewn
trough underlined the stillness of the perfect morning.
    "I'm dressed, let's have breakfast." Erika swung the

front door wide open. "Brrr, is that cold! You must be an icicle." She pulled me in.

In the *Stube* Hilde poured steaming milk from the morning milking into our cups and handed us each a slice of bread with butter and jam. Frau Schmidt and Gaby took a break from their chores and joined us, dipping dry bread into their mugs. In the beautiful Bavarian style, both women wore their blond braids like wreaths around their heads. Even Hansl crawled from his hiding place behind the ceramic oven, with a kitten in his hands, to get his share of bread and milk.

Kittens! After breakfast I snuggled into his corner. There the five cutest, furriest kittens played in a pile of blankets and pillows. Soon their frisky little bodies were everywhere, even in my hair.

The following day we took the train to Bischofswiesen to start school. Hilde had already enrolled us. That small, two-story house was a school? One classroom on the lower floor housed the first six grades, the room on the upper floor the other six grades, all with one teacher. As we entered the lower room, he interrupted his teaching. "Class, we have two new students. They are from far away, from Düsseldorf." He strutted up and down in front of the children. "The *Rhein* by Düsseldorf is so wide you cannot see the other side." I bit my lip, didn't dare to look at Erika. Did he really believe that?

"You, Margot, that is your correct name, *ja*? Good. You sit here," he pointed to a small desk in the back of the room, "while I take Erika upstairs to the upper class. I'll be right back." I spotted Hansl a few rows ahead of me. I couldn't believe it, two classrooms and one teacher for all twelve grades! *Herr Hauptlehrer* ["main teacher"] was a heavy, swarthy man with a mean temper, as I soon found out.

I shook the school pack from my back, lifted the top of the desk and started emptying it into the space when somebody called, "Hey you, what grade are you in?" "I'm in fourth grade." A salvo of laughter followed. I busied myself with my books.

The same voiced asked, "Where is whatever that name was?" I hardly understood his question, spoken in heavy dialect, so I didn't answer—just continued to shuffle things.

"Hey", the same voice, more irritated, asked again, "we want to know where you come from."

I wanted to say, "If you'd speak German I'd understand you," but since I had to live with them for a while, I changed my mind. "From Düsseldorf."

The boy, a big, heavy guy, got up. "Düsseldorf? Where's that?"

I mumbled, "It's north of here."

He stepped up threateningly close. "Hey, look, if you want to live with us here, you'd better do it our way." My stomach tightened. I looked at him as innocently as I could manage. "Sure. Don't worry." He grunted and shoved off.

Herr Hauptlehrer came back and resumed class, asking questions about arithmetic. I was dumbfounded and sick to my stomach. Did I have to live with that? All of a sudden I hated school. I hated being in Bavaria. I wanted to go back home. I could hardly understand these kids. But—Erika and Hilde could, they would help me, I would learn.

The bell rang. Everybody stormed out. I followed slowly just as Erika came down the steps, her face annoyed. "Darn them all. They don't understand me and I don't understand them," she muttered under her breath.

Outside we found ourselves surrounded by kids from my class, including the big bully. That spelled trouble, and there was no time to clue Erika in. And while we hardly had any training in what followed, it came naturally. Words flew back and forth, the bully waved his fist in my face. In sudden anger Erika seized his wrist with an iron grip. He was caught by surprise and unexpected strength. I knew it well from our wrestling matches, which I lost every time.

Herr Hauptlehrer stepped out of the school, boomed out the guy's name, caught him by the neck and marched the squirming and whining bully behind the building. The air exploded with loud screams. Horrified I looked into the grinning faces of my classmates. Later a sullen bully sat silently in his seat.

In the afternoon we learned that we had to memorize a poem by Adolf Hitler within the next two weeks. "It's long, so start well ahead of the deadline," *Herr Hauptlehrer* warned. "Don't let me catch anyone not knowing it."

After school we followed for three-quarters of an hour the slightly cleared road between *Berchtesgaden* and *Bad Reichenhall*. In Winkl we left the road and ran through knee deep snow to the house. Hilde looked up from her book. "How was school?"

Our frustration poured out like a torrent through open floodgates. "If these people would speak German, we could understand them." Horror-stricken Erika stopped. The Schmidt's sat at the table.

Hilde reassured her. "Don't worry, they don't understand you either. You sound just as strange to them." She smiled. "And if you two speak any faster even I won't understand you. Now, what's your homework?"

"Imagine, we have to memorize the 'Credo' by Adolf Hitler." I was appalled. "Hitler's Credo! Who cares?"

"Wait a minute. If you have to learn it, you'd better learn it well. Guess who's going to be asked to recite the whole thing? How many verses does it have? Fourteen? Well, you both know what to do." She left the *Stube* to start our dinner. She was right. We were forewarned.

By the next morning the weather had changed. The crispness was gone, the air heavy and oppressive. The snow looked dark and wet.

Frau Schmidt sounded happy. *"Der Föhn* ["south wind"] has come. Soon we'll see the first flowers." Once the *Föhn* established itself in the valley, the snow had no chance of staying. Soon the first grass peeked out, giving the meadows a welcomed green hue. But with the disappearance of the snow, the time to learn Hitler's poem also disappeared.

We four decided to walk in a big loop, at even distances, from the house across the meadow and back, poem in hand. This way we didn't disturb each other. Erika and I mastered the poem quickly, but the boys had problems. Especially Hansl was tongue-tied speaking in high German.

The day of the deadline arrived. All the way to school we recited the poem out loud over and over, walking single file along the road.

After the ritual of saluting the flag and singing the *Horst Wessel* song, *Herr Hauptlehrer* promptly asked, "Well, who wants to recite the 'Credo' by Adolf Hitler?" Silence. His eyes darted from one student to the next, looking for the unfortunate one he knew couldn't do it. He almost called on Hansl when his glare fell on me. He smiled. A hush fell over the class, an ominous silence. My stomach twisted into a knot.

"Margot, why don't you say it? It will be so nice to hear you recite it." Somebody snickered.

I got up from my little bench in the back and started,

"Ich glaube und bekenne…"

["I believe and confess…."]

Everybody turned around. I didn't think I sounded funny, after all the poem was written in German, but most of them chuckled, poking each other.

Herr Hauptlehrer beamed at me. "Why don't you come

up to the front, Margot, where we all can see you and hear you better?" Anger made the heat rise into my face. I got up, walked to the front, stood before the class and, focusing on the picture in the back, I recited all fourteen verses carefully, slowly. I had no intention of giving that man a chance to gloat over a mistake.

"*Ich glaube und bekenne*
dass ein Volk nichts höher zu achten hat
als die Würde und Freiheit seines
Daseins..."
["I believe and confess
that a people has no higher aim
than the dignity and freedom of its
existence..."]

"Very good Margot," Herr Hauptlehrer acknowledged almost reluctantly, "you've learned it well." I stalked back to my desk, head high.

Each day looked more like spring. The Ache lost its playful murmur and became a fast moving, gurgling stream, ready to sweep with it everything in its path. The muddy brown waters gushed by, pushing along earth, rocks and tree limbs torn from the mountains.

Palm Sunday was approaching. It would be a festive day in church with a procession in which all children carried hand-made 'Palm trees'. To create them promised to be lots of fun.

We picked up fresh curled wood shavings from the sawmill. Their sour smell soon permeated the house. Then we bought ribbons in various colors.

"Next we cut pussywillow branches," Gaby told us.

Friday afternoon we followed the winding path along the Ache in search of the best pussywillows.

"There, that big tree, that looks just right." Gaby pointed

to an old willow. Plump, silvery pussywillows shimmered in the sunlight. But—it stood in the middle of the swirling, icy water with a huge, gnarled tree from the mountains, stripped bare, jammed against its branched trunk.

"I'll see how deep the water is," Seppl volunteered. "Let's make a chain." We piled shoes and socks on a flat rock. Cautiously Seppl waded into the gurgling water, testing each step. "Oh, is this cold."

"Wouldn't it be better to find another tree?" Hilde suggested.

"Let's try this one first." Gaby tiptoed in after Seppl with Hansl reluctantly following her. Erika wanted to go next. Hilde held her back. "No, Erika, I'll go next. You and Margot stay at the end of the chain."

The rushing current swirled and foamed up to Seppl's rolled up knickerbockers. Suddenly he slipped. Gaby screamed, but held onto his belt and leather pants. With flailing arms he finally caught himself, reached the tree, swung himself on a low hanging branch and climbed higher.

"Get going and cut, my feet are numb," Gaby urged as she stepped deeper into the water to catch the branches he tossed down. She passed them on, we piled them up on a rock. The silvery buttons on the reddish young bark looked perfect.

"Hurry up, come down." Gaby's voice was full of pain. "I've got to get out of this water." He hurried down. Gaby groaned with each step, could hardly make her way back across the rocks, when she lost her footing. She slipped and fell forward into the water onto her hands. "Ouch, that hurts." She limped up the grassy slope, her feet and legs fiery red. "My feet, oh my feet," she moaned, searching for a dry spot on her heavy woolen skirt to rub them.

Each of us carried home an armful of branches and piled them on the bench in front of the house.

Gaby handed us cord and a freshly stripped stick. "Here.

Fasten the best willow branches to the stick. Then tie ribbons and shavings on the branches wherever you like."

Holding the stick between my knees I alternated pink and purple ribbons with the long wood shavings. The result was amazing. A beautiful, colorful 'palm tree'. Hilde ran to get her little box camera.

That Saturday, the house and we got a thorough cleaning. Gaby and Frau Schmidt scrubbed on their knees all the wooden floors in the *Stube*, the entrance and the hall, the steps and the big table and benches. No shoes were permitted in the house until evening. Hilde cleaned our rooms.

Finished with the scrubbing, Frau Schmidt and Gaby baked rolls, bread and, for dinner, *Dampfnudeln* ["steam noodles"], one of my favorite meals. Still warm, the sweet yeast rolls are broken into bite sized pieces and dunked into a bowl of vanilla or chocolate sauce, or, even better, into elderberry sauce.

Hilde brought water for our thorough and very cold sponge bath. By now we had gotten used to it. Scrubbed clean I felt good.

Downstairs I slipped out of my shoes and into the *Stube*. The house was peaceful and quiet. The creaking of the upper floor told me Hilde was still working, Erika was in our room. The boys helped their father outside. Gaby's and Frau Schmidt's voices came from the stable. The promising aroma of freshly baked bread filed the house.

With a contented sigh and my favorite book I curled up in the snugly place behind the stove. The story transported me twenty fathoms under the sea in a boat that could stay under water for a long time. What a fantasy.

"Get up, you lazybones. It's Sunday morning, you wanted to walk to church." Hilde came into our room, dressed in her new *Tracht*, the Bavarian national costume. "Hilde, you look beautiful!" Hands at her slender waist, she twirled around. The black bodice, laced in front, topped her white, puffy sleeved blouse. A fringed scarf in a lovely rose print covered her shoulders. A light green taffeta half-apron over the dark green, long skirt completed the dress.

"And you changed your hairdo." Her hair was now long enough to be worn in a roll low at the nape. Even Erika sat up in bed. We both inspected our pretty sister.

"I like it. You look wonderful," Erika agreed. It gave Hilde's face an even gentler, sweeter look.

"Now get up, you two." Against Erika's loud protest Hilde pulled off her featherbed. We washed and dressed in a hurry. Hilde brushed my hair, helped me with my new green wool jacket. Erika braided her long braids herself.

Gaby called up the steps, "Hurry up, we've got to go." I raced down. All the others wore their *Trachten* too.

In bright sunshine with a cool wind from the mountains, we followed a winding path through lush meadows. Other children, carrying their palm trees, joined us with their parents. Each palm tree looked different, each looked pretty.

At a bend in the path we passed one of the many road side crosses. The carved, weathered crucifix hung under its own steep little roof. A glass jar packed with fresh pussy-willows stood beneath the cross on a shelf. Reverently the men took off their green felt hats.

At the church the procession had already formed. The melodic call of the church bells echoed through the sunny valley. When the bells were silent, the chatter of the people quieted down. The musicians, distributed throughout the procession, started the first hymn with lots of lungpower, sunlight bouncing off their shiny instruments.

Flowers and birch branches in their lovely spring green decorated streets and houses. People lined the road singing hymns of the Passiontide with us as we passed by.

The procession wound its way through Bischofswiesen along the main road, closed off by the police, then back to the church.

After the long winter, spring rushed into the valley. Flowers popped up everywhere. The meadow in front of the house turned into a yellow carpet of primroses. The gentle breeze filled the valley with their sweet fragrance. Big clumps of deep throated, dark blue *Enzians* ["gentians"] bloomed beside the white stars of daisies. The meadow larks sounded as happy as I felt, climbing higher and higher, singing their little hearts out.

Without the restriction of snow and heavy clothes Erika and I ventured into new territories. For hours we played at the banks of the Ache, once again the meandering brook. Its crystal clear waters splashed over moss-covered rocks, chasing brook trouts.

One day, when we got back from playing, Frau Schmidt and Hilde stood in the *Stube* talking. Their serious looks reminded me that somewhere a war was going on, a fact that I successfully screened out of my mind.

"Is something wrong?" Erika asked. I held my breath, I didn't want to think about the war.

Hilde filled us in. "The German army moved into Norway and Denmark last week. Frau Schmidt just heard they also marched into the Netherlands, Belgium and Luxembourg. And there is talk that Chamberlain might resign." Where did Frau Schmidt get her news? I had seen neither a radio nor a newspaper being delivered.

"Herr Entmoser stopped by this morning." Frau Schmidt answered my unspoken questions. Could she read my thoughts like Mama? Herr Entmoser was the game warden and a high partei official.

Hilde smiled at us. "You look pretty with your wreaths

in your hair. Where did you go?"

"Oh Hilde, you've to come with us and see. We discovered Grenzwiesen. It's beautiful. Here, they are for the dinner table." I handed her a bunch of deep blue Enzians. Gaby brought Hilde a vase from the open cupboard.

"I have more bad news." Frau Schmidt sounded angry. "We're supposed to have another house guest." Surprised, we looked at her. "We all were told..." she waved her arm to include Winkl and Bischofswiesen, "...we all were told to house some of the *SS* officers that are everywhere. As if we needed them. They make life difficult enough." She opened the door. "We don't know when or who it will be." Still muttering she stomped to the stable for her evening chores. The stable door slammed. Slowly Gaby followed her.

I looked at Hilde. "What's wrong? I've never seen her that angry."

"Let's sit outside on the bench."

On the bench in front of the house, Hilde smoothed the folds of her apron. After a while she looked up. "You both have seen the blond little boy around here?"

I nodded. "Greggy, with the big blue eyes and blond curls? Of course. What about him?"

"He is the son of a relative of Frau Schmidt and of an *SS* officer stationed in Berchtesgaden." She looked at her hands, twisting her small gold ring. "The *SS* has a house there. And, I guess, young women of the area are invited to visit them."

Erika whistled through her teeth. "Now I understand. I've heard remarks about that house. But, if Greggy's mother isn't married, who pays for him?" As always, Erika thought of the practical side of things.

"That's part of the problem. The *SS* pays the women and they pay for the child, or children, too."

"But why?"

"To bring up Aryan children. The young women are all blond and blue eyed, Aryan looking."

Erika grinned. "They have a special word for those houses, don't they?'

"Yes, and it's not a nice one," Hilde said sharply.

"What is it?" Now I was curious.

"Breeding station," Erika answered quickly before Hilde could prevent her. She chuckled and pulled on her heavy braids. "Am I glad I've dark hair."

"All right, enough about it." Hilde got up. "Oh, one more thing…" She turned back to us. "Don't talk about this."

We walked back into the *Stube*. Now I understood Frau Schmidt's anger.

A few days later Erika and I remembered a task for the *Bund Deutscher Mädchen—BDM* ["League of German Girls"]. We had to collect primrose blossoms, dry them and bring them to the weekly meetings for tea for our soldiers. We told Hilde.

She nodded. "Start picking them when you are done with your homework. They'll be in bloom for another week."

We ran out. The thick grass felt like a cool carpet under my bare feet. Squatting in the middle of the meadow, I was surrounded by the sweet fragrance of the yellow blossoms. I hated to nip off the pretty flowers but I knew in a few days they would die anyhow. Now they might help our soldiers.

We emptied bag after bag of the fragrant blossoms to dry on newspaper on the floor of the upper balcony. Forgotten was the war, forgotten the possibility of an intruder. The joy of being was all that mattered. I envied the meadowlark for expressing its joy and happiness by filling the air with its jubilant song.

A few days later Hubert Entmoser, the son of our game warden, bolted into the door, out of breath. "Hitler has been announced. Come quickly, let's see his train."

Frau Schmidt looked up. Without a word she continued

to sweep the floor. We ran to the tracks in time to hear the guard rails clang down.

Unexpectedly, in a cloud of dust, two troop carriers roared up and blocked the road on both sides. Soldiers in *SS* uniforms jumped off. With their backs to the tracks they faced us, guns pointed. Startled, I moved back into the shadow of the trees, staring at the gun barrels. With an excited grin, Hubert inched as close to the troopers as he dared. I withdrew even further.

The shrill sound of the train whistle came closer. The soldiers with their guns pointed at us stood motionless. A huge, shiny locomotive appeared around the bend, trailing white steam. I covered my ears to block the incessant noise.

Long, shiny cars, marked with swastikas, moved slowly by. Men in uniforms, some looking out, some with their backs to the outside, stood behind closed windows. Then the train was gone, swallowed up by the bushes along the track. Following a sharp command, the troopers jumped back into the trucks and roared off.

Slowly I followed the others back to the house, saddened by the intrusion into my paradise. No matter how desperately I banned from my life the thought of the war with its uncertainties and pain, its shadow had again fallen over my sunny path.

A few days later Lieutenant Kirchner, the new house-guest, joined us at the dinner table. His young face with baby-blue eyes and blond, wavy hair did not fit the black uniform, for me the frightening symbol of Hitler's power.

"*Heil Hitler*," he saluted as he stepped into the Stube.

"*Grüss Gott*, Lieutenant, sit down." Frau Schmidt pointed to the empty chair.

"I have good news. The German army marched into Paris today."

I dropped my spoon, stared at him. Into Paris? Does that mean…? I still could hear Papa say, "You come home as soon as Paris falls." I looked at Hilde who was as startled as I was, then back to the Lieutenant. "Does that mean…? Will the war be over soon?" My appetite was gone, I didn't want to know the answer. I didn't want to know that our time here was running out.

He smiled at my question. "No, I'm afraid that will take a while. There is stiff resistance. The French are so foolish. As if they could resist us. And I'm sure the war won't be over with Paris, or with France, for that matter."

Nobody answered. We busied ourselves with eating. After a while I could not endure the silence any longer. "Hilde, when are we going to climb the Watzmann next week?" I had been asking this question ever since the day on the Königsee when Hilde promised we would climb it. Also I was glad I could focus on the mountain.

She looked at Herr Schmidt. "What do you think?"

He shrugged, took a few more bites. "Maybe Tuesday or Wednesday. Weather should be all right then."

Finally the day of preparation arrived. Hilde handed me a brown rucksack borrowed from the Schmidt's. "Tomorrow noon we'll leave. Here are the things you need to pack."

I stuffed socks and underwear into the rucksack. "Erika's still not coming with us?" She steadfastly refused to do any climbing. "Who else is coming?"

"Gaby and Seppl as our guides, since they've been up there, Hansl, you and me and…." She stopped.

"And, who else?" I looked at her. "Oh no, don't tell me the Lieutenant is coming too." I had realized he liked to be around Hilde, searched her out, which made me uneasy.

"He asked if he could come with us if he had that day off. I couldn't say no without a reason."

"Hope he doesn't have off. Hope Hitler needs him," I blurted out. I didn't want a stranger with us and certainly not him, an *SS*. I didn't trust him. And I did not trust him around my big sister.

"Margot, that's not nice. He's pleasant and polite."
Hilde defended him? How could she? I jammed my stuff
into the rucksack. "I don't mind him so much, he seems all
right. I do mind his uniform, what it stands for. Hitler's
henchmen!"
"Margot, for God's sake, be quiet."

Hilde made arrangements for us to spend the night in an
Almhütte ["meadow hut"], so we could sleep on the mountain and at sunrise start out fresh for the summit, to make it
down and home before the next nightfall. An *Almhütte*, a
primitive, one-room hut, shelters the farm hand who stays
with the cattle from early summer to late fall up on the lush,
high meadows.

The train took us into Berchtesgaden. The Lieutenant
came with us, but since he insisted on carrying my rucksack
in addition to Hilde's and his own, his presence didn't
bother me that much.

Tired and hungry after zigzagging up grassy slopes for
hours, we welcomed the sight of the little hut, tucked away
in a sheltered corner below the tree line. Smoke curled from
the chimney. Heavy rocks weighed down the wood shingled
roof.

Franzl, our host, took us to the barn. He made space for
Hilde, Gaby and me in the front part, while Seppl, Hansl and
the Lieutenant climbed up the ladder to sleep in the loft. We
tossed our gear into the hay and met in the hut for the special
treat I had been looking forward to all the way up.

The glow of the fireplace shed a warm light on the
roughly hewn table, two chairs and a wooden cot, covered
with blankets. The aroma of wood, and butter and cinnamon
added to the coziness. Gaby held a stack of plates that Franzl
filled from a huge iron pan with *Kaiserschmarren*, THE
specialty of an *Almhütte*.

The souffle-like egg mixture was made with rich, fresh

cream and lots of butter, sprinkled with cinnamon and sugar. With it Franzl handed us a loaf of his freshly baked bread.

After our feast we emerged in time to watch the sun dip behind a distant range. Deep shadows swallowed up the valleys while the mountaintops and streaky clouds glowed in the last golden light. I had seen *Alpenglühen* ["the glowing of the mountains"] from the valley, but up here it was much more beautiful. As the rosy glow slowly faded, a cool wind from the darkened valleys swept up the mountainside. The sound of cowbells drifted through the stillness.

Softly Hilde started to sing, then stopped abruptly. Of course, we had a stranger with us. Franzl came out to remind us that we had a strenuous day ahead of us.

I looked forward to sleeping in the hay. Wrapped in blankets we burrowed ourselves deep into the sweet smelling fluffiness.

"Get up, Margot, it will be light soon. Come on, get washed outside." I never understood how Hilde always woke up on time. Did I really have to leave my warm little nest? Outside, in the silvery light of the moon, the mountains loomed foreboding and so clear I could see every crevice. The first tinge of a cloudless, cold dawn spread along the sharply edged horizon. The air, already filled with the melodic sound of the cowbells, smelled of wood fire and spicy grass. I shook the hay out of hair and clothes and braced myself for the ice cold water as the boys appeared, yawning and sleepy.

"Breakfast is ready!" Franzl announced from the open door. A hearty breakfast of eggs, rolls, fresh butter and thick milk prepared us for the exhilarating climb. By the time the sun emerged above a ridge, we were on our way. Thick layers of white clouds separated the valleys from the crisp, clear morning.

Bright red paint splashes marked the path. Seppl and Gaby made us aware of special sights, warned us, coaxed us.

This was the fun part of our expedition, the part I especially looked forward to.

Single file we crossed a steep boulder field. Far below us the decline ended in a rock ledge jutting out from the side of the mountain. My foot slipped. A rock was thrown loose and fell bouncing off the wall, taking other rocks with it. The clatter grew more distant until it died a long way down.

Hilde behind me warned, "Margot, watch your step, don't look around so much."

After a few hours we reached the saddle, the crossover from the lower mountain to the main Massive and the summit.

Gaby stopped to instruct us, especially me, to watch our step, to go slow and to hold onto the iron cable. I glanced across. Our narrow path led to a spot where only a few inches connected one mountain side with the other, with nothing right and left but a sheer drop of thousands of feet—nothing but the wind whistling around us. A thin iron rope stretched across it.

Seppl and Gaby crossed over swiftly. I held onto the rusty rope and stopped. Suspended in air, almost weightless, I looked down. The drop on the one side was straight, sheer, lost in dark nothingness, the other side had a slight slope to it. Way below, large birds circled in the warm updraft.

"Margot, for heaven's sake, go on. Don't look down, you'll get dizzy." Hilde's voice sounded alarmed. No, I was not dizzy, I was fascinated! With a firm grip on the rope I continued to solid ground, then looked back. Above me the rocks rose to the summit in clear sunshine, below my feet lush green woods laced the valleys. I could have soaked it up for hours.

Steadily we climbed along the ridge toward the summit.

"There are the wild flowers!" Tiny white stars on mossy cushions, blue bells with blossoms larger than I had ever seen, hid in the cracks of huge boulders, protected from the sharp wind. Further down, also in the windbreak, I found *Almrausch*, low bushes like mountain laurel, covered with small red flowers. Later we crossed a whole field of *Almrausch*. Ahead of us along the ridge, Seppl stopped and waved his arm. I ran up to him. He pointed over the edge down to a rock ledge. An *Edelweiss*! How beautiful! The fragile silvery petals on the slender stem swayed in the icy wind. Its roots and gray leaves nestled close to the rock.

"Don't get too close to the edge," Seppl warned as I tried to see it better. The side of the mountain below the ridge was still in deep snow. Reluctantly I moved to let Hilde have a closer look.

"Thank you, Franzl."

A shy smile lit up his serious face. "I knew you wanted to see one."

An hour later, the wooden cross of the summit loomed above us against the cloudless sky. I remembered the cross of the *Shesaplana* in Voralberg, when I learned that the highest point of every mountain in the Alps is marked by a tall wooden cross. Only another few more yards.

At the top a sudden wind caught me with such ferocity it almost toppled me over. On all fours we scrambled behind a boulder to get out of the icy blast. Here in the windbreak we welcomed the warmth of the sun.

"Munching time," Gaby announced. Out came sandwiches, fruit and, my favorite, *Landjäger* ["salami sticks"]. The Lieutenant tried to sit close to Hilde but Gaby inched him out.

Before us the Alps unrolled mile after mile of snow capped peaks. Like frothy layers of lace, ridge upon ridge stretched along the clear blue horizon. Below our feet the deep valleys added their lush green to the snowy toppings. I leaned against Hilde.

"Like it?" she mumbled with a full mouth.

"Like it?" I searched for words. "It's the most beautiful sight I've ever seen." I pointed to a valley way below us. "Those little dots must be cattle. And there, see the smoke of that *Almhütte*?"

Gaby nodded. "*Freili*, ["of course"] it's Franzl's, where we slept last night." She pointed to the sharply etched line along the horizon. "See how clear it is? The weather's changing." A few minutes later she got up. "Let's start back. We need to be down before dark." We packed empty bags and bottles back into the rucksacks. "Let's go," Gaby urged, getting restless. She decided to take a faster route down. Soon I realized why we hadn't come up this way. It was steep. It would have been a tough climb up, but downhill was wonderful. I jumped from rock to rock, making sure not to lose the trail. Downhill was fun and so much faster, but it still took us hours to reach the valley. The worst part was the walk to the station.

Waking up in my bed the next noon I remembered nothing of the train ride or how I got home. I had not wanted to eat anything, just sleep.

All morning Erika and I played at Grenzwiesen, rolling down the grassy hill into the meadow, then running back up to roll again. What fun! That our dresses were dusty and my bare legs and feet scratched didn't bother me.

"We've to go home, should be lunch time." As always, Erika was practical and hungry. I shook the grass out of my hair, straightened my apron.

"I'll race you home." She took a shortcut through the meadow, ducked underneath the log fence, raced across the road and the railroad tracks to the bridge. I followed her as fast as I could, knowing I could not win.

Hilde waited in front of the house, a letter in her hand.

"Vater wrote." Her voice and her shoulders dropped. Erika asked, "What's the matter? What did he write?" "Mama plans to visit us." I took a deep breath. "Mama? Why? We are fine. She doesn't have to come." "I don't know why, but she's coming next week." I stared at Hilde. "Next week? Oh, Hilde, what if she wants to stay here and you've to go home? Then I won't stay here. Hilde, I don't want her to come." I could not hold back my tears. Hilde put her arms around me. I sobbed. Mama never put her arms around me. Why did she have to intrude into our paradise?

Hilde brushed the hair out of my face and gave me a peck on the cheek. "Come on, *Stöppchen* [no translation, an endearment]. It'll be all right." I took a deep breath and nodded.

A few days later, we returned from playing in the Ache when Seppl called from the stable. "Somebody's waiting for you." We looked at each other. Mama!

Erika eyed me quickly. "Brush the sand off your legs and straighten your apron." She smoothed her hair out of her face. We opened the door to the *Stube*. Mutter sat with her back to us facing Hilde, who looked as joyless as I felt.

"Oh, there you are." Mama surveyed us and, I was sure, didn't miss a thing. "Are you glad to see me?"

Awkwardly we came forward and shook hands with her.

Hilde tried to end the inspection. "Come and sit down, you two," but Mama was not to be interrupted.

"Why aren't you wearing any shoes? You can't walk barefoot. What if you step into some glass?"

"Don't worry, Mama, nobody here wears shoes in the summer." Erika's voice was light and convincing. "How was your trip?'

While Mama talked, I looked at Hilde. Her usual radiance and gentleness had turned into a sullen defensiveness.

The defensiveness came out more and more as Mama seemed determined to check on every penny Hilde had spent during our six months' stay. Hilde had kept meticulous records. Mama asked over and over why Hilde bought this or that when we weren't wearing any shoes. I was glad Hilde had cleared with the parents the purchase of our new clothing and her *tracht*.

A few days later Hilde whispered as she tucked me in, "She's going to leave in two days."

"And are you staying?" She nodded. "Oh, Hilde, I'm so glad." I put both my arms around her neck, she fell flat on my bed. We laughed until tears ran down my face.

We took Mama to the station. Hilde carried her suitcase, Erika made conversation. I only relaxed when the whistle announced the train. We waved it out of sight, then linked arms and marched down the road, laughing and singing.

A few weeks later on the way home from playing, I stopped at the bridge over the Ache. Below me in the sun drenched water, two little trouts darted playfully upstream, flicking their tails. How they enjoyed their freedom.

Hilde stood at the front door. I ran up to her when I saw a letter in her hand. I slowed down. Would that be it?

"Vater wants us home."

I knew it! This beautiful time had to come to an end. Everything wonderful always came to an end while everything dreary and joyless went on and on and on.

"He mentioned something else." Hilde sat beside me.

I shrugged. "So, who cares."

"We have a new brother." That startling news made me lift my head to see if she was serious.

"His name is Ernst."

She was serious. I thought of my parents and shook my head. "Come on, Hilde. What're you talking about?" I was mildly curious.

"They have accepted a young man, Josef's age, to live with us while he finishes his training in Düsseldorf."

I lost interest. "When do we leave?"

"As soon as we receive the tickets, most likely in three or four days."

Upstairs I sat on my bed, kicked off my shoes. No more running barefoot through the dewy meadows. The front door banged, Erika was home. After a while she pushed the bedroom door open with her bare foot, plopped on her bed, still chewing her roll.

"Let's go over to Grenzwiesen."

That sounded good. We changed, ran out of the house and across the bridge to our hideout. The deep indentation in the grassy hill felt warm from the sun. With arms under my head, the news hit me with full force. Tears streamed down my face.

"Erika, I don't want to go home."

"I don't either. However, we knew this was coming. When Mama left I knew they would soon call us home."

We lapsed into silence, interrupted by my sobbing. I knew it was inevitable, but that didn't help. I tried to picture what I was going back to, what our place looked like, but I couldn't. Nothing came. No memories. Tears rolled again.

A high pitched, sharp sound like the cry of a sea gull pierced the quietness. I lifted myself halfway up and, raising my head above the rim, answered in the same high-pitched squeak. Hilde was looking for us. I couldn't remember when or how we had started this way of communication, it proved helpful. Only we two could exchange it. Not even Erika could make that sound.

Hilde sat beside us in the grass. "How are you two doing?"

"Terrible!" Erika's face was unhappy.

I sobbed again. "Hilde, I can't even remember what our

apartment looks like. I don't want to go home."

Hilde put her arms around me. "They're all looking forward to having us home again. And you'll get used to the city again, you'll see. It will be all right."

"Do you want to go back?"

Hilde took a deep breath. "No, not really, but we knew this was only temporary. We did have a good time here, didn't we?" As answer I snuggled into her arm. "Let's try to remember together our apartment."

As soon as she mentioned the kitchen with the covered bathtub, everything jumped back into place. Like unlocking a door, behind which I had pushed things I didn't want to think about. "That's right. Now I remember." The long, dark streets with gray apartment buildings, gray sidewalks, every-thing cement, nothing green. It all came back.

Hilde got up. "We've got to get back for dinner."

"Can I roll down the hill once more."

She smiled at me. "Sure, *Stöppchen*."

I ran to the rim of the slope, threw myself down, and with arms over my head rolled into the valley below. For a moment I lay there. A deep sadness settled over me. The sun had disappeared, the evening was gray and motionless.

Next day Hilde got our papers transferred back to Düsseldorf, even though we didn't know which school I would attend. When the tickets arrived, we packed.

After the last dinner I sneaked out, sat on the bench in front of the house. I needed to be by myself, to listen to the larks sing their evening prayers, to the goodnight chirping of the robins. Slowly the valley darkened. The last rays cast a golden glow on the mountains as if to say good-bye. The glow lingered for another moment. Then the day was gone.

FALL, 1940

CHAPTER 3

After a long dreary ride, our train screeched to a halt in the huge vaulted station. "*Düsseldorf*, this is *Düsseldorf*," the stationmaster's voice boomed over the speaker. Doors swung open, spilling out travelers and luggage. The blackened bulbs of the station added to the gloom of the rainy fall evening.

As I followed Hilde out of the train I heard shouts, "There they are. They're coming out." Vater and Josef ran to greet us. Mutter followed with another person at a slower pace.

"You look good. Did you have a good ride?" Papa shook my hand, gave me a quick kiss. So did Mutter.

Even Josef gave me a shy peck. I was glad to see his boy-ish grin again. He gestured to the visitor. "Here is somebody who wants to meet you."

A pleasant looking young man, Josef's height and age, stretched out his hand. "My name is Ernst. *Guten Abend*."

Oh yes, our new "brother" Ernst. We shook hands, picked up our luggage and moved with the stream of travelers down the steps. In the parking lot we all squeezed into the back of our old faithful Opel Olympia.

I pressed my nose against the window and saw nothing but houses, their silhouettes dimly visible against the darkening sky. The heavy air smelled oppressive, dirty.

"Tell us, how was your stay? What did you do?" Papa was eager to hear, and I was eager to talk about our wonderful time, about *Grenzwiesen*, the cows, the Ache and our attempts to catch trout. Papa and Mama listened, asking occasional questions.

Watching Papa drive, I marveled how smooth the slow traffic flowed in the darkness. The headlights were blackened to a small slit to let only a thin shaft of light hit the road in front of the car. Glowing phosphorous buttons floating through the dark streets showed where people hurried by.

We pulled into our street. How different everything looked, as if I saw it for the first time. The huge apartment buildings rose enormous and dark from the wide cement sidewalk. No trees, no grass.

As soon as the car stopped, I jumped out and rang storm on Oma's doorbell. Of course, she was waiting for us and gave us a hug.

"It's so good to have you all home again. You look wonderful." We sat around her table, talking of all the marvelous things we did.

"No, I didn't learn to milk, I couldn't do it, but I learned to make kindling."

Mutter looked alarmed. "Margot, you used an ax?"

I nodded proudly. "I also learned to use a sickle to cut grass." A sharp kick from Erika silenced me.

"Hilde, how could you let her do such dangerous things?"

"Don't worry, Mama," I said quickly, sorry to have gotten Hilde into trouble. "Herr Schmidt taught me, he watched me, it wasn't dangerous for me at all."

"Can we go upstairs, I'm hungry," Erika changed the subject. Oma had offered cake and coffee, but Mutter, as I expected, categorically declined.

Our parents had long planned for us to move to Benrath,

to get out of the city and to have more space. Benrath was an old established suburb of Düsseldorf, famous for its eighteenth century pink rococo hunting castle, the *Benrather Schloss,* ["Castle of Benrath"] and for its beautiful park with many ponds.

Ever since I could remember, Oma's presence in our family was a constant sore spot for Mutter. As the only son, Papa's devotion to his mother irritated Mutter no end. She wanted Vater to get a separate apartment for Oma. However, Oma was going to move in with us, have a room on the second floor. In bed at night Erika and I often heard angry voices, slammed doors.

The houses, a brand new street with blocks of two story homes on both sides, were the last ones permitted to be built during the war and Papa feared they might not be finished. Every Saturday afternoon he worked on the house to do whatever he could.

By October, without a paved road, without sidewalks, without front yards, Papa decided we had waited long enough. Time to move in. The movers had to thread their way around potholes and puddles. So did we for the next weeks.

Erika and I shared a bedroom in the built-out attic. Our window looked towards a field that was still being farmed at the end of the street.

Behind the house our spacious *Veranda* overlooked a bare space that I hoped, one day, would be a lovely little yard with a wooden fence and trees and flowers.

Papa spent a lot of extra effort on our two-room shelter in the basement. He reinforced the ceilings of both rooms with thick iron plates, supported by heavy iron beams. The larger room contained our bunk beds, the narrow one our chairs and a small table. Airtight wooden doors separated the shelter from the rest of the basement and from the outside. I felt secure and confident that nothing could happen to us unless we got a direct hit.

Having missed the start of the *Höhere Schule* ["high school"] in Benrath, I enrolled for the rest of the year in the *Hans-Schemm Schule,* ["Hans-Schemm school"] the local elementary school. The spacious modern facility had been confiscated by the Nazis from the Roman-Catholic Church, as had happened all over Germany. The school had been renamed and was used as a public school.

On Sunday morning we walked to our new parish church, St. Cecilia. A massive, dark brown structure with a tall tower and a clock with golden bars, it dominated the center of the town, affectionately called *Dorf* ["village"]. Our fifteen-minute walk led through tree lined streets of individual two story apartment buildings and spacious old single homes with attractive front yards.

After the service we stopped at the adjacent rectory. *Pfarrer Antheck* ["pastor"], who had preceded us from our former parish, sounded enthusiastic about his new parish.

"It's a large congregation with lots of programs. Hilde and Josef, come Wednesday evening. I'll introduce you to our young people. Herr Füsser, with your interest in charitable work, I know you'll like our *Charitas* ["charity"] group. It's well organized."

After road and sidewalks were installed, more people moved into the street. The family in the neighboring corner house had one daughter, Alize, about Josef's age. Her father, Herr Leimbke, a high Nazi official, wore his required round Partei button proudly. Since Papa refused to join the Partei, his unadorned lapel broadcasted that fact loudly. Each time he encountered our neighbor, Herr Leimbke stared at the empty buttonhole and made some remark about Vater some day being sorry for being so blind.

Another family moved in across the street with their daughter, Annemarie, who was my age. We sometimes played together, but her parents were unfriendly. They had lost house and job in Saarbrücken when Hitler annexed the Saarland and in their anger and bitterness reacted negatively to everybody, especially us, their new neighbors.

"Mutter, I need a Martin's lantern. Friday is St. Martin." I flung my school bag on the floor of the entrance hall. Ever since I could remember, Erika and I participated in the St. Martin's Parade, commemorating the patron of beggars. Every year we watched the re-enactment of the story, when the knight shared his cloak with a freezing beggar by slicing it in half with his sword. In the parade we all carried a home-made lantern, hooked to a stick, with a burning candle inside. "St. Martin even has a white horse for the parade."

Mutter stopped peeling potatoes. "I don't want you to go with that parade. Talk with Vater tonight."

"Why not? We've always gone."

"Don't you remember what happened two years ago? You are not going if I have anything to say."

"No, I don't remember. What happened?"

"As I said, ask Vater." As usual she referred any non-routine decision to Vater. I knew she did not like the local custom of *grippschen* ["collecting treats"], when we kids would go from house to house to sing for treats.

The afternoon went by quickly as I constructed my lantern. When Erika came home, I asked her for help assembling it. "Mutter doesn't want us to go. Do you know why?"

"*Ja*," Erika answered slowly, "that fear is still in her. She hasn't gotten over it. Neither has Josef."

"What happened?"

"Two years ago, on November nine, 1938, the main parade, the big one in the *Altstadt* ["old town"], turned into a horrible clash with the Jews."

By evening our lanterns were finished. We proudly showed them to Papa and Josef. "Papa, we can go, can't we?" I pleaded.

"Is the parade in Benrath?"

"Oh yes, with St. Martin on a white horse."

"Josef, I don't want them to go." Mutter looked at Papa. "You know what happened two years ago."

My brother Josef, the dark fuzz on his upper lip showed his sixteen years, stood quietly in the doorway, listening. I looked at him. "What happened, Josef?"

He shook his head, was silent.

I prodded him. "What happened?"

"It was terrible." He dug his fists deep into his pocket. "Haven't talked much about it." He took a deep breath. "We were in the *Altstadt* going toward the Market for the re-enactment, you know. Suddenly I heard glass shatter behind me. Then I heard screams. At first I thought somebody fell into the glass. But then, right beside me, a store window gets smashed. And I mean smashed, on purpose, with a rock."

"On purpose? Why? Weren't there any police?"

Josef laughed bitterly. "Police? They were there all right. But what can they do if the criminals are the authority, *SA* and *SS* in full uniform? Stand by. Watch. Police!" Josef spit the word out. "Police doesn't dare to tell these hoodlums anything. Nobody dares to."

I stared at my brother. His ruddy face was pale and taut with anger, his nostrils flared. Hilde looked at me, laid a hand on Josef's arm as if to restrain him, but he went on. "Things were flying all around us: clothing, books, linens, furniture, everything. Whatever the store sold, they threw out. The *SA* and *SS* ran into apartment buildings, threw stuff through upstairs windows. Stuff like crystal, china, every-thing."

"How did they know where to go?" Erika asked.

"They knew. The Jews had long been singled out. That yellow star was on every smashed window. Or *Jude* ["Jew"] was smeared in yellow across it. And not only did they throw the new stuff into the streets. They burned it."

He stared at his shoes. Slowly, testing his voice, he continued. "Beside... beside one burning pile stood a woman with her baby. Tears ran down her face as the *SS* threw her dowry linen, you know, it still had the little blue ribbons around it, they threw it into the fire. My God, did she cry when the flames shot up."

Josef stopped again, his jaw clenched. To hide my tears, I backed into a little corner beside the sink, my stomach hurting. Josef sniffed and continued. "Down the street a man, white hair, bent shoulders, stood beside a pile of furniture from his antique store. You know, one of the beautiful old ones in the *Altstadt*. His whole body shook as he mumbled something like 'it took my whole life to build this up.'"

Josef ran his hands through his thick hair. "Why do they hate the Jews so fanatically? What have they done to the Nazis?"

The question hung in the air. Nobody could answer it.

"And the worst was...." His voice broke, he fumbled for a handkerchief, blew his nose, "...the worst was I saw it all and could do absolutely nothing. One young man grabbed the arm of an *SS* as he tossed a crystal lamp onto a pile to stop him. They threw the man to the ground, kicked and beat him unconscious. Of course, they continued. And that young man was not a Jew." With white knuckles he rubbed his tense jaw line. We waited.

"And in the midst of the screaming, the splintering of glass and crystal and furniture, people just stood there, shocked. How is this possible? I saw in their faces what I felt. Utter powerlessness."

A heavy silence hung over us. With my sleeve I wiped my wet face. The ache in me, would it ever go away again? Why? Why were they so hateful, so brutal?

Hilde broke the silence. "Of course, later we found out that the same thing happened in other cities. Same event, same purpose. It was all planned, all orchestrated."

Finally Vater coughed, cleared his throat. Our verdict was about to come. He looked sternly at us. "You can go, but only if you promise to stay together and to come home immediately if something happens."

"*Ja*, Papa, we'll watch out," Erika assured him.

Relieved to move, to get away, I scooped up my lantern to run out of the kitchen. Papa's voice stopped me.

"One more thing." He searched for words. "Don't tell anybody, not even to your best friend, what we talk about here at home. Understand?"

"*Ja*, Papa."

He rubbed his bald head, cleared his throat again. "There have been cases of children telling in school what their fathers or mothers said. The Nazis got wind of it and picked up the father during the night."

Telling on parents? I couldn't imagine it.

Papa eyed us sternly. "And these were harmless little remarks, you understand. They didn't intend to tell on their parents, they only repeated what they heard at home. In some instances teachers even asked the children what the parents said about the war or the Partei. So, keep your mouth absolutely shut. Not one word. Do you understand, Margot?"

My heart hammered in my throat. "*Ja*, Papa." Did he think I would say something? Tears welled up again. I choked them down. Papa got up. We were dismissed.

In our room I tossed my lantern on the dresser and plopped on the floor to clean up the mess we had left. My head swam. Did he really think I would say something? Cause him to be picked up? What if a teacher asked me? What would I say? Lying was our greatest offense at home, one that brought out Vater's full wrath and fury. I took a deep breath.

Erika stopped crumbling up scraps of black paper. "Quite a sermon for one evening, huh? Are you all right?"

Tears spilled down my face. I wiped them with my apron. "Erika, could that really happen? That a child says something and the father gets picked up?"

"*Ja*, I know it happened in our old school in the city. A boy told the teacher that Jews were people too and when the teacher asked, he said his father thought the same. A few nights later the Gestapo hauled the father away. Nobody has heard from him since."

I shuddered and vowed never to say one word to anybody about anything.

Late Friday afternoon, armed with extra candles, matches and a roomy gym bag for treats, Erika and I lined up at school in a loosely formed parade. Parents accompanied the smaller children, some even in strollers. A police car, followed by a band, waited at the entrance of the school driveway.

A murmur ran through the excited crowd. "There's the horse. St. Martin's coming." The white stallion tossed its mane, the rider in a knight's armor held his sword high in salute as he rode past us. The band struck, "St. Martin, St. Martin...." With the help of some of the adults we lit the candles, carefully hooked the lanterns to the sticks, picked up the tune. The St. Martin's parade was in motion.

The colorful column of glowing, swaying lanterns wound its way through the dark night of low hanging clouds and raw wind. We walked slowly, carefully, watching the burning candles as we sang. A second song, *"Last uns froh und munter sein, und uns heute kindlich freuen...."* ["Let us be happy and joyful today like children..."] alternated with the St. Martin's song.

Some of the lanterns were elaborate. One boy carried a replica of our pink castle with its many glowing windows. I liked my lantern. Yellow candlelight shone through black circles, stars and triangles. Erika's looked lovely too with the red glowing through her cut out flowers.

In front of the castle, the parade stopped beside the huge stone lions on their square pedestals. We fanned out around the steps and up the curved drive, singing once more, "St. Martin, St. Martin rode through snow and wind...." Then all was quiet.

Hushed expectancy hung over the children. I shivered and was glad I wore my wool mittens and hat. Then we saw St. Martin. His white cape blowing behind him, he galloped on his white stallion down the walkway. From behind a stone lion, a beggar in dirty rags threw himself into the path of the horse and held up his trembling hands. St. Martin reined in his horse, swirled down his mantle, brandished his sword and after slicing the cloak in half, threw part of it to the beggar. Gratefully the old man wrapped himself in it. The knight disappeared into the night before the beggar could thank him.

We all applauded. The official part of the parade was over. The band marched back to school. Now to the fun part, the singing for treats.

With burning lanterns Erika and I, with a few of her friends, walked to the houses and apartments of people we knew. We sang until the doors opened and we received a treat or a hot cup of chocolate.

In the dark streets groups of glowing lights danced from house to house, filling the night with singing, bursts of laughter and with loud "*Vielen Dank*" ["many thanks"].

By the time we finished canvassing our neighborhood, I was cold and glad to get home. When Mutter opened the door and I saw her anxious look, I remembered what could have happened.

We poured our loot on the big kitchen table, but kept it separated. I sorted my sweets into heaps of candies, chocolates, apples and nuts. "Mama, look what I got."

She shook her head. "Make sure you brush your teeth after all this sugar. People must have saved their sweets for months. There certainly isn't much on the ration cards."

After offering our treats to the rest of the family we packed them into individual bags and stored them in our bedroom drawers.

The sirens wailed incessantly. Coming out of deep sleep I pulled my featherbed over my head to escape the painful sound.

"Get up! They're here!" In the dark Erika tore my cover away, pulled me off the bed and threw my clothes at me.

The rumbling of *Flack* ["anti-aircraft cannons"] came closer. Overhead I heard a thick humming. I grabbed my little red suitcase and slid down the banisters to the ground floor. Just as we reached the cellar door the flack in the field at the end of our street bellowed round after round. We stumbled into the shelter. Oma sat quietly in her corner. Mutter in her chair glared at us.

The height of Vater's eyebrow showed his anger. "What took you so long? Didn't you hear the siren?" I was too tired to explain that we must have fallen asleep again.

"British planes in formation are entering our airspace. Direction: Düsseldorf," the precise voice informed us. An attack on Düsseldorf? We looked at each other. So far we had been lucky, Düsseldorf had not been singled out.

Papa checked the airtight doors. My heart pounded in my throat. Was this the night we were going to die? I fumbled with my wool dress, trying to get it over my head.

Hilde helped me. "We'll be all right." She patted me on the back. After fastening my wool stockings and shoes, I threw the coat on my bed and climbed into the top of our triple bunk beds. Erika stayed below me, Hilde at the bottom.

I opened my little red suitcase. Mutter had said, "Make sure you have your important things always with you in case of emergency." But what was important to me? I finally had assembled my passport, according to Mutter the one document I needed, added a little celluloid doll with big blue eyes that opened and closed and a picture book about a little prince.

That picture book I took out. For a long time I looked at the little blond prince, sitting alone on a branch, surrounded by stars and quietness. I wanted to crawl into somebody's lap, wanted to have some arms around me, to hold me, to reassure me. But Mutter's eyes had been cold and angry because we were late. They were always cold, even when she smiled. Hilde seemed preoccupied. I took a deep breath, tucked the suitcase beside me against the wall, nodded and smiled at the lonely little prince, hugged the book on top of me, and closed my eyes.

Our Flack shot more rounds and woke me again. Under me I could feel the wooden slates through the thin straw filled paper sacks, but I didn't care. All I wanted was sleep.

At a lull in the rumbling that like a tide swelled and ebbed, Papa raised the two long handles on the shelter door to have a look outside.

Mutter frowned. "Josef, you can't go outside now."

My brother Josef jumped up from his bed across the room. "Papa, can I come with you?"

"No, you stay here, I'll be back in a moment. Maybe it's over." Soon he came back. "*Ja*, it was an attack on the city. It's burning."

After the end-of-raid siren we ran up the steps to the back yard and stared at the northeastern sky, aflame in various places.

"What about Bilk? And what about the Brass?" Mutter asked anxiously. Oma Brass lived in the center of Düsseldorf and Vater's business was in Bilk.

"I don't know about Brass, but it doesn't look like Bilk is burning. That's further east."

Murmuring voices came from every back door of our block. We all had relatives or business in the city. But nobody knew anything specific. The following evening Papa brought the news that Oma Brass and the aunts were all right. So was his business.

Only a few more weeks and we would celebrate our first Christmas in our new home. Erika and I waited for the right moment to approach Mutter with a suggestion. One evening after dinner she sat down in the kitchen and picked up the *Düsseldorfer Nachrichten* ["News of Düsseldorf"].

"Mama?" Erika and I stood beside her, waiting.

"Hmm?" She looked at us, annoyed at the interruption. "What is it? What do you want?"

Erika boldly stepped forward. "Mama, can we this year celebrate Christmas Eve instead of Christmas Morning? We are both old enough to stay up."

We two had talked it over. The Christmas tree with candles would be much more beautiful in the dark.

"Let's see what Vater says." She looked back down to the paper and thumbed to the next page. We knew, if she was on our side half the battle was won.

"I can take a nap in the afternoon," I offered.

"Hmm." She looked at us again as if she was sizing us up. Finally she nodded. "*Ja*, that would be important, so you stay awake during Midnight Mass. All right, let's see what Papa says."

We knew we had won.

"But until then we have a lot of work. Monday is wash day. After school I need your help. Then we have to do the baking."

"Can I cut the cookies and decorate them?" That was one of my favorite tasks.

"*Ja*, you both can help," Mutter agreed. "We also have to

clean the house. I do miss Frau Müller who helped me in the *Ruhrtal Strasse*. This house is a lot of work."

"I'll do the vacuuming," I volunteered. Vacuuming always inspired me to sing at the top of my lungs.

The following Monday after school, I dropped my coat and school bag in the hall and called for Mutter. Her muffled voice answered from below. I opened the door to the top of the basement steps and hot, sudsy-smelling steam streamed into the house. I groped my way down the long flight of steps.

Through a fog I saw Mutter lifting with a wooden pole clothes from the copper kettle, full of boiling suds, into a huge galvanized tub overflowing with cold water. Her face gleamed with perspiration, her hair stuck in wet strands to her skin. In heavy rubber galoshes and a black rubber apron, she looked like the seamen cleaning the boat. She handed me a second stick.

"Here. Separate the clothes and move them around." She stoked the fire, threw a new load of presoaked garments into the bubbling suds and closed the kettle with a flat lid. Slowly the air in the basement room cleared.

"That can boil awhile. Let's go upstairs for lunch." In the kitchen she lit the fire under the prepared potato soup and slumped into a chair, her face drawn and pale. Erika came in from school, we sat down. It was my turn to say the prayers.

"How was school?" Mutter's routine question unleashed a fury in Erika.

"Oh, Fraulein Knops made a terrific fuss today. She talked about the Hitler *Jugend* meeting on Sunday morning." Erika looked at me. "You have been told too?"

"Sure." I knew and had tried to forget about it.

"And, of course, I know I'm not permitted to go, so I told her I couldn't come. Did she get furious. She said things like 'young people who are not participating in the Hitler *Jugend* are traitors'". Erika drew a deep breath. "And she said that in front of the whole class. I'm just as much a German as she is, even if I don't go to their stupid meetings." Erika threw her napkin on the table.

I looked at her, alarmed. If she was that angry, she might say something.

Mutter dropped her spoon and gripped Erika's arm. "Erika, for God's sake, don't say anything in school. Not one word, you hear? Let them say what they want but don't say a word." Mutter leaned back. "And you are right, you can't go on Sunday morning because we are going to church."

"I can't anyway. Papa won't let me have a uniform. And Fraulein Knops emphasized 'uniform is a must'." Erika flung her braids back and pushed her chair from the table.

I asked Mama, "Why can't we get uniforms?"

"You won't get any. That's it. *Basta.*" She pointed to Erika. "You sit down. We are not finished."

For us children it was a cardinal sin against etiquette to get up from the table before the adults, unless we were excused. Grumbling, Erika sat down again, her feathers still much ruffled.

Mutter emptied her plate. "Did Fraulein Knops say anything else?"

"She also said," Erika's heavy, black eyebrows knitted together over angry hazel eyes, "...she said—while she looked directly at me—'and some people even have their physician excuse their daughter from out-of-door activities of the Hitler *Jugend*. This is not the kind of spirit that wins the war'." Wagging her head, Erika tried to imitate her thin, sour classroom teacher.

Mutter nodded. "That's right. Dr. Zielhoff told the Nazis to excuse you from these activities. Remember, you got meningitis two years ago after they let you stand in the rain for hours, and we almost lost you. Of course, as an officer he did not ask them but ordered them to excuse you. And they don't like that. They don't like to be told anything." Slowly she got up from the table and stacked the soup plates in the sink. "Don't worry about it. Now get changed, both of you, and help me get the wash finished."

Strange, I thought while slipping a cotton dress over my head, why do adults always say "don't worry"? Of course we worried what our teachers thought of us. I let out a deep sigh.

"What's the matter?" Erika asked.

"If we only had a uniform. Or if there were other kids without one. We wouldn't be so obvious."

"*Ja*, I know. Would make things easier. But you know Papa and his darn principles."

"Oh, don't say that, Erika. He's right, I'm sure. It just makes things so difficult."

Erika snorted. Aloud she said, "Let's go before she yells at us."

In the wash cellar the huge copper kettle bubbled away. My job was to get the clothes rinsed and pressed in a water press so Erika could carry them into the backyard for line drying. Load after load she hung up in the correct order: towels together, napkins, bed linen, specific kind of underwear, all neatly in groups. Even if it meant digging for matching items or rehanging a whole line. Mutter insisted on a neat appearance.

"What will our neighbors think if they see that jumble out there?" was her standard remark.

Next day, ironing day, Mutter handed me a stack of dampened handkerchiefs to start with. After sliding the hot iron over a piece of wax cloth to make it glide easily I was ready.

I liked to run my hand over the smooth linen, thin like fine paper, to fold it neatly with edges matching and to pile one finished item on top of the other. Especially Mama's embroidered and lace-edged handkerchiefs. They looked so pretty afterwards.

With a stack of them finished, I tackled the tablecloths. "Tell me about your childhood, Mama. What did you do?"

This was the other part of ironing I liked. It was the only time Mutter talked about herself, the only time she let us get close to her, confided in us.

"Well, you know, being the oldest of ten was not easy." The sharp line between her eyebrows softened, her small eyes with which she ruled my life, looked almost gentle. "I was responsible for the younger ones. My mother needed me at home, but I really wanted to continue school."

"You did? Why?"

"I wanted to become a school teacher."

"And? Why didn't you?"

"My father said 'absolutely not!' Girls didn't do that in those days."

Erika came home. After a quick plate of soup all three of us stood at the extended kitchen table and ironed. The stacks of neatly folded linens grew. The smell of hot wax and damp, clean cloths filled the air as the baskets slowly emptied.

Mama continued to talk about her childhood, about the large family farm in Westfalia where her mother was born. As a child Mama had visited that farm often. She also talked about the French occupation of the *Ruhr* district and the *Rheinland* after the war, how the Germans chafed under it and the joy when Hitler brought that disgrace to an end. "At least he did one good thing. Too bad he couldn't also send the dirty *Polacken* ["Polish people"] home, who flooded our towns and took away our jobs."

Erika and I glanced at each other. Whenever Mutter launched into her tirade about "*die Polacken*", it took my fun out of ironing.

"Why? They needed to live just like we do," I said.

"What do you know about that? You don't know anything."

I slammed the iron on its end and unplugged it. I knew of the prejudice against the Poles in the mining towns and couldn't understand it. Why weren't other people permitted to come into our country and work? And why was I always told I didn't know anything? Did a fun time always have to end up like this? I never heard her talk that way to Erika. Did she not like me? That thought had occurred to me often, but each time I pushed that feeling way down.

I caught Mutter's angry glare. "You're not finished."

"I'll pack things away." I carried the linens, napkins and towels into the parents' bedroom and stacked them in the designated order on the shelves.

CHAPTER 4

Christmas Eve morning was bitter cold. The wind drove the dry snow so hard against my face it hurt, but it didn't bother me. Today was Christmas. In the village the stores sparkled with lights and decorations as Mutter and I got the last few items she had carefully saved on our ration cards. We even found beeswax candles and one orange for each of us.

This year Erika and I were permitted to help Mutter fill the Christmas plates with sweets. Each person's fluted plate stood in front of us on the table.

Mutter opened frantically every kitchen cabinet. "What did I do...? Where did I put the chocolate?"

Erika laughed. "Mama, not again! You mean we might find some for Easter?"

We opened the larger of the two tins we had filled the week before with home-made cookies.

"Make sure, you two, to count the same amount into each plate. And, Margot, don't let me catch you snatching *Pfeffernüsse* or something. You'll have to wait till tonight." That didn't bother me, I could wait.

When Papa and Josef came home from work, Josef sniffed the air. "Hmm, smells like Christmas."

Hilde and Josef helped Papa set up and decorate the tall spruce he was able to get from a customer. They clipped candleholders to the end of the branches. Papa checked them out, one by one, stepping back occasionally. Gently Hilde unwrapped shiny silver balls and stars and hung them into the tree. Josef added the final touch by draping long tinsel over the tip of each branch. At the end he placed a bucket of water behind the tree—just in case.

With everything accomplished, empty boxes removed, heaped Christmas plates waiting in the kitchen, a last vacuuming done, we all withdrew for a much-needed rest. Mutter was exhausted and irritable, as usual before holidays. Erika and I got permission to stay quietly in the little room in front of our parents bedroom, the only warm room of the house, where Josef had filled to the brim the cone shaped coal scuttle for the pot bellied stove. Soon the warmth and excitement of the day took its toll. On the couch with the soft oriental throw and lots of pillows I fell asleep.

Erika shook my hand. "Margot, wake up. We've to change."

Christmas Eve! Finally. In our ice-cold bedroom we washed and changed in a hurry. I selected a red knit wool dress with white wool stockings.

Back in the warm little room, behind the black shade I peeked out the window, screening out the reflection with my cupped hands. Snow filled the air, came down heavily, silently.

Oma opened her door across the hall and poked her head out. "How are you two doing?"

"Oma, come and wait with us."

A smile lit up her wrinkled face. She smoothed her brown wool dress over her round figure and hurried over. Her thin gray hair was neatly tucked into a tiny bun at the nape. I felt vaguely guilty for not visiting with Oma more often and was therefore uncomfortable around her. She lived in the front room on the second floor; we passed her door many times every day and yet she was not part of our lives. Vater had insisted that Mutter invite Oma for Sunday noon dinners, but outside of that reluctant routine, we had little contact with her. And each time I did talk with Oma, Mutter called me down under some pretext.

The door to the living room downstairs opened. "*Klingelingeling*," the silver bell rang. "*Klingelingeling.*" The butterflies in my stomach woke up, my heart pounded. "Oma, come on, let's go down." We helped her up, but she rushed back to her room. While Erika and I flew down the steps, I saw her follow with an armful of presents.

At the door I stopped. In the dark living room, warmed for the special occasion by a small black stove, the silvery Christmas tree glowed and sparkled in the warm light of the candles. Presents covered everything, the table, the desk, the armchair in front of the desk, the sofa. Something caught my eye.

"*Meine Post!*" ["my post office"] On the floor beside the desk chair I discovered the post office, the main item on my wish list. "Erika, look, I got the post office!" I inspected the sturdy tabletop set with slots for mail, for envelopes and for forms. It came complete with stamps, different color inkpads, letters and envelopes. On the chair beside it, I found more: a light brown leather attaché case for high school, two books— *Heidi* and *Julchen* and a navy training suit. Draped over the armchair was a lovely striped wool sweater.

How much I got. A warm glow spread through me. Mama and Papa fulfilled my biggest wish on the list that Erika and I had left on the kitchen table weeks ago.

Erika's globe, her first wish, stood on the table surrounded by books and clothing. Amid laughter we admired each others gifts, especially Mutter's potato peeler.

Erika tugged at my dress and motioned upstairs. We ran to our room to bring down the little presents we had acquired over weeks of secret shopping trips. Oma added her armful, so did Hilde and Josef.

"Oh, look what I got." I laid out all items for the others

to see and experienced the joy all over again. After we thoroughly exhausted all the oh's and ah's we shook hands and kissed warm cheeks.

Papa picked up his Bible and cleared his throat. We quieted down. Tall and straight, he looked impressive in his immaculate white shirt and heavy silk tie that complemented his charcoal wool suit. He flipped the worn book open to a marker and looked at us. "Let's not forget the most important gift to us, the birth of the Christ Child."

Listening to his raspy voice, I saw in front of my closed eyes the bright light from heaven shine on the small group of shepherds, saw them at the stable staring at the baby in the manger.

Hilde and Josef tuned their guitars. "*Stille Nacht, Heilige Nacht.*" My favorite carol. I squinted into the candles to keep from crying, yet soon tears rolled down my face. We sang one carol after another. Between the singing I munched cookies and pralines from the plate in my lap.

Papa watched the burning candles. "Josef, blow them out, they are getting low. I'll check the road." Coming back in, he stomped the snow off his shoes. "We can't drive, too much snow. Get ready, we need to leave soon."

All bundled up I braved the icy night with the others, trying to follow in Vater's large footsteps. The dry snow crunched under my feet. I took Hilde's hand. "Remember?"

Inside her shawl she nodded. Just like our arrival last March in Winkl. It was only months ago but it seemed like years. How I missed the mountains and the freedom I experienced for the first time in my life.

Barely visible in the grayness of the snow, others walked in the same direction. The bells of St. Cecilia rang out over the sleepy village. Muffled by snow, their deep sound called the faithful to worship.

Stomping and shaking snow from hats and shoes, people shuffled into the hushed church. Tall spruce trees surrounded the high altar and the life-sized nativity scene to the right of the altar. In our crowded pew I stood on my toes and craned my neck to see it.

"Let's have a closer look at it tomorrow, all right?" Hilde whispered. I nodded and squeezed her hand. She always knew what I wanted.

The organ started with all its might as the procession of altar boys and three clergy, in festive gold brocade vestments, moved up the aisle through the packed church. The most beloved service of the year, Christmas Midnight Mass, began. By sermon time my eyes would not stay open.

Erika kicked my foot. "Wake up! It's going to be your fault if we won't have another evening celebration."

"I'm tired."

I caught Mutter's sharp look from between her furry collar and black felt hat and sat up straight.

With Christmas anthems sung by the choir and more carols, the High Mass and the immediately following two quiet masses were over. Outside the driving snow was piling up against trees and doorways. With each step I sank into the fluffy coldness as we strung out across the street and stomped home through the night. "Silent Night, Holy Night," echoed through my mind, deepening my warm, happy feeling. Sensing more than seeing the dancing and whirling snow in the darkness, I wished the street lights were lit to illuminate the winter picture.

We rounded the corner and walked into the *Marbacher Strasse* before I saw the group in the middle of the road, blocking our way. Hilde beside me drew in a sharp breath. For an instant Papa hesitated.

"Erika, Margot," he called to us on the outside of our line, "move up on the sidewalk." With a shock I recognized the round caps and swastika armbands.

Hilde grabbed my hand. My heart raced. The picture of the *SA* at the train station beating up Willi's friend in front of his new wife flashed through my mind. My mouth went dry, my fingers and toes tingled. Papa herded us on the sidewalk away from the group. We were almost past when, in the thick silence, the mocking voice of our neighbor called out, "*Heil Hitler*, Herr Füsser."

I bit my lip. Would Papa answer? He got us safely by them before he turned around and tipped his hat. "*Guten Abend, Herr Leimbke. Und Frohe Weihnachten.*"

There was no answer.

The five minute walk to our house seemed like an eternity. I shivered. Why? Why now?

The front door closed behind us. We were safely inside. The Christmas smell of spruce needles, spices and cookies and the warmth of the house greeted us. Nobody spoke. Finally I couldn't stand the silence any longer.

"Papa, why were they there? What did they want?"

Mama shrugged. "How should we know. Don't ask so many questions. You can have a cup of tea, then up to bed."

Shortly after the Christmas holidays, Willi Alferding visited us again for a few days. His uniform called me back to reality. Yes, there was a war going on.

In the evening we all sat together in the living room as he talked about battles in Lyon and Nancy in France. I listened spellbound, sitting behind the table covered with wine glasses and ash trays. The gold embroidered, black table-cloth with long, golden fringes held a special fascination for me. I could listen to the adults for hours, while braiding the soft fringes. I watched Willi. Yes, I would marry him if Hilde would not. When he related the plight of the French civilians under the *SS* and *Gestapo*, Vater sent me to the kitchen to empty and clean the ashtrays. Behind his back I threw him an angry look, stomped into the kitchen, dumped the ashes and returned in a moment. I hated to be treated like a baby.

The next evening we again sat in the living room. Papa gently lifted his light brown evening cigar out of its wooden box, removed the gold band, carefully clipped the bottom part, wet the mouthpiece, tried it for fit and lit it with a match. Little puffs of sweet, aromatic smoke trailed from his lips. I liked this ritual, knowing that Papa was now in a gentle, relaxed mood. I braided the gold fringes and listened to the adult's talk when Mutter left the room. Moments later we heard her scream. Vater, Hilde and Willi ran out and found her, almost unconscious, in the bathroom in a pool of blood. With no ambulances available for civilian use, Vater and Willi managed to get her into the Olympia and rushed her to a hospital in the city. Hilde stayed with us.

The following day Vater told us that Mutter was very sick and needed a difficult operation. At one point he talked about a hysterectomy, but did not explain it. I did not ask.

The next week Hilde took us to visit Mutter. Her eyes looked deep and dark, her skin almost yellow. I stood beside her bed and didn't know what to say. With the swishing sound of her voluminous habit a nun served Mutter's dinner in large silver containers and disappeared. Mutter gave us a tired smile and closed her eyes. Hilde placed the thermos with a thick, delicious soup, (I knew, I licked out the pot), that Vater asked her to cook for Mutter on the night table. Vater motioned us to leave.

Outside I breathed deeply and shook off the gloom of the silent, long halls and smelly air. We beleaguered Hilde with questions. "What's wrong with Mutter? How long will she be there? What if we have an air raid? Will they take her to a shelter?"

"All right, all right, take it easy," Hilde stemmed the flood. "I'll tell you what I know. Mutter had a difficult oper-ation, a hysterectomy. She lost a lot of blood, but no blood is available. It all goes to the field hospitals. The doctor told

Vater her recuperation will be slow, may take six to eight weeks. Can they move her in case of an air attack? Not right now, maybe in a week or so. That's why Vater stays with her."

"Hilde, what's a hysterectomy?" I wanted to know. She looked at me embarrassed. "Margot, I don't know. Nobody told me, and I don't like to ask Vater." I was surprised but I understood.

It was getting dark and bitter cold. Finally the streetcar screeched around the corner. We three huddled close in the almost empty, rattling car. For six to eight weeks Hilde would again be in charge of us.

At home, while she made us a quick pancake for supper and I rubbed my frozen feet until they tingled, Erika asked Hilde, "Can you stay with us that long? What about your work?"

Hilde shrugged, sliding the large pancake onto a dinner plate. "Of course it interferes with my apprenticeship again. Last time when I took you to Bavaria I had just gotten ready for the exam. I had to repeat the preparations all over again. And this time?" She shrugged. "I don't know how long this will take. But somebody has to be here with you two." She smiled at us. "We had fun, didn't we? Let's try to have fun again, all right?"

It did not turn out to be fun. When Mutter finally lay in her upstairs bedroom, greatly weakened, the full burden of nursing her back to health fell on Hilde.

After Mutter's arrival, to let her rest, we sat down in the kitchen to a plate of pea soup. During prayer Mutter pounded the floor with Vater's hiking stick, her means to summon us, especially Hilde. Vater motioned to Hilde to go up. We ate. By the time Hilde, her face unhappy, came down again with Mutter's soup untouched, we were finished and

Hilde's soup was cold. Erika offered to heat it up. Hilde slumped into her chair. "No, no, that's all right. I don't mind." I turned on the radio. Vater clicked it off. "It disturbs Mutter." The stick pounded again. Hilde jumped up and ran upstairs. Vater followed her.

Erika looked after Vater. "This is going to be a heck of a circus."

The stick gave Mutter a twenty-four hour command. "Hilde, when are you going to cook?" "Hilde, I need some water." "Hilde, I can't eat this soup."

After many weeks, with longer days and warmer temperatures, Mutter recuperated.

In the spring of 1941, the war grew in dimensions and intensity. British planes attacked the *Ruhr* district and the *Rheinland* almost every night. Erika came running into the kitchen, flipped on the radio. *A Sondermeldung* ["news bulletin"]. The announcer talked about a sea battle in the Mediterranean, in which the British fleet suffered tremendous losses. No casualties for us. We listened intently.

Hilde shook her head. "Isn't it interesting that only the enemy loses, and we don't?"

Her remark surprised me. I always took things at face value, believed what we were told. "You think they're lying? Surely somebody would know?" How could they get away with it, since lying, at least at home, was a cardinal sin?

"Nobody would dare to contradict the High Command." Hilde answered. "Besides, they don't care. They'll tell us what they want us to believe."

On the *Ostfront*, Yugoslavia surrendered when Belgrad fell into German hands. The Greek army capitulated, British forces withdrew from Greece and the German army invaded Crete. West Europe, occupied by the *Wehrmacht*, ["army"] was quiet.

"I'm so glad Willi is in the West," Hilde commented after the news of one of the fierce battles in Greece.

A few days after my eleventh birthday in June of 1941, the radio brought another *Sondermeldung*. "*Das Ober-kommando der Wehrmacht* ["The German High Command"] —OKW announces: Today German troops invaded Russia." Speechless, we stared at each other.

Papa buried his face in his hands. "*Um Himmels willen, das ist unser Ende*" ["for heavens sake, that's the end of us"]. We can never win against Russia." After a long silence he mumbled, "Hitler has gone mad." Mutter stared at the floor without a word.

Shortly afterwards Hilde got a phone call from Willi. His unit was shipped to the *Ostfront*. He had a few days furlough, but could not come to Düsseldorf. Could she meet him for one or two days in Wiesbaden.

"I knew this would happen," Hilde moaned. "I can go, Papa, can't I? Willi mentioned his parents would come too."

We had gathered in the living room. As usual I sat behind the table. I braided furiously the soft golden fringes, not daring to look up. Vater would never permit Hilde to go. With her nineteen years she had great responsibilities, but no freedom and no life of her own. I connected their unrelenting strictness with a remark Mutter made to me a long time ago. "I don't want any one of you girls to turn out like *Tante* ["aunt"] Gerda." She glared at me. "You know what I mean. And Hilde reminds me of her." It was murmured that Gerda, a relative, had a child out of wedlock, an insult to the family name that Mutter neither forgot nor forgave.

Vater turned to Mutter. "What do you think, Trude?"

"I guess, with his parents there it would be all right. You could call tomorrow from the shop and talk to them."

Papa agreed. I breathed again and opened the golden braids done to perfection.

The *Wehrmacht* made spectacular progress on the

Ostfront in 1941. Day after day *Sondermeldungen* talked of Russian cities falling under the pressure of the *Wehrmacht*. When Kiev fell, the jubilant headlines cried: To Moscow! The German troops seemed invincible. It seemed everything Hitler undertook, every campaign, was successful.

That fall I started high school. Our lyceum and the boys' gymnasium occupied the left wing of the *Benrather Schloss* ["Castle of Benrath"]. The two wings of the stately baroque castle extended in a half circle around the large castle pond. The *Schloss*, an ornate pink stucco building with tall windows and white shutters, overlooked the spacious sweep of steps and cobblestone driveways.

Hilde and I had toured the castle. With a group of visitors we stepped into large felt slippers at the door, to protect the beautiful parquet floors, and followed the guide through rooms and halls of elaborate stucco work in gold and pastel. Glittering chandeliers and sparkling candle holders along the walls contrasted with heavy tapestry and deep blue and red velvet draped over the tall windows.

On my first day in Sexta, I realized to my great joy that my classroom faced the pond. I claimed the desk beside the window. Some of my new subjects I liked, like Biology, History, German, Physical Education, Art and Art History. Others like Physics, Chemistry, English and Math I knew I had to work for. In addition we had to change our penmanship from the Germanic *Sütterling* to the Latin cursive used for foreign languages.

After only a few weeks we heard rumors that our school would be evacuated to the Black Forest because of the increased air raids. One morning Fraulein Dr. Schulte, our homeroom teacher, handed out permission forms for relocation. They were to be signed by the parents. I took mine home with trepidation. Would Vater let me go?

"Absolutely not!" he answered in the evening. "You stay here."

"But I have to go. Everybody else is going."

"That does not matter. You stay here."

I was crushed. It would not help to ask again or beg him. It would only increase his determination.

On the day my classmates left for *Herrenalb* in the Black Forest in a whirlwind of excitement, I ran home and worked in the back yard. I kneeled on the ground and dug and tore at the weeds, feeling sorry for myself, angry and upset with Vater for being so unreasonable. The damp soil yielded to my relentless hacking. Slowly my anger disappeared. Maybe Vater knew what he was doing, maybe he was right, even if I did not see it.

Finished with my task I sat back, inspected my work. The patch looked clean and neatly raked, the soil dark and moist.

The next morning those of us still at home, all of them stayed home for medical reasons except me, met in one classroom. I was the only one from my class. The one available teacher gave us homework assignments for the next day and dismissed us.

In the next weeks I asked some of the mothers of classmates what they heard from *Herrenalb*. "They all love it. They are staying in a converted hostel. It's absolutely beautiful." Soon I stopped asking.

Then came the first news that some children were ill. Two days later it was officially confirmed. Scarlet fever had broken out in the camp. Many students were placed in quarantine in hospitals, the rest sent home. It took a while before regular schooling was possible again.

English, one of the subjects I had dreaded most, turned out to be fun because of the teacher, Fraulein Hennig. She was petite, young and lively, not as stodgy and boring as most of the other teachers. In pleasant weather she permitted us to move with books and paper to the steps behind the castle to learn "London Bridge is falling down" and "Poor Clementine". Laughing and pushing, we raced for the best place in the sun. In front of us stretched the Mirror Lake, long and narrow, reflecting majestic chestnut trees.

The air attacks at night continued. There was hardly a night we slept through. Especially hard hit was the old city of Köln, some 30 km south of us. Yet BAYER in Leverkusen and many of the surrounding chemical companies survived.

One evening Mutter pushed an official looking envelope over the table to Hilde. "Here. For you." The envelope was opened, even though it was addressed to Hilde. I had often seen Mutter opening Hilde's mail. It upset me and increased my feeling that Mutter did not respect our privacy and did not trust us. Hilde scanned the letter.

"I'm drafted into the *Reichsarbeitsdienst*—RAD ["National Work Service"]." She almost sounded happy.

"What's that? You mean you are leaving us?" I had heard of RAD before, but not paid much attention to it.

Hilde explained, "Women are drafted to replace the men on the fronts. Usually the women work on farms or in ammunition factories."

"You have to work in a factory?" I could neither picture her with grease and dirt nor cleaning out stables.

"I don't know."

Mutter's only comment was, "We'll discuss this tonight with Vater."

After Erika and I went to bed we heard angry shouting and the slamming of doors. "Erika, what's going on?" I sat up, too upset to sleep.

"I'm sure they don't like her to go. They don't like her to do anything but work. I hope she goes and has a good time."

"You want Hilde to go?"

"No, I don't want her to be gone, but she needs to get away. Maybe then they'll appreciate her. If she's drafted, there isn't much they can do anyhow. Of course, Mutter with four children could ask to have her deferred."

"How do you know all this?"

"Maria's family went through this with her sister."

"Did she get deferred?"

"Yes, for a while. But every girl over eighteen has to serve sooner or later."

The next day Mutter snapped at me every time I said something. Finally, I stayed in my room as much as possible. When Hilde came from work Mutter ordered her around like a child. Helping Hilde set the table, I nudged her. "What's the matter?"

She shrugged. "Go upstairs, I'll come up in a moment."

I went to my room. Soon she came in and sat beside me on the bed. "Why're they so angry?"

"They found out I volunteered."

I stared at her in disbelief. "You volunteered? Hilde! Why?"

"Margot, I've got to get away from here. I simply have to. I can't stay here any longer. And I didn't see any other way."

I shook my head, a sinking feeling in my stomach. Somehow it didn't make sense.

"I'm sorry, *Stöppchen*. Some day you'll understand."

Mutter's angry voice could be heard from downstairs. "Hilde, where are you? Come down immediately!"

Hilde sighed. "Will be hell 'til I'm gone."

"When's that?"

"In ten days." She ran down the two flights just as Mutter yelled for her again.

I was glad Hilde was gone all day. The evenings were difficult enough. I got a lot of weeding done. What would life be without her? I couldn't imagine.

One evening Erika and I talked for a long time. I needed reassurance. "I don't know how it will be without Hilde. Do you?"

Erika laughed angrily. "Don't worry, we'll live. You'll survive too. She needs to get away. Don't you make it more difficult for her."

Erika was right. I was unhappy for selfish reasons. If it was best for her to go, I didn't want to create more problems. "But I'll miss her." Suddenly I let go, the floodgates opened. I quickly crawled under the blanket, pulled it over my head so Erika would not hear my sobbing.

After a while she nudged me to move over and got into bed with me. She waited a moment. "Feeling better?"

I nodded, not trusting my voice. Her warmth and closeness melted the knot in my stomach. Just as we dozed off the sirens started.

"Darn sirens, darn planes, darn war, darn everything." Erika stomped out of bed, flung her clothes from the chair to the floor and picked them up again to get dressed. I almost laughed at her outburst. I envied her ability to be so outgoing, to deal with her emotions so much better than I did. I took my time to wash my face before going downstairs.

The dreaded day came. Before noon Vater, Erika and I took Hilde by streetcar to the *Hauptbahnhof* ["Central railroad station"]. Predictably, Mutter stayed in bed. The farewell had been icy. Mutter mumbled something about ungratefulness.

The entrance hall of the *Hauptbahnhof* was jammed. Vater pushed ahead of us, around people and luggage. On the announcement board he searched for the track number to Erfurt. Hilde found the number, pointed it out and on we marched, down the steps, underneath the tracks to the surface of the huge sooty train hall, Vater not turning around once to check on us. Hilde carried only a small suitcase, since she would wear uniform.

"I wonder how you'll look in uniform?" I grinned at her. "You also have to salute? To march?"

"Of course. All that we learn in boot camp. That's what boot camp is for."

Vater paced up and down the platform, up and down. Erika's gaze followed him. "I wish he would relax. He makes me nervous."

"He will once I'm gone. He is just furious that I volunteered. He doesn't understand that I have to go. He doesn't appreciate that twice I have been deferred because of Mutter's need for help. They think I'm showing disrespect and ungratefulness."

Erika kicked a pebble onto the tracks. "Ungratefulness for what? For all the work you had the privilege to do?"

Hilde shrugged. "Now you two have to be the helpers at home. You are old enough for that."

I happened to turn around. "Oh look, that train looks strange." I pointed to a freight train going by slowly on the very outside track of the platform. The freight cars were all boarded up.

"Put your hand down, don't point." Hilde spoke sharply.

"What is it? Those boxes are full of people."

"Margot, keep your mouth shut. Don't say a word." Hilde pushed the words through clenched teeth.

Car after car rolled by. The people in the freight boxes pressed their eyes to the slits to look out. Could they be prisoners of war? By the time the long train passed through, everybody stared at it.

Behind me a man's voice said, "Filthy Jews, they get what they've coming to them." I turned around and looked into the hard face of an *SS* officer.

Jews? To where?

The crackling of a loudspeaker interrupted my thoughts.

"*Fernzug* ["long distance train"] to Nümberg over Köln, Darmstadt, Erfurt, Weimar on track four is approaching. Please step back." The streamlined train raced in. Holding onto my skirt I stepped way back. Brakes screamed. When the train stopped we looked for the car marked "Erfurt".

"Here. Erfurt. Come on, come on." Vater impatiently waved his arm.

"What does he think we are doing?" Erika mumbled. Hilde just laughed. She sounded already freer than I had heard her in a long time. I was glad for her.

"Good-bye Vater." She kissed his cheek. He moved quickly away. "Bye, Erika. Bye, *Stöppchen*." For a moment she held me close. "Answer my letters, will you?"

I smiled at her through tears. "Of course."

"Hurry up, hurry up." Vater shoved her suitcase into the open train door as the stationmaster raised the signal.

Hilde climbed in, closed the door. She stayed at the window, smiling. "Take care, let me know what's going on."

"Everybody step back, the train is leaving." Two sharp whistle blows, the train glided smoothly and quietly out of the hall. Erika and I waved as long as we could see Hilde.

"Let's go!" Vater had enough.

Hurrying to keep up with him I thought of the people jammed into the boarded up boxcars. Did they have enough air? What a contrast to the elegant, shiny and sleek train Hilde left in.

I fought to keep my tears in check. The lump in my throat hurt. Hilde was gone. I felt alone, all alone. Don't think about it, not now, not here, I told myself. I stuffed my desperation down.

WINTER, 1941-42

CHAPTER 5

During the Fall of 1941 Hitler unfolded his vision for Germany. He saw a pure, strong Aryan race, the 'thousand-year nation', as the leader of Europe. This was the first time we heard the theme of the thousand-year nation.

Another theme we heard more and more: the lashing out against Jews. Daily they were lambasted in the news, in the paper. The 'Capitalist Jew' was blamed for everything that went wrong. They were folk enemy number one.

One Saturday morning my parents and I took the street car to Düsseldorf. Our faithful old Olympia stood on blocks in the garage for lack of gasoline for civilian use. We were walking down *Schadov Strasse* when the showcase for the *SS* newspaper *'Der Stürmer'* ["The Storm Trooper"] along the shopping windows caught my attention because of the cluster of people around it. My parents continued window shopping. Never having seen the paper before, I was at first fascinated by the clever and expressive caricatures until I realized they were all directed against the Jews. I was aghast at the ugly and insulting pictures and captions.

Suddenly Vater yanked me away by the wrist and pulled me into a store entrance, his face red with anger. "Don't you ever look at that paper again!" He forced his words through clenched teeth into my face so close that I could smell his cigar breath. "Do you understand?"

Mutter glanced around nervously. "Josef, be quiet! Not here in the middle of the street."

Vater still held my wrist. "Do you understand me?" Stiff with fear I nodded. What if somebody watched us? He let go of me. "Just remember!"

I felt as if I had been slapped across the face. No, I did not want to see those filthy and nasty pictures again.

Winter started early in 1941. Already in October the temperature hovered around freezing. Again Vater decided to heat the little living room on the second floor in order to warm the whole house. Oma, on the same level, had her own stove. Vater made sure she had enough coal.

Oma still joined us for our Sunday noon dinners, otherwise I saw her seldom. School and Catholic youth group activities kept me busy. Also Mutter's increasing dislike of Oma made me feel uncomfortable talking with her.

As the temperatures dropped, the frosted windows in school were tightly shut and I could not, to my great dismay, watch the ducks and geese on the pond anymore. Their swimming hole needed to be chipped open daily. Soon the *Schlossweiher* and the other ponds in the park had a thick layer of ice.

Mother gave me permission to use Hilde's cherished possession, her brand new ice skates. The shiny white leather boots were without a scratch. "Just make sure you don't lose your own shoes," Mutter called after me when I ran upstairs to try them on. I promised myself to be very careful with Hilde's treasure.

A few days later we watched as the police removed the sign "*Betreten des Eises verboten*" ["do not step on the ice"]. With jubilant shouts we streamed down the banks onto the slippery surface. In some places the ice was smooth, in others it was rough with leaves and twigs frozen into it. I ran home to get Hilde's skates.

As I entered the front door *Sondermeldung* music

stopped me. "The first German troops reached the outskirts of Moscow." Moscow! I envisioned windswept tundra, covered with a thick blanket of snow.

That evening I skated until late, oblivious to hunger, time or to my numb feet. Finally I realized that only a few young people, mostly from our youth group, still whirled around. I asked Jürgen, one of the boys of that group, "What time is it? I'm sure I have to go home."

"It's 8:30. If you have to go home, I'll go with you."

"Thank you." It was an unwritten rule of our groups that girls had to be accompanied home by whoever was available. Jürgen walked me to our street. We shook hands, I limped home, my feet still hurting.

"It's about time you decide to come home. You know how late it is?"

I expected Mutter to be upset, so I endured her scrutinizing looks. I took the lid off the pot. "Anything to eat?"

"Get cleaned up first. There's still some pudding soup for you."

Erika looked up from her book. "How was it?"

"Fun. Lots of people. Jürgen Freiholt brought me home."

Mutter stopped filling my plate and looked sharply at me. "Who's he?"

Erika answered for me. "He's a nice boy, part of *Kaplan* ["chaplain"] Kroll's group."

"And two classes higher at the Gymnasium," I filled in.

"Isn't his father a dentist?" Erika's question had a humorous undertone. We both knew Mutter's reaction to this.

"So, he is the son of a dentist. Well, well, isn't that nice." Mutter practically beamed.

I got my plate of soup, a bit thin by now, but sweet and hot. My feet started to tingle and itch. I remembered Hilde's advice to rub them to keep the circulation going.

I wondered how she was. Her letters sounded good, she

liked her group and her leader. I realized that the ache and emptiness of her leaving had become less painful. Maybe Erika was right, maybe I would survive.

A few weeks later we were told the schools did not have enough coal, that our schooling was reduced to two hours every morning to get our assignments for the following day. Now the afternoons and evenings were filled with ice-skating. With continued low temperatures some of our group even scraped and flooded the ice to smooth it out. By now my curfew on skating nights was nine o'clock, to which I strictly adhered. Usually Jürgen accompanied me home. I liked him, he was comfortable to be with. I could be myself.

"Any mail today?" I asked Mutter as I came home from school one day. I was waiting for news from Hilde.

"A letter for us from Willi Alferding's parents." Mutter looked preoccupied. She pointed to an opened envelope on the table.

"Why do they write to us? What are they saying?" I glanced at Mutter. "Something wrong?" She kept peeling potatoes. "Mutter, what did they write about?" Fear tingled through my body. I had the horrible feeling I did not want to know the answer. "It's about Willi, isn't it?"

She nodded slowly. "He was killed in the battle of Kiev. His parents didn't know how to reach Hilde. They want us to tell her."

Willi was dead. Poor Hilde. I walked upstairs, stared out of the window into the back yards. They looked empty, gray, lifeless, frozen in time and place. Dead. Newspaper pictures flashed through my mind: wind whipped, endless snow, dark figures, some laying half buried in the snow, some staggering around, soldiers on the *Ostfront*. Was that where he was? Lying somewhere deep under the snow? How will she take it? They had hoped to get married as soon as the war was over. She was only nineteen, he twenty-four. The blue eyes, the smiling face. Gone.

"Margot, I need your help." I pulled myself away from the window, burying the deep ache.

"Here. I need this ground up." Carefully Mutter poured a measured cup of wheat kernels into the old-fashioned coffee grinder that Vater had fastened into the door of a kitchen cabinet. Through connections he had brought home in the previous year a sack of whole-wheat kernels which, crushed and cooked into soup, supplemented our meager rations. But only with the weight of my whole body could I manage to move the handles of that grinder.

Later that afternoon I turned on the radio. *Sondermeldung.* We stopped everything. "The High Command of the Army announces: This morning Japanese aircraft attacked the American fleet in Pearl Harbor."

"The American fleet?" I thought I hadn't heard right. "They're not at war with Japan."

"They are now." Erika shook her head. "When will all of this end?"

In the evening Vater read Alferding's letter without a word. Later I saw him at his desk writing. I did not feel like ice-skating that night.

Erika and I were just in bed when the sirens went off. Mechanically we dressed again, went downstairs.

In the basement Mutter seemed to continue an ongoing conversation. "What's going to happen next?"

Vater was not only gloomy, he was angry. "By now the whole world is in this war. We cannot win it. And who got us into it?"

"You know what's going to happen next," Mutter repeated, glancing at Josef, who sat across from me on his bed, hunched over, listening.

"I know, I know. Josef will be drafted. I will not be able to defer him any longer." Vater's voice was hoarse with pain.

"But they can't draft him. He's only seventeen."

"Oh yes, they can, Mutter." Josef, who seldom spoke, got up and tossed his hair out of his face. "Classmates of mine have already been drafted. I think if they do their duty, I have to fulfill mine too and not hide at home."

"Just a minute!" Vater's fist came crashing down on the table top. "Don't you talk about hiding, about not doing your duty. Your duty is to work where you are needed, and that's in the shop. I have very few men left. Why don't they draft those…," he searched for a choice word but left it unsaid, "…those in their fancy uniforms like Leimbke here beside us. The *Braune Haus* ["local head quarters of the Nazi Partei"] is full of them. Why aren't they on a front? You will stay here and do your duty as long as that is possible." Vater stomped out, slammed the heavy door behind him, leaving a thick silence with us.

I lay on my bunk bed with my little red suitcase, listening, tears dripping slowly into my hair. Why didn't anybody talk about Willi, or at least mention his name? It had to be on their mind. But as usual nobody talked about their underlying feelings.

The next day brought the official declaration of war by the United States and England on Japan. A few days later Germany and Italy declared war on the United States.

Newspaper headlines branded America and England as the aggressors, as warmongers and capitalists. People in food lines and over neighborhood fences avoided looking at each other, were silent.

"Wear something over your head, it's bitter cold outside." I was on my way to school to turn in homework a few

days later. Mutter produced a wool scarf. "Here, use this."
"Oh, Mutter!"

"Go and see for yourself how cold it is." I opened the front door and stepped into the loose snow whipped against the door. The sharp air cut like razors into my face, the hair in my nose froze instantly. Reason prevailed, I bundled up. Close to school I caught up with Leonie, a friend from my youth group.

She moved the wool scarf from her mouth. "Heard anything from Hilde?" Her breath came out in little puffs. Leonie had been very disappointed when Hilde left for her duty in the RAD and would not be with us on our group evenings anymore.

"Uh huh. She'll be home for Christmas. Can't wait." I didn't dare to tell her about Willi. I didn't want to cry.

In the classroom we sat in coats, mittens and scarves, but they did not keep the chill from seeping into every bone of my body. "I need your attention." Fraulein Dr. Schulte, our homeroom teacher, waited for silence. "Dr. Göbbels has called on all students to collect warm clothing and blankets for our brave soldiers on the *Ostfront*. You have heard how bitter cold it is in Russia. We all need to sacrifice. Go to relatives, friends and neighbors and ask for anything they can give. Saturday morning, instead of homework, bring these items to school. I expect each of you to have your arms full."

At home Mutter was sweeping the kitchen. "Mutter, we have to bring clothing to school on Saturday."

She continued to work. "*Ja*, I heard. Göbbels told the whole nation to start a *Winterhilfe*. He sure is busy these days as Minister for Propaganda. He also wants us to have an *Eintopf-Sonntag* ["one-dish Sunday"] once a month and give the savings to the *Braune Haus*."

"A one-dish meal on a Sunday?"

"As if we had any choice. We hardly get any meat as it

is." On Sunday noon we had *Wirsing*, a cabbage type green vegetable, mixed with potatoes, without meat. A jar for the *Pfennige* ["pennies"] ended up in the corner of the cabinet.

Josef came into the kitchen. In spite of the turned up collar of his long and heavy winter coat, his face and ears were red. He rubbed his hands. "Imagine, the *Rhein* is going to be solid for the first time ever. It's already covered with ice floats." He warmed his hands over the hot pot. "We were down at the yacht club. The bank on the other side seems so close."

"Don't you go on an ice float," Mutter warned him. "Just yesterday the paper talked about three boys that the police had to rescue. They walked out on the ice, the piece broke off, was pushed into the current and ran against a bridge. One of them almost drowned."

I pictured Josef in the middle of the river, sailing downstream with no way to get to him.

"Don't worry, Mutter, I'm not that dumb." He took his overcoat off. "And how is our *Nesthäckchen* ["little nest hook]?" He tousled my hair.

"*Nesthäckchen!*" I played the insulted. "I'm not a baby."

"No, but you are the youngest. What're you doing these days?" He sat down at the table, obviously waiting for an answer.

I was surprised. I couldn't remember ever having had a conversation with my brother. He floated through my life, saying little at home, spending a lot of his free time with his friends. How manly his angular face had become. "Well, I go ice-skating a lot. We don't have school because there isn't enough coal."

He shook his head, his light amber eyes twinkled, amused. "I wish I had it that good."

"Don't you like your work?"

He looked at me for a moment and grew serious. "Yes, I like my work. But it's not always easy to work with Vater, to be the son of the boss."

"I can imagine." I remembered well how impatient Vater got whenever I was summoned to help him, to hand him tools or hold something for him.

"It seems as if I have to work twice as hard. He's a difficult taskmaster."

Mutter came back in from the basement. "What are you two talking about?"

For an instant Josef hesitated. "I just said it's not easy to be the boss' son."

"Vater wants you to learn as much as possible."

Josef took a deep breath and got up. "*Ja*, I know."

I was proud. My big brother had confided in me. "You know that Hilde is coming next week?"

He turned and smiled at me. "And you are happy?"

"Of course."

On the eagerly anticipated morning Vater, Erika and I took the streetcar to the station. The icy wind howled through the dark train hall. The loudspeaker boomed. "On track five the train from Erfurt is approaching. Please stand back." Finally! I tried to catch a glimpse of the faces behind the doors as the long, shiny train raced by. With screaming brakes it stopped at the end of the hall.

"There she is!" I spotted a waving arm and ran towards it. "Hilde! Hilde!" A young lady in RAD uniform jumped down. "Hilde, you look wonderful." After a loving embrace I walked around her and inspected her. With a beanie perched on lightly curled hair, she looked sharp and attractive. The long brown wool coat hung open and revealed a tailored brown suit over a white blouse. Brown military boots completed her outfit. But when she smiled her eyes were as gentle and loving as always.

That evening we sat together in the little living room.

The potbelly stove did its best to keep us warm. Even Oma came over. Hilde's eyes sparkled as she talked about her life in camp, about her small group of twelve young women, about her leader Ingrid, whom she liked. She did not mention Willi.

"It's unmercifully cold in Thüringen. Our barracks are heated, but at outdoor drills we stand in knee deep snow. Every morning at six I walk with Marianne, who is with me on outdoor duty, to *Schloss Wippach* ["castle Wippach, a large ranch"]. What do we do there? Clean pigpens and stables. Yes, Margot," she grinned at me, "we pitch the dung outside, hose down the stables, lay in clean straw, milk the cows and feed the animals. Whatever needs to be done, we are it. In the evening at six we walk back, dead tired. Once in a while we get a lift from soldiers driving along the road."

I saw Erika glance at Vater and Mutter, a hint of amusement in her eyes. What would they say, especially about Hilde's curly hair and lipstick? After a silence that we did not interrupt, Vater looked at Mutter, completely disconcerted. "Did you ever think Hilde would experience something like this?"

Hilde laughed, a free and uninhibited laugh. "Yes, I have changed. I had to. I've learned to express my point, to prevail and to succeed. And I'm glad." She smiled at them, challeng-ing. Mutter shook her head but said nothing.

I looked at my big sister with fascination. She had changed and I was glad. But part of her had become a stranger. That loss hit me unexpectedly.

"I hope you got the packages I sent? I hope they're helpful. Unfortunately I can only smuggle out small quan-tities of flour or sugar."

"Yes, they are helpful. But isn't it dangerous to send us food from your kitchen?"

Hilde shrugged her shoulders. "If I get caught, of course. But we have an enormous, well-stocked kitchen for the hun-

dreds of women in our camp. I know how little you have."
The next day we baked the only Christmas cookies for the upcoming Feast with the flour and sugar Hilde smuggled out. Mutter looked sadly at them and apologized. "There just isn't much available."

Christmas Eve 1941, Erika and I waited upstairs in the warm room for the bell. We had wondered what Christmas would be like without a tree, when Vater managed the day before to get a four-foot, spindly spruce. It wasn't much, but we had a Christmas tree.

Vater had told us, "In the depression, some fifteen years ago, we didn't have a tree one year. But for Hilde and Josef's sake, they were both very small, I drilled holes into a broom stick and stuck some evergreen branches in. It didn't look like much, but it was green and we could put some candles on the branches."

We had decided that it would be Christmas even without a tree, that the tree was not the most important part. But I was not prepared for what we saw or didn't see when the bell called us down.

In the glow of the sparsely lit tree I saw that things on the living room table were covered with a cloth. I looked around. No presents visible anywhere. Only something on the table and that was covered! I glanced at Hilde. She had a funny smile on her face.

"I thought," Vater began after clearing his throat, "I thought you're old enough to understand that the Christmas spirit does not depend on presents but on the real reason for the celebration. Therefore let us first sing some carols, I'll read today's gospel and then we can have a look at the presents."

I sat down, very disappointed and very dismayed. What a stupid idea!

Hilde and Josef tuned their guitars. As usual Hilde started with, "*Stille Nacht, Heilige Nacht.*" I tried to figure out what could possibly be under the cover, to make out a shape, but I couldn't. Vater read the well-known story. Even the account of the angels singing, "Glory to God in the Highest," could not overcome my sad feelings. After a few more carols, Vater suggested cheerfully, "Now let's take off the covers." I stayed seated. How could he do this?

"Margot, come, look for your place," Hilde encouraged me. Erika kicked my foot with a motion, "Don't make a fuss, get up." I did. I recognized my corner by the book that headed my wish list. *"Deutsche Balladen,"* the Best German Poems and Ballads. In school we had started reading them, the beautiful poems intrigued me.

From Hilde I got three lovely, embroidered hand-kerchiefs. Mutter had made a short-sleeved blouse for me. Somehow it looked familiar. Of course, this had been her pretty blue dress. "Mutter, you cut your dress apart for a blouse for me." The tears that stuck in my throat all evening rolled down my cheeks. I was so ashamed.

She smiled at me. "You are growing fast, you need some-thing new. I didn't wear the dress that often."

The evening went by quickly. As much as I tried, I could not overcome my disappointed feeling.

A few days after Christmas, Hilde brought the conversation back to Christmas Eve. "Papa, I know why you wanted to cover the presents, but that may not be a good way to focus us on the meaning of Christmas."

"Why not, what's wrong with it?" Papa was offended. I was surprised at Hilde's courage.

Josef jumped into the breach. "I agree, it was not help-ful."

Erika helped. "We all know the meaning of Christmas anyhow. It's not the presents that count."

I added my two cents. "I wondered the whole time what might be under that tablecloth."

"All right. I thought it would bring out the meaning more, but if it is…."

"…counterproductive it's not worth it." Mutter finished the sentence for him, summing up all our feelings.

Vater admitted defeat. "Well, all right."

Hilde had one more day of furlough. Coming down for breakfast, I found her already in uniform. "Where're you going?"

"I want to visit the Harbach's on the *Ruhrtal Strasse* before I leave. Their two sons were Willi's friends. I'd like to talk with them if they are home, or with Frau Harbach."

Hilde mentioned Willi's name! Why was it people didn't talk about important things, like Willi's death? Were other families the same? I had no way to compare. How did she feel about his death? Why didn't she at least talk to me about it?

With a slice of toasted dark bread with jelly and a cup of hot peppermint tea, I curled up in the warm room with my German Ballads. The poem "*Der Taucher*" ["The Diver"] by Schiller transported me into an era of kings, nobles and brave young knights. The beauty and rhythm of the language capti-vated me as I read it over and over again. In the "*Erlkönig*" by Göthe I could feel the brooding moor, sense the panic of the boy and the fear of the father.

But the one poem I returned to again and again was "*Füsse im Feuer*", ["Feet in the Fire"] by C.F. Meyer. It talked about forgiveness, that revenge belongs to God only. The story of the father and his two terrified children, who recognize in the late night guest the tormentor and murderer of their mother, and yet took no advantage of his helpless situation, but hosted him and let him go, that picture stayed with me. How wonderful to be able to forgive like that.

"Margot, come down and set the table." Mutter's voice tore me away from my thoughts, brought me back into the present.

Mutter was spooning cabbage and potatoes on my plate when Hilde came in. She rubbed her red hands over the hot pot. "That wind goes through skin and bone." She took off her boots. "My feet are like icicles." I slipped into her boots, they almost covered my knees, and traipsed around the table. "Margot, sit down and eat. Here, Hilde." Mutter handed Hilde her plate. "How are the Harbachs?"

We prayed and Hilde ate a few bites before she answered. "Frau Harbach sends her greetings. Hermann, the oldest, is on the *Ostfront*; George is in boot camp. Frau Harbach didn't know about Willi's death, it was a real shock to her. She is worried about Hermann, who is with the Infantry ["army"] also. However, she told me some bad news about some of our old friends on the *Ruhrtal Strasse*. You all remember Anna from across the street?"

"*Ja*, of course." I had not forgotten Frau Ackermann's panic and fear. "Why?"

"Frau Ackermann was notified about a year after Anna disappeared that she died of pneumonia."

"Pneumonia?" Erika asked. "Did she really die of pneumonia?"

Hilde shook her head. "No. That's the standard expression on a form letter some families get from the Nazis about relatives that were picked up by the *Gestapo*. They all die of pneumonia. But families of political prisoners get nothing. They've no idea what happens to their people, if they're alive or dead."

Mutter sighed. "I'm sorry for Frau Ackermann, even though I didn't expect Anna to return. Did anybody know where they took her?"

Hilde shrugged. "There are some theories, but nobody knows for sure. Unfortunately, I have more bad news."

Erika groaned. "What?"

Hilde continued. "You remember the Baumann family

with their four children?"

"Sure." Mutter looked anxiously at Hilde. "They lived just down the street. He had a good position as civil servant with the Justice *Ministerium*. Why? What happened to them?"

"Herr Baumann did not agree with the Nazis, just like Vater, and must have said so. He refused to join the Partei, even though as a civil servant he does not have that choice, he has to be a member. So he lost his job. Without proof of employment, he lost the right to ration cards for his whole family. No work—no food. It's that simple. And, no money —no housing. They lost, of course, their apartment."

Mutter leaned forward. "Good heavens, what happened to them? What are they doing now?" I had stopped eating. I remembered especially Gretchen, the youngest, who was in my first communion class. "Where are they?"

Hilde leaned back and wiped her tired face. "That's the horrible part. Nobody knows where they are. Even if they're still alive. The parish, St. Vinzenz, tried to take care of them, fed them and gave them rooms in a private home. But the Nazis threatened with *Sippenhaftung* ["imprisonment of the whole clan"] anybody who helped them, branding the Baumann's as traitors."

"Oh my God!" Mutter covered her face with her hands. We sat in stunned silence. Would that happen to us?

"Hilde, what is *Sippenhaftung*?" I shook off the silence. "I haven't heard that expression before."

"It means you make the whole *Sippe* ["clan"] responsible for the action of one person in that family. It must come from some primitive tribal custom, where whole tribes are wiped out in revenge. Like so much of what they're doing is primitive, tribal warfare," she added angrily. "It's nothing new. They have practiced this all along. And clan means not only sister, brother, parents and grandparents, but also uncles, aunts, nephews and nieces." She got up, walked in stocking feet to the stove and poured a cup of tea for Mutter and herself.

Sipping the hot tea, she stared into the cup. Without lifting her eyes, she continued. "With the Baumann's it meant if a member of St. Vinzenz helped with food or housing or work, whatever, the whole family of that parish member would be carted off. Under such circumstances people think twice of helping." She scoffed, her voice tired and monotonous. "It's a very effective measure in silencing your opposition. They've made a public example of the Baumann's. Nobody even dares to ask for them or talk about them. They might be hidden somewhere, they might be dead. Who knows?"

Erika shoved her chair from the table, got up. "A whole family—simply gone. It's unbelievable what they're doing."

Mutter pointed to Erika's chair. "Sit down. We are not finished. And keep your mouth shut. There's nothing you can do."

Disgruntled, Erika slumped into her chair. Mutter looked at Hilde. "Any other bad news?"

"Yes. You remember Dr. Hartmann, the Bible scholar?"

I remembered well Katie, their little girl. "Sure. They lived below us. Why, what happened to them?" Fear rose from the pit of my stomach. I sat there like a stone. The girl, her sweet and gentle mother, where they gone too? Was everybody gone?

Hilde wiped her face again, the strain of the morning showing in her tired eyes, in the deep lines between her heavy brows. "He was hauled away by the *Gestapo* one night. For whatever reason, months later, he returned, skin and bones, not saying one word about what happened. Not one word. Now they are gone, maybe moved to where no-body knows them and nobody asks questions."

Mutter shook her head. "I knew he had been picked up. That's why I'm always so afraid that one of you two says something that will in the end kill all of us." She fixed Erika and me with a glare. "Let that be a lesson to you. If you say one wrong word we're all in for it."

I nodded, a big lump in my throat. Erika stared gloomily at her plate.

After a long silence Hilde took her empty plate and got up. "I'm sure glad you live here and not in Düsseldorf anymore."

It was on my tongue to say, "They'll find us wherever we are," but I kept my mouth shut.

The following Sunday afternoon, Hilde had returned to her unit, Papa looked up from his newspaper. "Wonder where Josef is?"

Erika had whispered to me after Children's Vesper that Josef and his friends planned to walk across the *Rhein*. Neither of us said a word.

Papa switched on the lamps in the little room and adjusted the black paper at the window. "It's getting dark so early." He slapped the newspaper with the flat of his hand. "Listen to this nonsense. 'From the coasts of Canada to South America our U-boats are on the attack!' Here: Hitler said, 'The Bolshevist Colossus may never again touch the sacred plains of Europe'. This is even better, 'While they lie, the German Wehrmacht acts'. His voice took on a sarcastic overtone, new to me. "I wish we knew what the other side is saying." He got up. "It's time for Vesper. I thought Josef would be home by now to come with me. Wonder where he is so long."

I bit my lip, trying to breathe evenly. If only nothing happened to them. I pictured Josef struggling with a huge ice float.

"Are you coming, Trude?"

"No, I'll stay here." Mutter seldom went to any other

service but Sunday morning, but he always asked her. I remembered countless Sunday afternoons when coffee had to be over by 4:30 so everybody, including guests, could go to church.

Where was Josef? I was becoming very fond of him as I got to know him a bit better. There was a solidity about him, a dependability and honesty.

Coming down the steps I heard stomping of shoes to shake off snow outside. Josef! I ran down, tore open the door. With a big grin Josef blinked in the sudden light. Behind him stood Jupp and Walter, his two closest friends.

"We were worried about you. Come in." I breathed a deep sigh of relief as they filed into the center hall.

Mutter opened the kitchen door. "Where were you so long? Vater was upset when you weren't here for Vesper."

The three laughed. "Well, you can't imagine where we were." Josef hung up his coat. "We walked to *Oberkassel*."

Mutter looked puzzled. "To the other side of the *Rhein*, across the bridge? Why?"

Josef's smile became uneasy. "No, not across the bridge. Across the ice."

Mutter stared at him. "You crossed the *Rhein* on foot? You must be out of your mind. You too?" She glared at Jupp and Walter.

Walter nodded. "We all went, Frau Füsser. There were so many people crossing the river it looked like Sunday afternoon on the *Kö* ["*Königsallee*—most fashionable street in Düsseldorf"]. Imagine!" Walter warmed up to his task of diffusing Mutter's furor. "Frau Füsser, this is a historic moment. The *Rhein* was never frozen solid as far as anybody can remember. It may never happen again. This will enter history books!" He smiled into Mutter's angry face. "Besides, there was no danger. Believe me, Frau Füsser, Josef would not have gone if there would have been the slightest danger. He's very conscientious and careful."

Mutter was outmaneuvered. She threw Josef an icy look. "We'll see what Vater says when he hears that," and slammed the kitchen door behind her.

I stuck my head into the kitchen. "I'm gone. *Tschüs.*" ["A colloquial expression for adieu"] She nodded. With my scarf flung around my neck I tossed the skates, knotted together by the shoelaces, over my shoulder.

"Going to the *Schlossweiher* ["castle pond"]?" Walter asked.

"*Ja.* Want to come too?"

He grinned, threw himself into posture, offered his cocked arm. "May I have the extraordinary pleasure to accompany the young lady to the skating rink?" With a low bow he opened the door to let me go first. I laughed and accepted his arm. We waltzed out of the house.

CHAPTER 6

A few days later, when I came from school, Mutter hardly answered my greeting and did not look up. Something was wrong. I scanned the kitchen, nothing was obvious.

"Any mail?" Could something be the matter with Hilde?

"Only for Vater," she answered after a while.

"Did something happen?" I stood beside her at the sink and looked at her. She laid knife and potato down, wiped her hands on her blue half apron and walked away. My throat tightened, my whole body tingled. Did I do something? Hilde? Erika? I racked my brain. Josef? Josef! What if he got drafted? "Is it Josef?"

She nodded, facing the stove.

"Is he being drafted?" She nodded again. Was she crying? I had never seen Mutter cry. I wanted to rush up, put my arms around her. But what if she withdrew like always when I tried to get closer; what if she shook me off, walked away as if I bothered her? Each time I hit that impenetrable wall surrounding her I promised myself not to try that again.

Slowly I walked up to my room, leaned my head against the open window frame. Josef a soldier. He was eighteen, it was inevitable. Hitler had said we were in a total war and whoever would not stand up to the task would be eliminated. What did total war mean? What more could we do?

The cool air felt good on my hot face. Why did Mutter always push me away? Did she not like me? I heard Erika's footsteps. She joined me at the window. "What's going on down there?"

"Josef's drafted."

"Darn it all! I knew it would happen." Her down-to-earth manner felt good after Mutter's silent withdrawal. We stood at the window, following our own thoughts. After a long pause, Erika wrapped her's up with, "Well, let's not mope about it. I'm sure Jupp's going to be drafted too. Let's go down and lighten up the scene."

Erika set the table and talked about school. "Got another lecture from Fraulein Knops. She said we all have to pull on the same rope, especially we, the German youth, have to stand up and be counted. We have to stand behind our soldiers."

Mutter spooned some kale with boiled potatoes and a small piece of bratwurst on Erika's plate. I shook my head to the bratwurst which I disliked and got, after a few moments, a fried egg instead. It earned me Erika's sarcastic remark, "The pale little girl needs her little egg," but I was used to that.

"*Ja,*" Mutter sat down, smoothed out her apron and in her typical fashion continued a conversation we were not part of, "it's one thing to stand behind our soldiers who give their lives, it's another thing to pull on the same rope with a regime that's wrong, that you can't believe in."

Surprised I glanced at her as she stabbed at her food without eating. I had not heard her speak out that way against the Nazis. She always left that to Vater and worried more about us, that we might say something in school that would get all of us into trouble.

In the evening, after Papa and Josef came home, washed up, scrubbed their greasy hands and clothing, Mutter handed Vater the envelope. He studied the letter, then called Josef down. "Here, that's really for you."

Josef looked at the already opened envelope with a

frown, took a breath as if to say something, swallowed and decided against it. The official look told him enough. "I'm being drafted." His nostrils flared with excitement but he kept his voice even as if to cover up his joy for the sake of our parents. His eyes flew over the lines. We waited. "In ten days I'll have to be in a boot camp in the Eiffel."

"Get ready, we can eat."

For a long time the clinking of our forks and knifes was the only sound in the dining room. Finally Erika repeated Fraulein Knops' admonition. Vater just nodded, Josef didn't seem to listen at all. As soon as he emptied his plate he asked to be excused, threw his jacket over his shoulder and was gone.

Later that week another letter arrived. *Pater Angelinus*, a Franciscan monk and a friend of our family, invited Mutter and me to spend two weeks in July or August in a convent in Belgium. We would get out of the air raids, get a change of pace and rest. Was the invitation the result of our recent visit to the little monastery in Düsseldorf, where *Pater Angelinus* was Abby? Nobody had mentioned the possibility of my being sent away again and I didn't feel like asking, but I was less than thrilled to go to a convent and even less about going there with Mutter.

That night the wailing of the sirens tore me out of deepest sleep. Our flack blasted away. I swept my clothes from the chair, grabbed shoes and suitcase and bolted downstairs, with Erika right behind me.

"British bombers entered our air space, direction Düsseldorf." I groaned, quickly dressed and lay on my bunk, wide-awake. The announcer came back. "We have a correction in course. The planes are headed for Köln ["Cologne"]. A second wave entered our air space."

Köln was as far south from us as Düsseldorf was north, about 30 km.

"Let's hope they don't drop the two-ton bombs which

they used last month on Essen," Papa said. I stared at our reinforced ceiling. A two-ton bomb? The wave of rumbling grew louder, came closer. The radio crackled, the announcer was back. "A third wave is entering our air space. Direction Köln. "

"Good God." Papa opened the airtight door. "I'll have a look."

"Josef, not now!" Mutter called. He was already outside, locking the door behind him. Mutter shook her head and mumbled something about "...*keine Ruhe im Hintern* ["no peace in the posterior"]."

"Mutter! What about *Tante* Ellie? Doesn't she live in Köln?" I sat up, suddenly remembering the heavyset younger sister of Mama who was, for reasons unknown to me, the black sheep of her family.

"*Ja*, she lives in a suburb. Now lay down again and don't worry about that."

"A fourth wave is entering our air space in direction of Köln with a fifth wave following closely." I lay motionless. A fifth wave? All on one town? The poor people. How could anybody survive this? Would anything be left of the city? The beautiful Gothic Cathedral, whose tall spires looked as if they were fringed with lace, would it still stand come daylight?

The basement shook. The hair on my neck stood up. My eyes were glued to the ceiling as if I could will it to hold the house together.

Vater came back, his face pale and drawn. He cleared his throat. "The sky is burning south of us. Our flack is shooting like crazy and can't get them. They're much too high." I lay still, surrounded by heavy silence.

Four agonizing hours later the monotonous siren told us the deadly raid was over, the longest one we had so far. I dragged myself up the stairs and into bed. Not even a slice of bread with peppermint tea could entice me into the kitchen. I was only glad to have a bed and a roof over it.

The next morning the newspaper denounced the saturation bombing of Köln by over a thousand planes as a 'cowardly attack on helpless and unarmed women and children.' Ninety percent of the city was destroyed, thousands of people killed. The Cathedral was severely damaged. For a few days we wondered why Köln when most of the chemical industry on the outskirts remained intact. And, who is next? What city? Will it be Düsseldorf?

"Don't worry about it," Papa told us. "We can survive anything but a direct hit. And against that...." He shrugged.

Again we stood in the train hall in Düsseldorf. It was Josef's turn to leave.

Erika and I had watched him upstairs pack a few of his personal things. As the last item he placed his slender green volume of the New Testament on top of his belongings and smiled at us. "I'll have this book with me at all times, wherever I am. It's my most important possession."

I nodded, not sure of my voice. My brother surprised me. I knew he often joined Papa and Hilde for weekday services, I knew he was active in his Catholic youth group, but I knew nothing about his faith. Was it as strong as Papa's? Did he not just go to church to please Vater, because he thought he had to? Did he not just take his faith for granted?

Once more Josef looked around his room. On top of his writing desk stood a framed saying:

'What Did You Go Out To See?
A Reed Shaking In The Wind?'

He picked it up, handed it to Erika. "Here. Hold this for me until I'm back, will you?" Erika's eyes lit up. She took and held it against her chest, placing both arms over it.

Vater called upstairs, "Josef, we have to leave."

"Ready!"

Mutter waited in the center hall. "Take good care of yourself, Josef." She shook his hand, hardly looking at him. He put his arms around her. I walked out to blink away my tears. Down the street he caught up with us. The platform at the station was packed with soldiers, many with bandages and crutches, some in wheelchairs. One young soldier beside us leaned against a post, his head heavily bandaged, his left sleeve flapping around. Red Cross ladies distributed hot coffee and sandwiches. Josef took a cup. His face was as shiny and expectant as the faces of the young soldiers I had seen on the Autobahn in August of 39.

The loudspeaker announced, "Stand back, the train to Saarbrücken is arriving on track two."

Josef handed me his cup with the remaining coffee. "Are you going to write to me?"

I nodded. Erika promised enthusiastically, "Everyday I'm going to write to you." He hugged and kissed us both, shook Vater's hand and kissed him, picked up his bag and pushed himself into the crowded car. Two shrill whistles, the train slid noiselessly out of the station and was gone. On the plat-form the people turned to the steps, many with tears in their eyes.

In our English class in school we beleaguered Fraulein Hennig. "Please, can we go outside and sit on the back steps of the *Schloss*? It's much too nice to be inside." She wholeheartedly agreed. Armed with books, notebooks and pencils we raced down the narrow curved hallway to the school door.

"If you can't behave like young ladies we'll go back immediately," Fraulein Hennig warned us. We calmed down.

I ran up the steps to the castle to find a sunny spot. A warm breeze flowed over us. The chestnut trees along the

Spiegelweiher ["mirror lake"] held up their white flowering cones like candles in a Christmas tree. The shiny, soft grass along the pond and at the bottom of the steps swayed in waves in the breeze. I closed my eyes and with a deep sigh I felt a heavy weight slide off my shoulders, a weight I did not know I carried. The singing and chirping of the birds—when did I hear that the last time? I could hardly remember.

"...but we cannot sit out here and daydream." Fraulein Hennig's voice cut through my thoughts. She looked at me. "Margot, can you conjugate the verb?"

I felt heat rise and knew I was blushing furiously. My classmates laughed. "I'm sorry, I didn't get the verb."

"Of course you didn't get it. You were gone. Now please pay attention," she said good-naturedly and turned to somebody else. I tried to concentrate. English grammar wasn't my thing anyhow.

She concluded the lesson. "Let's sing the English songs we know by now." We started with 'London Bridge" and finished with 'Clementine'. How strange, we sang English songs and learned English words, when at night English bombers were trying to kill us. It didn't make sense. Nothing made sense. The heavy feeling returned. I stuffed it down and shrugged. After all, it was war.

During supper that evening a *Sondermeldung* interrupted the program. "The OKW announces: The heroic fight for Sevastopol has come to a successful conclusion. As of this afternoon the city is in the control of the German *Wehrmacht*."

Mutter sighed. "I hope Josef doesn't have to go to the *Ostfront*."

Papa tried to console her. "Trude, we know he'll be sent there. I'm sure of it. But let's not worry about it. It's not in our hands."

"Mutter, we're having a special Hitler *Jugend* Rally on Sunday morning and I HAVE to be there." I dropped my school bag into the hall.

"You HAVE to be there?"

"*Ja.* Fraulein Dr. Schulte said we have to be at the Exhibition Halls. And in uniform! Walter von Schirach, the National Youth Leader, is going to speak to us." I let that sink in. "What am I going to do? I have no uniform."

"When does it start?"

"At ten."

"Of course, at church time. If you go beforehand to the seven o'clock Mass, you can go."

One hurdle overcome. "What about the uniform? Fraulein Dr. Schulte made a point of it. No civilian clothing. So now what?" Heat rose into my face. "Why is Vater making it so difficult for us? Why are we not permitted to—"

"Be quiet. Not another word from you. You are not getting a uniform, *basta.*" Doorknob in hand to leave the kitchen, she turned. "Don't worry about it."

"Don't worry about it!" I threw up my hands. That was it? The issue of the uniform had given me a lot a derisive remarks from classmates and questioning looks from teachers. Not only did it make me feel inadequate and poorly dressed, it scared me.

I was still stewing in the kitchen when Erika arrived from school. "*Ja*, we all have to be at ten at the Exhibition Halls in uniform." We went up to our room together. "Erika, what are we going to do? This time we'll really get into trouble because of Vater's stupid stubbornness."

"Let's see. We need a brown skirt, white blouse, brown scarf with a leather knot and a brown velvet jacket with all the insignias. The jacket we'll have to dispense with, I know we won't get that. Maybe it will be too warm anyhow. Scarf and knot, we may get permission to buy those. We both have

white blouses. That leaves brown skirts. Do you have one?"
I unearthed a brown wool skirt in my wardrobe. So did
Erika, even though they weren't the official color.
"See, no problem. Already taken care of." Erika closed
our wardrobe. I laughed with relief and gave her a quick hug.
Sunday morning Pfarrer Antheck was surprised to see us
that early. After mass we took the streetcar to the Exhibition
Halls at the *Rhein* Promenade and followed the stream of
uniformed youth, all wearing their smart, tailored velvet
jackets. With Mutter's permission we had bought scarves
and braided leather knots. While our makeshift uniforms did
not look authentic, they came close.
Loud, brassy march music told us we were heading in the
right direction as we approached the giant complex. As we
turned the corner of one of the many exhibition halls, the
inner court presented an impressive picture. In front of the
square facade of the main building, rows upon rows of red
flags formed the background. Countless standards surrounded the podium, the eagles and swastikas on the tip of
the shafts glistened in the bright sun. On the upper part of
the building, above the whole scenery, a giant eagle spread
its wings against a solid red background.
When we found our troop from Benrath, my BDM
leader, Frau Bartram, the wife of a Nazi official, moved us
around until we stood in straight, even rows. All teachers
were in uniform and stood close by to keep an eye on us.
The music stopped. A hush fell over the thousands of
youngsters in brown. Intoning the National Anthem, the
mighty band began,
Deutschland, Deutschland über alles,
über alles in der Welt....
["Germany, Germany, above everything,
above everything in the world...."]
We sang with our right arm lifted up. I liked our German
anthem and sang it with conviction. Yes, for me Germany

was above everything in the world. As always the national anthem was followed by the *Horst Wessel* song, the battle hymn of the *SA*.

Somebody stepped to the podium. "Let us greet our *Führer: Sieg Heil; Sieg Heil; Sieg Heil.*" I was surprised to spot our neighbor, Herr Leimbke, close to the podium. Then I remembered, he was Assistant District Leader. The District Leader introduced Walter von Schirach.

The Youth Leader gave a dynamic address to the German youth, summoning them to their honor, calling them to faith-fulness and loyalty to our *Führer* and to our great flag. He reiterated the word honor over and over. To honor our *Vaterland*, the greatest country, the leader of the world, is our duty, our obligation. He talked about the unsung heroes of glorious battlefields and about one specific hero, Reinhard Heydrick, who died of the wounds received in a 'shameful, coward assassination attack,' to whom this rally was dedicated.

After a pause the music started a song I loved and dreaded because it always moved me to tears:

"Ich hatt' einen Kameraden,
einen bess'ren findst Du nicht.
Die Trommel schlug zum Streite,
er ging an meiner Seite
im gleichen Schritt und Tritt.

Eine Kugel kam geflogen,
gilt sie mir oder gilt sie Dir?
Sie hat ihn weggerissen,
er liegt mir zu den Füssen
als wär's ein Stück von mir.

["I had a friend,
a better one you cannot find.
The drum called to battle,

he walked alongside me
step after step.

A bullet came flying,
is it for you or for me?
It tore him away,
he lies at my feet
as if he was a piece of me."]

Tears welled up. I tried hard not to think of Willi or of Josef.

The tempo of the music changed, with it the mood. The songs became more rousing, more challenging. By the time the rally was over we were charged up and ready to stand up for our *Vaterland*.

"Mutter, a letter from Josef."

Mutter tore it open. In the short letter he told us that his boot camp would be over soon. Before being sent to the *Ostfront* close relatives could visit them for two days. Would Vater and Mutter like to come?

"How nice. You are going, Mutter, aren't you?"

"I'll talk with Vater about it." She drew a deep breath. "To the *Ostfront*. I was afraid of that." Later, I was reading the newspaper, she continued the conversation. "It's good we can visit him next week because in two weeks you and I are leaving for Belgium."

"We are? To that convent? Why?" I hoped they had forgotten about it.

"You need to get away, to sleep through the night, so you can fully recuperate from the hepatitis."

"Mutter, I am all right. I really don't want to go." The more I thought about it, the less it appealed to me.

"It has all been arranged. We are going."

I ran upstairs, resisting the urge to slam the kitchen door.

I knew I could do nothing to change that decision. I plunked down on my bed, brooding. Maybe something would happen, maybe I could get sick, or get into an accident. Spending two weeks in a convent with nuns, and, worst of all, with Mutter. If only Hilde would be here to talk to.

Erika came in. "What's the matter?"

"I don't want to go to that convent."

Erika laughed. That needled me.

"What's so funny?"

"Well, it isn't the end of the world, you know. Besides, you may like it."

I jumped up. I had enough. "You are an idiot. Why don't you go?"

For a moment she was silent. "Because nobody asked me. It's you they are concerned about."

That stopped me. "Do I detect a funny note in that?"

She looked at me, shook her head. "No, Margot, not at all. But you are being ridiculous. Stop making such a fuss." She left the room.

Heat raced into my face. I hastily changed, by-passed the kitchen and ran through the basement into the yard, picking up tools for weeding. The yard looked lush and green, most of it weeds. I attacked them with all the furor I felt. The crumbly, moist soil gave up willingly the intruders. Anger started to flow out of me. Was I really being ridiculous? If they were concerned about me, not that I knew why, but did they have to choose a convent? And to have to be together with Mutter all by myself for two weeks! I felt the heat rise again.

"Margot, come in, dinner is ready," Mutter called through the open kitchen window.

"Coming." Sitting back on my feet I surveyed the job. I needed much more time to get the yard in shape before leaving for two weeks, at least a couple of hours each day, now that summer vacation had started.

Our parents left to visit Josef. Every day I spent a few hours in the yard. Working in the rock garden around the water basin and the blue spruce was my special joy. The patch of chick and hens was bulging out of its corner beside the basin. Their dainty pink bells on tall stems contrasted with the rich lavender blossoms of the fleshy sedums.

I cleaned out the fieldstone basin. Papa originally intended to have three spitting frogs as fountains, but instead the water spurted out of the end of three copper pipes. The refreshing sound reminded me of the beauty of the mountains and of the water trough in front of Schmidt's house in Winkl.

After two days our parents returned from the Eiffel, bringing greetings from Josef. He enjoyed receiving Erika's constant flow of letters and encouraged her to keep them coming. He was assigned to a repair troop within an antitank patrol unit because of his specialized mechanical training. But where on the *Ostfront* he would be sent nobody knew. We prayed it wouldn't be Stalingrad.

SUMMER, 1942

CHAPTER 7

A few days later Mutter helped me pack. "Where exactly is this convent?"

"West of Aachen in the Ardennes, a woodsy, hilly area. You'll need your sweater and your solid shoes." I finally had gotten a new pair of shoes but I still needed to grow into them.

The train ride to Aachen was uneventful except for the constant *Gestapo* patrols that opened the door to our compartment after every stop with a stern, "Your papers please." In Aachen a local train took us to a little railroad station out in the country.

The clatter and rattle of a horse drawn wagon stopped alongside the station. A white haired man in a blue overall climbed slowly down. "Frau Füsser?" Mutter nodded. "And this is Margot?" He knew my name. "I'm Albert." His German had a Belgian accent, but I had no problem understanding him. He dropped our luggage over the side onto the loading platform and invited us to sit beside him on the driver's bench.

Sitting up high behind the horse, I felt the cool breeze of the sunny afternoon. The dusty road wound through green fields, dotted with large trees and an occasional farmhouse. Each building had a gigantic white B painted on its roof.

Albert pointed up the winding slope to a clump of trees with red roofs peeking through. "There is the convent." On top of the hill, he turned the horse toward a cluster of houses. A door flung open, a group of children ran up to meet us. Albert pulled on the reins, climbed down, helped us get off. Children in a convent?

A black haired girl about my age, with long braids, stretched out her hand. "I'm Katarina, you must be Margot."

A nun stepped out of the main building. Her white habit bounced with each step. "Welcome to our convent, Frau Füsser. Welcome, Margot. I am Sister Margaret. I hope you will spend an enjoyable time with us." With a sunny smile she shook our hands. Mutter beamed, pleased with the friendly reception. Sister Margaret conversed with us as we walked towards the next building. "Supper will be served in the dining room at seven o'clock. Oh, Frau Hauser!" Sister Margaret introduced us to Frau Hauser and left us in her care.

Our room was bright and friendly. We just finished unpacking when Frau Hauser knocked to pick us up for dinner. In the large dining hall, two long tables with high backed chairs were set for dinner. About ten children of varying ages, including Katarina, still played around the tables, while most of the mothers had taken their seats. Sister Margaret introduced us and showed us our places.

Katarina came over, her dark eyes looked intently at me. "Can you play with us after dinner?" Before I could answer she quickly said, "I'll be waiting for you," and dashed to join her mother and younger sister at the other table.

After prayer two nuns set dishes with soup, vegetable and potatoes in the center of the tables, desert on a side table. Frau Hauser, sitting beside Mutter, filled us in. "A few years ago this Belgian convent opened its house to guests. It's like a refuge here. The nuns are loving and kind and wonderful cooks. As you see we get plenty of food. We can help with chores if we like. The children especially have fun picking fruits. The convent has a good-sized apple and cherry orch-ard and extensive gardens with lots of vegetables and fruits." She looked at me. "Do you like to pick berries, Margot?"

Before I had a chance, Mutter answered for me. "Margot does our yard at home. She loves to be outside." After dinner I played with Katarina and the other children until dark.

"Well, are you now glad we came?" Mutter asked as I crawled into bed, tired but feeling good.

"*Ja*, it's really nice here. Everybody is so friendly. I never expected children in a convent."

The next morning Katarina knocked on the door, two pails in her hand. It was strawberry picking time. One long row after another of plump and juicy berries rested on dry straw, easy to pick. My pail filled up quickly.

"They don't mind if you eat one," Katarina laughed as she stuck a dripping fruit into her mouth.

I shook my head. "No, I'm fine." I had not gotten into the habit of eating while picking.

In the afternoon we picked red currants. Frau Hauser, Mutter and two other women prepared the fruit for jam. Pass-ing the women for the umpteenth time to empty my pail, Frau Hauser smiled at me. "You are a good little worker. I haven't seen you stop and eat or rest yet."

"Don't overdo it, Margot," Mutter beamed. "Yes, she is a hard worker." Mutter had something good to say about me? I was surprised and happy and increased my effort.

The following day we picked cherries on the other side of the hill, where the trees were loaded. The higher I climbed the darker and sweeter they were. This was fun.

Standing on a branch peering through the leaves I had a beautiful view over the Ardennes. Densely wooded hills in one direction, open farmland and houses in the other. And a gigantic white B on every roof. Then it came to me. Of course, the B stood for Belgium. These houses were marked so the British bombers knew they were still over Belgian territory.

That night I woke up from the sound of planes overhead. Hearing voices outside, we slipped into housecoats and went out. The sky in the east lit up over and over as with lightning, accompanied by faint rumblings.

"Look, that's Aachen, Aachen's being bombed. Those are detonations," Frau Hauser whispered. "My God, the poor people there." The redness of the sky spread out and intensified. Wave after wave of planes flew over us into Germany. Here we stood, protected by giant B's, on foreign soil, and watched a German city being destroyed. I felt almost asham-ed, guilty, even though I knew I could do nothing about it.

"Is there light in that little chapel?" I thought I saw something flicker behind the stain glass windows.

"Yes," Frau Hauser, who seemed to know everything around here, answered. "The nuns are praying. At every air attack they spend almost the whole night in the chapel. Isn't it amazing, with them being Belgians?"

The next morning we heard Aachen had been heavily bombed.

Saturday afternoon brought a surprise visitor, *Pater Angelinus*. It turned out he was the spiritual leader of the convent. He spent the afternoon with the nuns, but we ate supper with him in the special guest dining room.

That evening I broke out into a rash with red welts over my whole body. Food poisoning. Sister Angelique, a young and pretty French nun who was medically trained, nursed me for almost a week with bitter tea to reduce the itch and the rash. By the time our vacation was over I was fully recovered. We tried to find the cause for the food poisoning but to no avail. As far as I knew I had eaten the same food everybody else did, including the fruit.

We thanked the nuns and said good-bye to those still vacationing in that lovely refuge. Katarina had returned home during my illness. On the train ride home, I thought over the last two weeks and realized I needed to revise my feelings about nuns.

In Düsseldorf, Papa and Erika picked us up. Mutter's first question was, "Any news from Josef?"

"Good news. He is in Romania, not in Stalingrad."

"Thank God," Mutter's relief was obvious in her voice.

Erika grimaced at me. "You survived the convent?" I laughed, a bit embarrassed. "*Ja*, it really was fun, at least the first week."

"Uh huh, we heard from *Pater Angelinus*, you got yourself again into trouble."

"Any news from Hilde?" I had not heard from her in a long time.

"Yes." Erika filled us in. "She is leader of her group for the next six months. She stays in *Markwippach* until she comes home in October."

"For good?" I couldn't wait. I still missed her.

At home Oma poked her face out of her room when I came upstairs. "Oma, you look well. How are you?" I put my arms around her. She looked good, her round face as animated and her eyes as clear as always.

"I'm fine. I'm glad you're home again." She patted my cheeks.

Later in bed Erika and I continued to talk. Jupp, her friend, was in boot camp. Yes, she had talked with Jürgen, he wanted to know when I would be back. I looked forward to seeing him again.

"Let's turn in," Erika suggested with a tired voice. "Let's get some sleep before they come."

Too late. The sirens went off. In the shelter we heard the familiar voice. "British bombers in our airspace. Destination: area of Düsseldorf."

Our flack went into action. I lay down. What was that? Was our basement shaking? In a flash I climbed down and crawled into Erika's bed. The wave of rumbling came closer, couldn't be stopped, seemed to roll over us. Suddenly it felt as if the air was being sucked out of the basement. Still the rumbling relentlessly rolled on. A gigantic boom followed. The shock wave of the detonation made me shiver. Every nerve tingled, adrenaline pumped in every toe and fingertip. I visualized the ceiling collapsing. Nothing happened. For a moment, a deadly silence.

Vater let out his breath. "That was close."

I poked my head out from under Erika's blanket. "You don't think we were hit?"

"No, I don't think so, but it was close. I better check." Mutter did not bother to protest.

Soon he was back, carefully closing the airtight doors behind him, his face tense. "Looks bad over the city, lots of flames, but nothing here. They're still dumping."

The announcer came back. "Another wave is flying in, same destination."

Erika beside me mumbled, "This is going to be a long night and I'm deadly tired. I've got to sleep." She turned around and pulled the blanket over her head. Could she really sleep with this going on? I couldn't. I was glad to be beside her.

Two more waves flew in. Our flack bellowed without success each time the planes turned around after dumping their deadly loads on the city. The poor people in that inferno. How lucky we were to live south of it.

Vater came back from another inspection. "They're still dumping. You can smell the burning, it's that close."

I looked at the thick iron plate overhead. What would it be like to have the house blown to bits right on top of us? Would our shelter hold? I heard stories of people being buried for days in the rubble. How long would one be able to survive? Erika was right. It was better not to think but to sleep.

It calmed down outside. Just as I dozed off I heard the

faint sound of the end-of-raid siren.

Next morning Papa left early, not knowing if the streetcars functioned. They didn't. In the evening, after walking home, he told us the city was hit hard, whole blocks lay in rubble. His business was not damaged. Also the area where Oma Brass lived was spared.

Within days the roads and public transportation functioned again. A new sight appeared on the streets: long columns of walking bundles of dark clothes and rags, working with pickaxes and shovels. These foreign laborers, mostly Russian and Polish men and women, were the work force behind the fast repair of the roads.

In late summer of 1942, school started in our old classroom. All fifteen students were back. On the first morning, our homeroom teacher, we had again Fraulein Dr. Schulte, appeared in the uniform of a Hitler *Jugend* leader. As usual we stood up as she entered the classroom. *"Heil Hitler*, girls."

"Heil Hitler," we greeted her, arms outstretched. After singing the partei song we sat down expectantly.

"Girls, we are starting a new academic year. I want us to be disciplined, courteous, studious and most of all loyal to our *Führer*, to our *Vaterland* and for what we stand."

I groaned inwardly. Not again. Standing beside her desk she looked attractive and trim in the tailored uniform. Her blond hair was short and nicely styled. It was her face that gave me a problem as I watched her. She still talked about loyalty and honor. Then it hit me. She conveyed no warmth, no genuine interest in us. Her blue eyes were cold, her smile insincere.

"...please feel free to come to me with any questions or problems you have. I will always take time for you." She looked at each one of us. Did I imagine it or did she look at me longer? I stiffened in my chair, my body tingled with a sense of danger that made me wish I sat away from her in the last row instead of my preferred first. I glanced at my classmates. With open faces they acknowledged her interest in them. She turned and started the lecture.

When we came out of school the weather was mild with a light overcast, a pleasant early fall day. I breathed in deeply the warm air. Maybe I could take a detour through the Flower Garden. Sauntering towards it I passed a group of boys in front of the Gymnasium. I scanned them quickly, yes, Jürgen's class. He spotted me, came over.

"Hello, glad you're back." We shook hands. I had hoped to see him. "How was Belgium?" His light brown eyes in the slender face smiled whenever his boyish grin appeared. We talked for a while.

"Want to come with me through the Flower Garden? I haven't seen it in a long time."

"Sure. I do have to be home by two for dinner. Mom doesn't like to keep food warm after that."

We crossed in front of the castle and entered the Garden. The hush of the park engulfed us. Huge rhododendron bushes lined the winding path leading to the small kidney shaped pond. Lush, manicured lawns, bordered by azaleas, box-woods and more rhododendrons surrounded it. The soft air was heavily scented by the innumerable azalea bushes, although they were not in bloom.

I pointed to the pond. "Let's go to the bridge." An arched bridge with attractive wrought iron rails spanned the narrow part of the pond. We stopped in the center. Below us the goldfish rushed together, almost pushing each other out of the water. Jürgen dropped in a few pebbles. The fish scattered. Walking along the soft path I drew a deep breath. "It's good to be home."

"How was Belgium? What did you do at the convent?" Jürgen asked again, brushing his straight, dark blond hair out of his face with a familiar gesture.

"It was fun. Much nicer than I expected." I didn't feel like talking. The peace and beauty surrounding us were too important to talk away. "Let's sit down. I'd like to soak all of this up, listen to the birds."

We sat quietly. The air, saturated with fragrance, felt humid like air in a conservatory. A squirrel scurried about, brown bushy tail stretched out. At a sudden noise it froze, the tail flicked up, the shiny black eyes darted back and forth. With danger passed it leaped along the path to an ancient beechnut tree where it scratched the loose ground for some nuts.

"Let's bike to *Urdenbach* or *Garrath* this afternoon," I interrupted the tranquillity. "The fields look so pretty, all lined with poppies and cornflowers. How about it?"

"Would be fun. What time?"

We decided I would whistle at four thirty opposite his house. Jürgen hurried home, it had gotten late.

I picked him up in the afternoon and in minutes we were in farm country. On both sides of the tree-lined road, wild flowers laced the golden wheat field. We swung into a small dirt road. The narrow, deeply rutted path was lined with bright red poppies and steel blue cornflowers. What a delightful summer picture.

We found an indentation in the wheat field, dropped our bikes and sat in the grass. A lazy wind rustled through the field, bending down the heads of the wheat, heavy with plump kernels. It smelled of warm earth, dry grass.

Jürgen reached behind him, stripped the head off a tall stem, rubbed it, blew off the chaff and held out his hand. I picked a few kernels, chewed them and told him about my stay at the convent, about getting sick.

We lapsed into silence. With arms around my knees I listened to the humming of the bumble bees, the rushing of a field mouse in the furrows, the meadowlark with its enchanting songs spiraling higher and higher into the sunlight. Each sound contributed to one symphony, the symphony of life.

The war, the fear at night, the worry about Josef, the tensions and complexities of my family, it all receded in the loveliness of the sunny afternoon.

Reluctantly I consulted Jürgen's watch. "We'll have to leave soon, but first I want to pick some flowers." I ran to a growth of poppies. The crinkly red petals, tissue fine, encircled a black star deep in the center. I mixed them with tough stemmed cornflowers.

"How will you get them home?"

I looked at my bike and discarded the idea of pinning them underneath the clamp of the stand. "I'll hold them in my hand. It'll work." We pushed the bikes back to the road. To protect my delicate poppies from the wind I held them in my lap. Across from his house we shook hands. I raced home to be on time.

"Mutter, Fraulein Dr. Schulte asked us to bring old news-papers to school to study them. Do we have any?"

Mutter shrugged. "Maybe in the basement. They sure aren't worth keeping for posterity."

I scouted around the cellar. It would be fun to find some real old ones since I did not remember much about the first years of the war. Under a frayed blanket on an old dusty chair I discovered a stack of *Düsseldorfer Nachrichten* from 1940. I lugged my find upstairs and dumped them into the center hall amid a cloud of dust.

"Margot! Don't get everything dirty! Wash your hands and set the table. We can eat soon."

Next morning I proudly carried the papers to school, dropped them on my desk. Another cloud of dust spread through the classroom.

Gisela looked at the papers with envy. "Where did you

unearth those? I couldn't find a single one."
"Want one?" She nodded eagerly. I handed her a paper.
"I couldn't find one either." Hannelore held out her hand. I handed out all but one for myself.
Fraulein Dr. Schulte entered the room. We stood up. "*Heil Hitler.*" We went through the usual ceremony.
"Who has found some old newspapers?" Six hands went up. "Very good. Give me the newspaper's name, date and the headline, starting with the oldest one. Anything from 1939? Nobody. 1940? Go ahead, Margot."
"They are all *Düsseldorfer Nachrichten*:
'2/1/1940 Critical Days for the Balkan Nations:
'Questions of Destiny for the Balkan'. 'Weakness of the British Position: Against the British Tyranny', a quote from Dr. Göbbels.
'New British Infamous Action—Watusi. English Pirate Trick'.
"Thank you, Margot. Ute, I saw your hand."
"Also *Düsseldorfer Nachrichten*: 2/25/1940 'Hitler speaks to the Old Guard '...and if the world were full of devils we still would succeed. We must triumph and therefore we shall triumph'. ["Old Guard, *Münchener Hofbräuhaus*"]
'...that they hate me is my greatest pride...' '...God did not create the world alone for the British...' "
"Thank you, Ute. Annemarie."
"Also *Düsseldorfer Nachrichten*: 2/29/1940 'The German Nation will end the Plutocratic World Tyranny', a quote by Dr. Göbbels.
'The Great German Nation is unconquerable'. 'Polish Sadism—in 20 years over 1.5 Mill. Ukrainians murdered'.
'3/13/1940 Terrible Defeat of the War Mongers, those that ignite the Flames of War'. "
"Thank you, Annemarie." Fraulein Dr. Schulte pointed to Hannelore. "Do you have something?"

"Yes. Also Düsseldorfer Nachrichten: 3/23/1940 'London dares to touch the Honor of the German Air Force: Infamous Suspicions'."

"Thank you. One more. Gisela?"

"Düsseldorfer Nachrichten: 8/10/1940 'Germany secures the Neutrality of Belgium and Holland. English and French Invasion of Holland and Belgium planned to march against the *Ruhr* district. It was averted in the last hour by Germany'."

"Thank you, girls. I think that is sufficient. What do we learn from these headlines?"

"That our *Führer* deserves our loyalty and our trust."

"That our enemies cannot overcome us."

Everybody had something good to say. I remembered Vater's remark. "We don't know what it looks like from the other side." I wished I had somebody to ask, somebody to talk to. Was it all propaganda? A conversation I overheard in Belgium came to my mind, how the German soldiers invaded that country for no reason whatsoever.

"Margot, you have not given us your conclusion."

I got up slowly, fighting back a rising fear. Did she try to trap me? "Everybody said it just the way I would have expressed it."

"And that is?"

The coldness of her blue eyes washed over me, forced down the heat and the heartbeat in my throat. I swallowed, and said with a light shrug, "That we can't lose."

"You are right. We can't."

Slowly I sat down, folded the newspaper nonchalantly together while my knees felt like jelly and my hands shook. She was out to get me, I had not misread the danger signal.

At the end of the class, I tucked my newspapers under my arm and strolled by her as she dismissed each one of us with a smile.

A few days later Mutter interrupted my homework. "Margot, come with me to the village to shop. I need you to stand in line while I continue to look." I sat at the desk in the living room, cramming English vocabulary which I hated. "Sure I'll come with you." I jumped up, closed the book and promised myself to have another look in the morning before the test.

In the kitchen Mutter studied our ration cards. "Two more weeks to go and not much left for the month. Let's see what we can get. I heard the butcher on Main Street has horse meat."

"Horse meat? What does that taste like?"

"Don't make such a face. It's meat. You wouldn't know the difference, especially as ground meat or in sausage."

No wonder I didn't like sausage, I thought.

On our way to the village, we overtook a group of foreign laborers. Even though it was mild, they were bundled up in dark clothing. As we passed them I was aware how dirty they smelled. Mutter rummaged in her purse. Out of the corner of my eye I saw a piece of paper flutter out.

"You lost something."

I was about to stop and pick it up when she said sharply, "Leave that. Just continue to walk."

We walked rapidly. "What was it? What did you drop?"

"A bread coupon. These poor people have even less to eat than we have. And they are forced to work hard."

"What if they don't realize it's for them?" I thought of the wasted loaf of bread.

"They know. They're very much aware of it. Next time at *Zinsheim* watch them observe from a distance everybody going into the bakery. They're forbidden to beg or stand close to the door, but they'll pick coupons off the pavement. You can't see their faces because of the scarves and caps, but they notice everything."

"How do you know? Have you done this before?"

"*Ja*, when I was sure nobody saw it. Even though it would be difficult to prove I didn't just lose it."

I looked at my mother, utterly surprised. She really cared. Mutter cared for the foreign workers. I saw a dimension of her I did not know existed.

"Do they have money for the bread?"

"They may get some money. But, if they go with a coupon to *Zinsheim*, he'll give them bread without money."

"Doesn't that get him into trouble?"

"He's careful."

At the butcher a line around the corner and up the side street indicated he had something special. "You stay here. I'll find out what they have." Mutter spotted a neighbor close to the entrance and talked with her. She came back. "They have horse meat, double the amount of the card. Here." She handed me money and the needed coupons. "Get two pounds of ground horse meat. I can make a meat loaf for Sunday and have cold cuts for Vater." She continued her shopping.

The clock from the church tower struck once, three fifteen. Since all shops closed between one and three, the butcher opened fifteen minutes ago. If he started with a fresh load of meat, maybe I had a chance to get some. I was glad it wasn't cold, it looked like a long wait.

Hilde wrote she would come home in one month. The year had gone by fast. I was already twelve, but nobody had remembered my birthday or my names day.

What might Hilde be doing? As leader was she doing paper work, ordering supplies for her 'well stocked kitchen'? Remembering our empty shelves, cupboards and potato bin, I wondered what a well-stocked kitchen looked like? Will she bring some food with her? Only a few times had she been able to send a package with a pound of flour or sugar or cornstarch. Once she surprised us with precious cinnamon and pepper. I loved cinnamon and sugar on sour milk and rice pudding, which I hadn't had in years.

Somebody tapped on my shoulder. "You can move ahead."

In front of me was a wide space. "Sorry," I mumbled embarrassed, looking at the woman behind me. "No harm done." She sounded friendly, but did not smile. Nobody smiled. Also, like me, nobody spoke to the person next to them. I studied the people around me. Their faces deeply lined, they looked straight ahead, avoiding eye contact with others.

Mutter came down the street with packages wrapped in newspapers in her shopping net. Good, she must have gotten something. For the first time I realized that she had lost a lot of weight. Also her face was deeply lined, especially the frown lines between her eyebrows.

"You stay here, I'll go home. Hope they have enough. Come directly home with the meat."

The clock on the tower struck again. Four fifteen. I caught a glimpse of a familiar tall, lanky figure. Jürgen! My heart leaped. I wished I could tell him how much I liked him, how important he was to me. With Josef gone he was a real brother to me. I felt warm and comfortable with him, able to confide in him. We had a lot of fun together. I did not feel lonely anymore, did not miss not having a girl friend. He was my friend. Maybe I related better to boys than to girls. They often behaved so silly and giggly, like some in my class. They either pouted or whined or whispered behind their hand about others.

When Jürgen was across on the other side, I whistled softly. His eyes searched the line. He waved and came over. "Hello. What are you waiting for?" When he heard it was horse meat he crinkled his nose. "What are you doing afterwards?"

"Mutter wants me home with it right away. Done with

homework?"

"No, I need to do math tonight. Just had to get out. You mind if I stay with you a bit?"

I chuckled. "Mind? No. Maybe you can find out how much they've left."

He came back with a reassuring smile. "I know the kid that stocks the counter. There's plenty."

Finally we reached the door and were inside the store. I smiled at him. "I'm glad you're here. Waiting with you is much more fun."

He looked embarrassed. "Well, I just came by."

I grinned. "Of course."

"How much would you like?" the butcher's wife asked me.

I handed her the ration coupons. "Two pound of ground meat please. I'm glad you had enough."

"Doesn't happen often." She handed me the neatly wrapped package. Jürgen walked with me to the corner.

"See you tomorrow. *Tschüs.*"

FALL, 1942

CHAPTER 8

A few nights later we rushed again into the shelter as we did every single night. Oma sat as usual in the furthest corner of the small room, her eyes closed. I was convinced and comforted to know she was praying.

Again waves of planes flew in, again we heard the dreaded word, "in direct formation towards Düsseldorf."

I just finished getting dressed and lay on my straw bed with my little red box when I felt the house shaking. My bunk bed vibrated. In a flash I crawled again into Erika's bed. The lamp with the white enamel shade that hung suspended from the ceiling swung wildly. I glanced at the reinforced cover over the basement window, with which Vater bolted the window shut. Would it hold? Or would it blow open and fly on top of us?

"A new wave is entering our space." Listening carefully it was difficult to sort out the detonations from the bellowing flack. "God, please don't let anything happen to us," I prayed.

"Another wave is approaching Düsseldorf."

Mama buried her face in her hands. Vater sat motionless, I could see his shiny head and stooped shoulders as he stemmed his elbows on his knees and his chin into his hands. Then, the momentary silence was torn apart by a sharp whining sound. Instinctively I pulled in my head. The deafening blast of the detonation shook the foundation of our house. The air in the shelter was being sucked out. I gasped for breath. Then the air was pressed into the room merci-lessly. I covered my ears, the waves of pressure went on and on.

"Please let it stop," I heard myself say over and over, holding my ears. Finally the pressure subsided. It was quiet.

"Whew." Erika let out a sigh. "What was that, Papa?"

He shook his head. "Don't know. They are dropping bigger and bigger bombs."

"You think we still have a house?" I asked.

"*Ja*, I think so." After a while he got up. "I'll have a look." Carefully he closed the shelter door behind him. Again our flack went into action.

Mutter opened the door. "Josef, for heaven's sake, come back."

After a moment he came in. "That was just a stray plane. Didn't take them long this time, but they sure did a lot of damage. We've some broken windows, but Düsseldorf is burning badly."

At the end of the raid, we ran upstairs. In the kitchen both windows were shattered, the floor littered with glass. Up-stairs the windows to the yard were smashed, but not to the front.

On hands and knees, carefully feeling across the carpet, we swept the glass together. I was grateful we still had a roof over our heads. After cleaning up we congregated in the kitchen.

"I'm hungry, Mama."

"I know Margot, so is everybody else. I'll heat up some wheat soup." The sack with wheat kernels seemed to be holding forever, now the labor of grinding them through the coffee grinder was shared by only Erika and me. Mutter dished out to each of us half a plateful. "I've added some of our plums."

I tasted the soup. "Ugh, is that bitter."

"Bitter?" Mutter looked unhappy. "I don't have any

sugar. That's why I added the fruit."

"That's all right, Trude," Vater said sternly. "Margot, stop making such a fuss. If you are hungry, eat, if not, don't. But don't complain!" I shrugged, I was hungry and ate it, but it pulled my mouth together and left an awful aftertaste.

The newspapers gave glowing reports of the 'fantastic advances' of the German troops in the East. They reached the Caucuses. Heavy house-to-house fighting was reported from Stalingrad. Where were the people, I wondered? What happened to them? Were they in their basements? And where was Josef? How was he? The last we heard he was all right, we should not worry about him. I couldn't envision his life as a soldier. As mechanic with the repair unit, he was behind the fighting lines. Erika still wrote to him every day. I marveled at her persistence. I wouldn't know what to write. Even to Hilde I had only written a few times. And now, in two days, she would be coming home, her year finished. We had not seen her since Christmas, ten long months.

Finally the much-awaited day came. Vater, Erika and I took the streetcar into town. Mutter, who had no passion for train stations, stayed home. The streetcar rattled through street after street of rubble. I pointed to a stretch that had been lined with attractive apartment buildings. "They are gone. Nothing left. What happened to the people?"

Papa nodded. "Those that survived live mostly with relatives. Wait till you see something you won't believe. Remember the pressure we felt during the last attack? That was a two-ton bomb. There is the crater now." He pointed to a hole big enough to sink a whole apartment building into it. Everything around it was gone, disappeared, erased, not even rubble, nothing, just one huge hole.

"Nothing? That's it? Disintegrated?" Erika asked. This was incredulous.

"Let's say, pulverized."

I stared at the hole. Pulverized, including the people. I nudged Erika. "One way to go fast."

The area surrounding the railroad station was especially hard hit. The devastations were enormous, ruins everywhere. The old elegant hotels—heaps of rubble. Part of one entrance facade was still standing, the shattered windows looking like empty eyes.

"How come they haven't hit the station yet?" Erika wondered. "Obviously they tried often enough." In the entrance hall as well as the train hall, lots of glass panels were missing. On the platform Red Cross workers handed out coffee, helping the wounded soldiers.

I looked around. Would we see again a boarded up freight train? "Erika, remember the train we saw over there?" I pointed to the outside track.

"With the Jews? Sure do. I'll never forget that."

"Can you two talk about something else out here?" Vater said sharply.

We stood around waiting, when I realized something caught Erika's attention. On the next platform, the train had just left. A *Gestapo* officer walked briskly to the exit, followed by a well-dressed gentleman with white hair and a white beard, accompanied by an equally well-dressed young lady with dark hair and a dark complexion. Behind them marched two soldiers, rifles with mounted bayonets slung over their shoulders.

"They caught somebody again," Erika whispered.

The intercom crackled. "Please stand back, the train from Erfurt is arriving." I stepped way back. With a surge of air and screaming brakes the train raced in. Would Hilde be wearing her civilian clothes with which she left? Doors swung open, people spilled out like ants. Standing on tiptoes, I tried to look over the heads of the crowd.

"There she is!" Erika spotted Hilde toward the end of the train, stepping out of a car.

"Hilde! Hilde!" Yes, she wore new civilian clothing. She looked good, relaxed.

She greeted us with hugs and kisses. "I'm so glad to see you, that you're all well. *Stöppchen*, did you grow! I can't believe it. You're almost a young lady."

I laughed happy and embarrassed. "Not quite, not really."

Papa picked up her suitcase. On the way out she bought a newspaper, folded it, put it under her arm.

"How do you feel in civilian clothing?" I asked her.

"I've to get used to it. I liked the uniform. It looked nice and made life much simpler." We stepped out of the entrance hall. Hilde stopped abruptly.

"Good heavens! It's all gone!" She looked around. "The hotels are gone! Nothing but ruins! I heard about the attacks, that is was terrible, but I didn't expect this." She shook her head. "How are things at home?"

"We were lucky," Erika answered, "had only some windows blown out." From the streetcar Vater showed Hilde the devastation of the two-ton bomb.

Slowly Hilde nodded. "I've seen a lot of destruction, but nothing like this. They really want to flatten Düsseldorf as they have done with Köln."

Irmgard, the fourteen year old, who was doing her year of duty with us and had started a few weeks earlier, slowly became a real asset to Mutter. She lost some of her shyness, was friendly and quiet. She knew what was expected of her and had the confidence to do her work. On washdays she came extra early to get the work done.

Coming from school I was greeted by the smell of sudsy

water. Washday! I hated it. Washing was a drudgery. Each time Mutter was so worn out she was even more short tempered than usual.

I dropped my school bag in the hall. "Anybody home?"

"*Ja*, down here." Irmgard's voice sounded muffled by the sudsy vapor.

Slowly Mutter came up the steps, wet hair hanging in her face. "How was school?"

"The usual. Another litany. We have to be the best for the greatest *Führer* of all times, blablabla. We also got a litany about the *Judenfrage* ["Jewish question"], that 'race politi-cally seen' half Jews are unacceptable. They are even prohibited to greet with *Heil Hitler*, which was new to me. It's a desecration of the greeting!" I sprawled in the chair. "I would rather learn more about poetry. Like the other day, we talked about Annette von Droste-Hülshoff's poem *Der Knabe im Moor* ["The Boy in the Bog"]. We have to learn it. I like it.'"

I got up, walked to the kitchen window, pulled my blouse and sleeves down and recited with a low, whispering voice,

"*Oh schaurig ists über's Moor zu gehn*
wenn es wimmelt vom Heiderauche...."

["Oh, how shuddering it is to walk through the bog
when it is filled with fog from the heath...."]

"All right, all right, that's enough. Go set the table, we can eat." After a while Mutter stopped. "What did you say about half Jews? They are unacceptable? Are you sure? So far half Jews have been safe. Good heavens, that means an awful lot of people."

"That's what we were told. What does 'race politically seen' mean anyhow? I don't understand the whole thing. Why does Hitler hate the Jews so much? What have they done to him?"

"Don't worry about it. Set the table." Erika came home

from school. As soon as Irmgard came up, we ate. Cleaning up afterwards I heard Irmgard hammer a nail into the wall of the wash basement below us. "What's she doing?" I asked Mutter. "We need more clothesline to dry the wash downstairs in poor weather. Maybe you can help her." I walked downstairs. The wash kettle boiled furiously. In spite of the closed lid, the room was full of steam. With both hands around my mouth I hollered, "Irmgard, where are you?" I saw her standing on a chair beside the boiling kettle. "Can I help you?" I jumped up behind her on the same chair.

"Watch out, I'm going to hit you," she teased me and swung the hammer back as if pounding in a nail with all her might. I ducked and—instead of hopping to the floor I leaped up onto the rim of the wash kettle. The lid tipped over and I sank to above my ankles into the boiling suds. A blood curdling scream came out of my mouth as I jumped back on the rim and down to the floor. Irmgard still stood on the chair, horror stricken. Frantically I tried to get my shoes off. As I stripped off one sock the skin peeled off with it.

Mutter came down the steps. "Did you hear that terrible…." She looked at me. "Oh my God! Margot, it was you who screamed. What happened?" She rushed in, sat me down, carefully eased off the other sock.

"The skin's coming off." My voice was shaky.

"I know, but the sock has to come off."

My feet were burning so badly, I thought my whole body was on fire. "It hurts, oh it hurts." I pleaded through clenched teeth, "Can't you put some cold water on them?"

Mutter shook her head. "Makes it only worse. Can you walk upstairs?" She helped me up the two flights to the little living room. "Irmgard, quick, run to the Apotheke to get burn ointment and bandages. I don't have enough."

In agony I sat on the sofa and stuck out my red feet. They looked horrible. The left-over skin around the ankles looked pleated; where the skin was gone, it was shiny. Mutter ran over and over to the bathroom window until she saw Irmgard with a package.

She hardly could get the words out from running so fast. "The Pharmacist said to put the ointment first, then the bandages, so they won't stick."

Carefully Mutter started to apply the cream. I winced. Irmgard stood in the door, tears in her eyes. "I'm sorry, Margot, I didn't mean to scare you with the hammer." "You didn't. I moved to the wrong side. Not your fault." I squeezed the words out. Lying back I bit my lips. The burning was so intense I couldn't even cry. It took Mutter a long time to bandage both feet.

Erika came upstairs. "Margot, what happened? What did you do?" Mutter sent her to the doctor to get more ointment. She gave me two aspirins.

Vater shook his head when he came upstairs. "I don't know, Margot, you have a knack for getting into trouble." They were standing around, looking concerned and sympathetic when Hilde came up.

"*Stöppchen*, what on earth did you do?" I started to cry. She sat beside me on the sofa. Mutter told the story for the third time. "Poor *Stöppchen*." She brushed the hair off my sweaty forehead.

I was glad Hilde was with me. "Did you have a good day?" I managed to ask her. I needed for somebody to talk to me, to distract me. After her return she had quickly found a good job with a local company in their finance department. She told me she walked to work that day, that she liked her new job, working with numbers.

I slept on the sofa. Without sufficient medication it was a slow and painful healing process. After school Erika always came upstairs to fill me in on what happened. She even let me brush and braid her hair, and made funny faces when I pulled on it, to get me to laugh and forget my pain.

After three weeks I started to hobble around. At the window I knelt on a chair to look out. The leaves were changing, the air got chilly. Mutter found an old pair of socks from Josef to keep my toes warm. After some more days I limped downstairs to eat with the others.

We listened to the news. "Heroic fighting in North Africa. General Rommel solidifies his lines in Egypt. With the start of winter on the *Ostfront* ["battle line in the east"], the Russian army began their counter offensive."

Finishing her soup Hilde shook her head. "Another winter in Russia. How are our soldiers going to survive?"

Papa cleared his throat. We all waited. "The *SS* came to the shop today," he started.

Mutter put her spoon down. "Why? What did they want?" We all stopped eating.

"They told me to join the partei."

Mutter grew pale. Her hands gripped the table. "Oh my God. Josef, what did you say?" My heart hammered so loud I could hardly hear Vater's low voice.

"I told them the truth. I told them I did not have the time. I told them I did all I could for our country by doing my work. However," Papa paused to rub his bald head, a faint smile pulling the corners of his mouth, "I was able to show them an official letter from the *Wehrmacht* that we got only a week ago, naming our business a war-important business, that the army depended on us in this district."

"And? What happened?" We all hung on his words.

"They read it. First the one, then the other, they looked at each other, then read it again. One of them even examined the stationary to make sure it was authentic. They didn't like it but there's nothing they can do."

"The letter is that crucial?" Erika asked.

Vater nodded. "As a war-important business we fall under the protection of the *Wehrmacht* to maintain their vehicles. The Nazis and the *SS* have no control over us."

"You mean now they can't force you?" Mutter could not believe it. "You mean we don't have to worry anymore?"

"Not as long as we are in business."

"Huh, what a narrow escape." Hilde breathed a deep sigh of relief. So did we all.

Mutter leaned back in her chair. "I can't forget the Baumann family, what the Nazis did to them."

"I think," Vater said slowly, "I think they came with the intention to force me to join or else. That letter from the *Wehrmacht* saved all our lives. We are very fortunate and I am grateful." His voice broke, he stared at his big, meticulously cleaned hands. In the deep silence I sniffled, tears running down my cheeks.

"I have an idea what 'or else' implies," Hilde said quietly. We all looked at her. "One day in Thüringen we visited another camp. On the way we passed a road construction. The people working on it were obviously prisoners, guarded by soldiers with mounted bayonets. They looked terribly thin, haggard, heads shaven, only dressed in light prison clothing, despite the bitter cold. Somebody in the bus said, 'those are *Konzentration Lager Häftlinge, K.Z. Häftlinge*, ["concentration camp inmates"]. Somebody else asked, 'What do you mean with K.Z.?' The explanation was, 'they are from concentration camps the *SS* has built for the enemies of our country.' My guess is those are like forced labor camps."

In bed that evening I struggled with my confused feelings. How could Germans do this to their own people, to my people? Landsman to landsman, even if some of them happened to belong to a different race, like the German Jews. What gave the Nazis the right to feel so superior? Was Papa, because he did not believe in the Nazi partei and in Hitler, an 'enemy of his country', of our country? It seemed a piece of paper saved us all, this time. What would happen next?

CHAPTER 9

Christmas of 1942 approached rapidly. We heard from Josef. It was bitter cold, especially during watch at night. He thought of us all. Otherwise he said he was all right.

Christmas Eve we gathered around the small tree with a few candles. The exchange of gifts, each one of us got one item, took five minutes. We sang a few Christmas carols. Then it was over. It didn't feel like Christmas at all.

The following afternoon Hilde and I relaxed in the warmth of the little room, reading and writing while the parents took a nap and Erika visited Maria. The radio broadcast the All-Request-Christmas program for our soldiers with Zarah Leander and Marlene Dietrich singing their latest hits. In one 'greeting' Marlene Dietrich breathed into the micro-phone,

Ich bin von Kopf bis Fuss auf Liebe eingestellt...

["I'm geared for love from head to toe..."]

I laughed out loud. "Doesn't she sound funny the way she sings that? And what stupid words."

Hilde looked up from her letter. "It may sound stupid to you, I like the way she sings that."

The next hit, *In der Nacht ist der Mensch nicht gern alleine, denn die Liebe….*

["In the night one does not like to be alone, because love…"] sung with lots of feeling by Marlene Dietrich I found even more amusing. "You probably like this one too", I teased Hilde.

She threw me an angry look. "Stop being a brat. Read your book."

The music switched to operettas. Those I liked. *Land des Lächeln* ["Land of Smiles"] by Franz Lehar was the first one. A soft tenor pealed:

Immer nur lächelns und immer vergnügt,
immer zufrieden wie's immer sich fügt,
lächeln trotz Weh und tausend Schmerzen,
doch—wie's dadrin aussieht geht niemand was an.
["Always only smile, always happy,
always content, whatever happens,
smile in spite of grief and a thousand pains,
but—what it looks like in here is nobody's
business".]

I liked that. I had never listened to the words before. '...smile in spite of grief and a thousand pains, but—what it looks like in here, is nobody's business'. Somehow that spoke to me. I wanted to remember that.

Various waltzes brought the finale. The concert was over. I got up. "I'm going to make some peppermint tea. Would you like some?" I looked at the letter. "To whom are you writing?"

Hilde smiled wistfully. "To somebody I met recently."

"Oh, really?" I plopped into the chair beside her. "Who is it?"

"You don't know him, maybe someday you will. Yes, thank you, I'd like a cup of tea. Now go and let me finish," she said with emphasis. I trudged off with a big sigh. Secrets! Why did grownups always have secrets. At least she wasn't sore anymore. I hummed while I brewed the tea. How much fun to be the bratty little sister.

The beginning of 1943 brought a lot of snow but not the terrible cold like the year before. Our news was filled with the heroic fighting of our troops in the face of heavy Russian pressure and the bitter cold. One question was on everybody's mind: will our troops be able to hold out? Soon we got the feared and disastrous news: Leningrad was lost. Shortly thereafter Stalingrad was lost. Two cities for which the blood of thousands had been shed. For nothing! Would Josef be involved in this 'heroic' fighting, maybe loose his life, for nothing?

Fraulein Dr. Schulte stood beside her desk, in uniform as always. "*Heil Hitler*. I want to remind you girls that our *Führer* through Feldmarschall Göhring asked our nation to mourn for two days the death of our heroes in Stalingrad. I need not remind you that we are involved in THE epic battle in history. We Germans are a superior race. As such we must rule with discipline and equity. The Bolshevist and Jewish menace must be eliminated. The Jewish World Coalition must be destroyed. We also must be prepared for greater hardships, for greater sacrifices. I ask all of you, every single one of you, to do your utmost in school and in your family lives to support our brave soldiers, our heroes, and to support the leader of this nation, Adolf Hitler. Please stand as we sing our National Anthem and, for our fallen heroes, '*Ich hatt einen Kameraden*' ["I had a friend"].

Tears blurred my vision. Would I some day sing this song with Josef in mind?

In Spring of 1943, Erika finished elementary school.

"How does it feel being finished with school?" I asked as she tossed her school bag into the bottom of our wardrobe.

With a big grin she answered, "Wonderful! No more school! No more horrible teachers."

"Never?"

"Not necessarily. Some day maybe a business school, I don't know. Right now I have to do my year of duty, like

Irmgard. I like to go to Frau Schuller, a relative of Maria. She qualifies for help and has applied for me. Now I have to wait for the official confirmation."

That confirmation came a few days later. With a smile Erika tore open the envelope. "Good, it's close by, not even a five minutes' walk, and Frau Schuller's really nice."

I missed Erika greatly. Not only did I have to take on all of her chores, but there was nobody to share with coming home from school. Talking with Mutter became increasingly difficult. Her questions were often perfunctory, she didn't wait to hear the answers. And I learned not to confide in her. Whatever I told her, she turned it around and used it against me, clobbered me with it.

The news from North Africa had not been good all spring. "Battles to the last piece of ammunition and with bare bayonets", the newspaper said. Finally in mid May the OKW announced the formal end of the African campaign. "The most heroic fight in Tunisia honorably finished!" "The task to its fullest extent accomplished!" the newspaper headlines shouted. Feldmarschall Rommel, the Desert Fox, was decorated with the highest honors ever bestowed on a German soldier, Oak Leaves with Swords and Diamonds to the Iron Cross. The remnant of the *Afrikakorp* surrendered and was taken as prisoners of war to America. They were lucky, they got out of this mess. Was is worth the lives of thousands of men? What was accomplished?

"Hilde, Mother's Day is coming up in a week and I have no idea what to give Mutter." It was Saturday afternoon, Hilde mended piles of bed sheets for the umpteenth time on the old Singer treadle machine in the little room.

She shrugged. "I don't have anything either. Let's think what we can do."

"We can't even get flowers. They are too expensive."

"Hmm, inexpensive flowers. Maybe we can get some wildflowers?"

"Of course. That's it." The more I thought about the idea, the more I liked it. "The Flower Garden in the park is full of blooming azaleas and rhododendrons. Absolutely beautiful. Jürgen and I just saw them yesterday."

"We can't do that! With guards walking around constant-ly. Besides," Hilde smoothed out the sheet to patch another tear, "what if we had an air raid? And we would be gone."

"We don't have air raids in the early morning."

Erika came in. "What are you two doing? Concocting something?"

I laughed. "We are. You think we can get some of those gorgeous azaleas and rhododendrons from the Flower Garden for Mother's Day? I can't think of anything else."

Erika's face broke into a wide grin. "What a splendid idea. Of course we can do that. I don't have anything either." She thought for a moment and laughed. "Can't you just see Mutter coming into a room full of lovely flowers, knowing perfectly well they're all stolen! Not to talk about what Vater will think."

"At least we have flowers and we remembered her."

"You are absolutely right. That is the important part. Where they come from is of no concern." That decided it. I got the task to scout out the guard situation and to know where the best flowers were.

It was not a difficult task. A few afternoons later Jürgen and I strolled after school through the Flower Garden. I told him of our plan.

He looked at me surprised and laughed. "You really want to cut flowers here on Sunday morning?"

"Sure. Why not? After all, the park belongs to all of us. We pay taxes. And the few stalks we take won't be missed in this mass of flowers."

We sat on a bench close to the entrance and watched. Soon an elderly gentleman in dark blue uniform slowly made his way to the Garden and disappeared into a path almost hidden from the rest of the park. We waited.

After a long time I nudged Jürgen. "You think he is sleeping on one of those benches in there?"

He got up. "Let's go and find out."

We entered the narrow path. The spongy, black ground absorbed our steps. The air smelled musty as if never a ray of sunshine penetrated the thick green ceiling. Jürgen grinned and pointed ahead. The guard, sitting on a bench, his head slightly fallen forward, snored softly.

I laughed. "That much for him. And we don't have to worry about the others, they are in different areas."

After deciding to meet on Saturday to check out the flowers we shook hands. "*Tschüs.*"

Saturday afternoon was cool and windy. Heavy, dark clouds moved rapidly across the sky, letting the sun through only sparingly. A typical May afternoon.

"Well, here we are, checking out what you can steal on Sunday morning," Jürgen greeted me.

"You don't have to put it that way." We laughed and entered the park. As always the hush, the filtered light, the lush beauty had a profound effect on me. I wanted to tread more softly, speak more quietly, so as not to disturb the mysterious silence. The air was heavy with the spicy fragrance of masses of flowers.

We sat on the bench in front of the *Hexenhäuschen* ["little witch hut"], deep in the shadow of the tall trees. In front of us spread the beautiful array of hundreds of blooming azaleas and rhododendron bushes on the sunny banks of the Garden. As if a painter with a preference to pinks and purples had slapped colorful splotches into the lush green, they ranged from delicate lavenders to burning pinks and deep reds. Some of the tall rhododendrons carried huge purple clusters of deep throated, bell shaped blossoms. I pointed to one area. "Those lavender ones are my favorites, even though I like the hot pinks and deep purples almost as much. They are mainly on that one path up there. No problem."

For a moment we were silent. I turned to Jürgen. "I want to ask you a question. Promise you'll answer honestly?"

He looked surprised. "Sure. I'll try."

I had thought about this question often and had waited for an appropriate time. "What does your mother say about our being together this much? I assume she knows about me?"

He laughed a bit uneasily. "Well, yes, she does, she asked me at one point about you. First of all she made clear that I cannot neglect my homework. With that I agree. She knows who you are, even though…." He stopped.

"…even though what?" I encouraged him to go on.

"I think she would be happier—oh, I don't know how to say it." He looked helplessly at me, blushing.

"I'm sorry, I didn't mean to embarrass you."

"No, I'm not embarrassed. She should be." He took a deep breath, started again. "I think she would be happier if you would come from an academic family."

I chuckled. I could still see Mutter, her face beaming, when I came back from ice skating. "So, his father is a dentist? Well, isn't that nice." Aloud I said, "Doesn't surprise me one bit. How do you feel about that?"

His boyish grin spread again over his face. "I don't care. I like you. You're a wonderful friend. Period."

"I'm glad, I like you too. You are like a brother to me. I just wish our parent's generation wouldn't be so class conscious. My mother's the same way. If your mom thinks

I'm below your class, too bad, not much I can do about." I laughed. "Come on, we have to go."

Saturday night the air raid lasted only over an hour. As we climbed wearily up the stairs, Hilde whispered, "Sleep fast, I'll wake you at four."

It seemed I had just fallen asleep when she shook my arm. I was dead tired.

Erika grunted, "Whose crazy idea was this anyhow?"

"Be very quiet, wear your dark warm-up suits and your gym shoes. I'll wait in the center hall."

She was ready with pocketknives and pruning shears. "We've to be back in an hour, so let's move."

Like dark shadows we ran on soft rubber soles to the nearest park entrance, passed the playground with its two giant sandboxes and entered the Flower Garden. Hilde pulled us behind an ancient, gnarled beechnut tree whose heavy branches touched the ground, hiding us completely. "If somebody comes, slip in here. Margot, if you hear the guard, squeak as high as you can. Now let's listen." I held my breath, hearing only my thumping heart beat.

"All right, let's go." We stepped out of the protecting branches into the quiet, cloudy night, no moon, no stars, and walked noiselessly around the corner, my eyes having adjusted to the darkness.

From the first bush, the lavender azalea with large, fluted blossoms, I carefully clipped a few blooming stems. How sweet and spicy they smelled. Back on the path I bumped into Erika. We both stifled a scream.

"Hurry up, we haven't much time left."

I listened for Hilde. No sound, only my heart in my throat. At the tall rhododendron with the large purple blossoms, she suddenly stepped out of its shadow, making me jump. "Here, I'll cut some for you. You can't reach them." She glanced at my loot. "We've enough. Let's go."

We collected Erika who was still cutting. Each of us had two ample bundles.

Suddenly Hilde froze. We heard a scraping sound. "Run to the exit!" Cradling the fragile blossoms in my arms, I followed my sisters. "Hurry, it's getting lighter." We ran straight home.

Unobtrusively we had prepared the living and dining room the evening before. Now we placed lavish arrangements of purples and pinks on tables, buffet and desk. After the last sprig was secured, we surveyed with critical eyes our accomplishment. Yes, the room looked as colorful and beautiful as spring itself and was already filled with the spicy fragrance.

"What if Mutter comes down while we get dressed?" Erika thought ahead.

"You're right." Hilde wrote a quick note, "Mutter, please do not enter living and dining room," and taped it to the first door. After a final look we tiptoed upstairs, dressed and waited. When Mutter opened her door, we followed right behind her. Hilde motioned to Papa to come down too.

Mutter stopped at the note. "What does that mean?"

I squeezed past her and opened the door wide. "Happy Mother's Day!" Sweet fragrance streamed out of the room. We congratulated and kissed her.

"How nice, thank you." She went from vase to vase, sniffed all of them. "How nice of you. Thank you. I don't think I've ever gotten this many flowers." She sounded genuinely pleased. We were glad and ignored Papa's questioning looks.

A few minutes later Oma came down to go to church. We pulled her into the room. "Happy Oma's Day, Oma." Erika handed her a lavender and purple arrangement made especially for her. I did see a twinkle in her eyes and a wistful smile before she mumbled, "I better get to church and pray."

Saturday evenings Hilde usually went to St. Marks, a beautiful Gothic Roman Catholic church in the old part of Düsseldorf, for Evensong and Benediction. Hundreds of young people flocked to the Vesper, chanted in Gregorian style. Often she took me along.

Afterward we sat outside in the grass in large circles and sang folk songs, accompanied by as many guitars as were present. We shrugged off the danger of an air raid, we seldom had one in the early evening hours. These Saturday evenings became special for me. As one of the youngest of our group, I was happy to be accepted. That I often saw *SS* and *Gestapo* in the vicinity of the church watching us did not disturb us. We were used to their presence.

"Do you really have to go there every Saturday night?" Mutter asked Hilde in a disagreeable voice as Hilde slung her guitar over her back.

"Sure, why not? We have fun. The Evensong is lovely."

"I think Margot is too young to be out every Saturday night." I became alarmed, looked at Hilde.

"Too young to go to church?" Hilde laughed. "That's a first. Don't worry, she's safe with us."

"What if we have an air raid? I don't think that is safe," Mutter insisted. I kept quiet, I had to leave this to Hilde.

"Then we'll all go into a shelter as does everybody else on the streetcar and be home somewhat later." Mutter shook her head and gave up for the time being.

One of the next Saturdays, we had just boarded the streetcar after the service, the siren wailed. Without stopping but with ringing its clanking bells incessantly, the streetcar drove through to the next shelter, a huge, ugly cement bunker.

"Everybody out and into the shelter." Our group of six girls linked arms, marched toward the bunker, laughing and singing.

"Break up those lines! Two by two, move!" The *SA*

official by the door waved his arm furiously at us. We unlinked, filed into what looked like a black hole. A dimly lit immense room with rows and rows of simple benches swallowed us up. The air was musty and damp, the thick cement walls oppressive. Hilde selected a corner close to the exit. One light bulb dangled high above us. On the hard wooden bench, we moved close together as Hilde started to play softly. One by one we fell in with singing quietly, some only humming. The Nazi official from the door walked by, frowned disapprovingly. Hilde continued to play. The bunker filled with hundreds of people as streetcar after streetcar deposited its load. On the bench behind us two small children sat on their mother's lap, being cradled and gently rocked, almost asleep.

Hilde stopped for a moment, smiled at me and started my favorite song, *Wildgänse rauschen durch die Nacht mit schrillem Schrei nach Norden...*' ["Wild geese soar through the night with shrill cries toward the North..."] Whenever I sang these words the walls around me disappeared. A feeling of freedom, of endless space, of boundless soaring permeated me. We sang the three verses quietly. The *SA* official marched by again. My eyes were riveted to the floor. The highly polished brown boots came to a sudden stop beside Hilde. My heart skipped. She continued to play so quietly I had to strain to hear the chords over the low hum of the place. Finally the boots marched on, clicking angrily with each step. I glanced up, Hilde smiled.

Finally the end of raid sounded. Stiff from sitting tensed up so long, we filed out past the official. Hilde ignored his irate stare. I was glad to leave his area.

"Well, it's about time you decided to come home," Mutter waited at the door. It was way beyond my curfew.

Hilde shrugged. "Nothing we could do, we had to stay in the bunker."

"My first time in a bunker. Interesting," I added.

"Interesting!" Mutter said reproachfully. "I want you to be home during an air raid."

I took a deep breath, pulled myself up to my fullest height. "Mutter, I can't stay home all the time because there might be an air raid. Life does go on, you know. I am not a baby. As a matter of fact I'm going to be thirteen in a few weeks." She looked at me, taken aback and shook her head. Round number one won!

"One more day and we have vacation." I dropped my school bag in the center hall on the floor.

"How was school?" I knew Mutter expected no answer to her perfunctory question.

"Fine." I went upstairs to change. One more day and Jürgen and I could ride our bikes to a lovely spot we recently discovered, where gnarled willows grew almost to the river's edge. But first, tomorrow was report card day. I knew I had not done well, had not studied enough.

Next morning Fraulein Dr. Schulte stood beside her desk, a stack of report cards in her hand. "Girls, we have come to the end of the academic year. Since all of you continue to the next grade, the *Quarta*, we will move together into a different classroom...." Oh, I'll loose my window seat. What will school be like without watching the ducks and the swans? She reminded us of our duty to the *Vaterland* and handed out the report cards. I glanced at mine. As expected, I got a poor grade in English and Math.

"*Heil Hitler*, girls." School was officially closed.

Jürgen was hanging around his school. "How's your report card?" I asked.

"Not particularly good. My parents won't be happy."

"Will you get into trouble?"

"Don't know. I may not be able to do as much bicycling as we like to do," he smiled ruefully. "We'll see."

At home I laid the report card on the table. "No more school. What can I help you with, Mutter?"

A week later all Hitler *Jugend* groups were summoned to the *Braune Haus*. Action: Yardage and shoe collection. When I arrived the group leader stopped me. "*Heil Hitler*. Where is your uniform?"

Heat and anger rose up. I glanced around, all other children wore theirs. "It was not specified on the summons to come in uniform."

"Of course not. That is understood. Don't come again without wearing one. *Heil Hitler*."

We each got a district assigned, each received a package of flyers to distribute on Monday to every family in order to collect the items on Friday and Saturday.

In my district were approximately twenty apartment houses, each with four stories, each story with two apartments. One hundred and sixty apartments. All Monday long I walked up and down the flights of steps to distribute the flyers.

Friday morning, I remembered to wear my makeshift uniform, we met again at the *Braune Haus*. It always amazed me to see so many men in *SA* uniform standing around idle, just talking. I could not remember that Vater ever stood around, doing nothing, just talking.

In the opening rally the district leader congratulated us for "being elected, for having the privilege to participate side by side with our heroes in the battlefield to win this struggle against the Jewish menace and the Bolshevist colossus". Then we swarmed out to start the collection.

Answering the first doorbell a little girl opened the door, her mother right behind her. She handed me an armful of clothing. "Thank you very much. Good day." Then I realized I was in uniform. I either needed to use the Nazi salute or nothing at all. I decided on nothing at all, just thanking the people.

I deposited the donated items beside each door on my way up and collected them on my way down, dropping them outside the entrance for further pickup by trucks. It was obvious people wanted to help. Most of the items were in good, if not perfect condition. At noon instead of going back to the *Braune Haus* for a sandwich, I went home and fell into a chair. "I'm exhausted. Up and down and up and down."

"How far are you?" Mutter set a plate of soup in front of me. "You'll get there. You still have plenty of time."

"*Ja*, I wished I had also plenty of energy." By Friday evening I had rung all one hundred and sixty door bells. Saturday I planned to go back to those on my list I had not reached. At the final rally we were informed the action was a huge success.

During the following week we prepared for Whitsunday, a major two-day feast day. Mutter started spring cleaning with only my help. With sunny weather and all windows open, curtains came down, we washed windows, beat the oriental rugs outside with a wicker carpet beater, scrubbed and waxed floors. Saturday afternoon Mutter even baked a *Stuten* with raisins for the feast day. Where she got the ingredients, I did not know, but the house smelled good, a Saturday smell. The home fried potatoes for supper tasted especially good. The others ate a heated slice of sausage, I got an egg. Erika grinned. "The poor pale faced little girl...."
A friendly kick under the table silenced her.

"Why don't you two clean up so we all can get to bed early to catch some extra sleep," Mutter suggested.

Erika protested. "Go to sleep? Marianne and I have promised Maria to meet her around 9:3O. It's Saturday evening, it's a holiday weekend and I have off for the first time." The dishes were done in a hurry.

"I'm gone," Erika pulled the front door closed. "Erika, wait!" Mutter ran to the door to catch her. "If you hear the siren you come home with the first sound, understand? Takes you only two minutes to run home. I'm not going to worry about you being somewhere else."

"Yes, Mutter, I'll be here." She was gone.

She is lucky, I thought, she has two girl friends. Upstairs in my room the open window let in the cool evening air. Leaning against it I watched the stars appear in the clear sky, one after the other lit up, as if a lamplighter worked his round. One star sparkled especially bright with a yellow hue. Could Josef see it? His last letter was from the Ukraine. He was so far away.

I closed the window, adjusted the black paper, flipped on the light and walked to Josef's desk. I ran my finger along the leather backs of his books lined up behind the sliding glass. I was sure he read them all. If only I knew him better. I promised myself to make a special effort when he came back.

As I sat down to open one of his books, the siren sounded. So early? If only Erika hears it and comes right away. A sudden burst of our flack tore the quiet evening apart.

"Margot!" Vater's voice sounded uptight.

"Coming." I swooped up my suitcase, slid down the banister rail to the second floor, jumped off, repeated the procedure to the first. "Is Erika in?"

"No, and we seem to be the target. Get down, I'll wait. Hurry."

What if Erika did not hear the siren? What if they went somewhere? The idea of not having her with us in an attack was unthinkable.

"The first wave is entering the *Ruhr* corridor, flying in close formation. Target: Düsseldorf," the familiar, precise voice announced as I stumbled into the shelter. God, please let Erika come home before anything happens. "Erika in?" Mutter asked anxiously. I shook my head. Just then the front door was being kicked and banged. A moment later Erika burst into the shelter, her face white as a sheet, Papa right behind her. She tried to catch her breath. "They dropped flares like Christmas trees. One is above our house. We're all lit up." "Good heavens, those are bomb indicators," Hilde jumped up. "They mark the periphery of a square target area." "I'll have a look." Papa opened the shelter door. Hilde slipped out with him. Returning only a moment later he called us. "Come, you have to have a look. I've never seen anything like it."

I hardly dared to follow him. He opened the heavy outside door to the backyard and to the loud humming of hundreds of planes and the sound of explosions. We crowded up the steps to a most amazing sight. Directly over our house hung a huge array of floodlights in the shape of a Christmas tree, lighting us up like a soccer field. Every branch of every tree was highly visible. Way over in the distance to the right and to the left we saw the same Christmas tree. If it was to be a square, the last one, the one furthest north, we could not see. So that was the target area. Maybe we were lucky. Maybe. Our flack bellowed, the explosions came closer.

Running back into the shelter we heard the second and third waves announced. "All right, all of you." Vater sounded businesslike and stern. "If our house starts burning, kick in the hole in the wall across from this shelter door. Remember, that's where the *Durchbruch* ["breakthrough"] was made months ago. Kick in the wall and run through as many houses as necessary until we can get upstairs and out. Otherwise we stay here and wait it out." We nodded. And waited.

"A fourth wave has entered our area." The rumbling of the explosions swelled up, came closer.

Hilde sat on her bed, the bottom one of our three bunk beds. With my little suitcase between my feet I moved close to her. She put her arm around me. "Don't worry." I tried to smile. "That's easy to say." Erika sat on the other side of me. I felt comforted and protected. What could happen? The worst was to die. And what was so bad about that? I had a vague idea there was a greater purpose to our life, but had not thought much about it. Maybe not dying but burning was worst. More and more incendiary bombs were being dropped. Knowing burns first hand I shuddered.

Hilde pulled me closer. "It's going to be all right."

"A new wave has entered the *Ruhr* corridor." We all groaned. Will it ever end? Düsseldorf must be decimated after this. Our flack shot bravely.

"I'll have a look," Vater left, Mutter shook her head. When he came back his face was like stone. "Düsseldorf is an ocean of fire. Everywhere it's burning."

"What about Bilk?" Mutter asked.

"That whole direction, one huge fire." So far his business in Bilk survived. What about Brass? Poor Oma, she was so frail and old. Would she get through this?

After three hours it calmed down. Vater went out and called us. "Come and have a look. They have done a thorough job for one night."

The floodlights above us were burned out. But the city was aflame. The whole sky north of us, from the west all the way to the east, nothing but a flaming inferno. At times the flames gushed up, intensifying the red of the sky only to collapse and to start somewhere else.

Like rabbits coming out of their holes our neighbors came up their steps. We could hear their hushed voices.

"I wish we knew how Oma is?" Mutter was worried

about her mother and sisters. I wanted to say 'They'll be all right,' but were they? Was anybody all right in that fiery square?

We stood silently in the balmy spring night, watching Düsseldorf burn. With so many people in the city we loved and cared about, here we stood, unable to do anything.

"Josef, isn't there some way we can find out?" Mutter's voice sounded strained.

"I don't think so, Trude. Phones won't be working even if we had one, public transportation will be down, we have no car, there's no other means of communication." He shook his head. "We'll have to wait."

Another attack was over and we were still alive, we still had our house. I hoped against hope that Brass family might also be alive by whatever miracle.

"If Brass survived I hope they come straight to us." Papa's words interrupted my thoughts. "We need to prepare for them. They could be here by morning or the latest by noon. It will take them that long to walk to Benrath."

"Walk to Benrath? Oma Brass walking fifteen miles to us?" I couldn't believe that would be possible. "And *Tante* Mia with her leg, walking to us with a cane?"

"It's amazing what you can do to survive. As soon as the air raid is over, I want you to go up and straighten out your rooms to have space for them if and when they come."

Good, that gave us something to do. The rooms all needed it, especially Hilde's.

At dawn the rooms were presentable. I opened the window to let some fresh air in, but closed it immediately because of the smell of smoke. The sun rose behind the opposite houses with a strange glow. "Happy Whitsunday," I thought angrily. What did Oma Brass and the aunts have to do with the war? Why were innocent people the victims instead of those that started them? The city lay under a thick layer of smoke and dust, with flares of fires shooting up.

I was surprised to see Vater come up to our room. "Why don't you two get ready for church? It's Whitsunday. I'll stay here in case they come."

"To church, now?" I had looked forward to this morning's service. Now it seemed so senseless.

"Especially now, Margot. Pray for all the poor people that are homeless or injured, and for all that have died during the night." Vater's eyes filled with grief and tears. He quickly left.

My bed was still untouched. It hadn't occurred to me that I hadn't slept all night. The cold water refreshed me as I quickly washed and changed into my one printed cotton dress that I had ironed especially for this morning. Mutter had sewn it out of curtain material. Now it seemed unimportant and meaningless.

Erika and I walked in silence to church. People met at the church not with happy shouts and greetings, but with anxious questions, "Have you heard anything from the city? Has anybody any news?" During Mass I prayed for Brass, for the people in the city, for Josef, for our soldiers. But wouldn't others, wouldn't our enemies do the same? To whom does God listen? Whose side does he take? Whom does he help? The questions confused and almost overwhelmed me. Still, I felt better afterwards.

After church we ran home. Papa shook his head as we arrived out of breath. No, nobody heard anything. Time went by agonizingly slow. Around noon, while I was on my way upstairs to look down the road for the umpteenth time, the doorbell rang. Mutter rushed up, tore open the door. Six people stood in front of us, unrecognizable.

"Oh my God, you are alive," was all Mutter could say over and over. Slowly, silently they filed in, scarves tied around their heads. Oma Brass, painfully limping, helped by *Tante* Hilde and *Tante* Grete. *Tante* Mia, leaning heavily on her cane, hobbled in behind them, followed by *Tante*

Franziska, holding tightly little Anneliese's hand. Their faces were smeared with smoke and soot, eyes red and tearing. *Tante* Grete's skirt hung in shreds, Oma's scarf showed burn marks, *Tante* Franziska's hair was singed. Anneliese's face wore smudged tear streaks, her pink dress sooty and torn. Their shoes were covered with ashes. They came without anything—not even handbags. Nothing.

"Sit down, sit down, let me make some coffee," Mutter urged them. They sat down on the first steps of the staircase. With them came a cloud of smoke filled air. *Tante* Franziska let out a deep sight. "Thank God we're here." She looked up, tried to smile, but it didn't make it to her eyes. "You know what saved our lives? The breakthroughs."

We spent the rest of the day filling bathtub after bathtub, finding clothes for them, getting food on the table and finding space to rest. Erika and I vacated our bedroom. We were in such a flurry of excitement and gratefulness that only in the afternoon did I realize how dead tired I was.

At that moment the doorbell rang. Mutter called me. I was astonished to see our BDM leader, Frau Bartram, in the door. Her bike leaned against our front hedge.

"*Heil Hitler.*" I waited. "You and Erika are expected to be at the *Braune Haus* tomorrow at eight sharp to help in the city."

"What do we have to do?"

"You will be told in time. *Heil Hitler.*"

"Erika, imagine, they are asking us to help."

She shook her head. "I can't go. I have to work."

"That's right. Did she say to wear uniform?" Suddenly I was angry with my parents. The skirt and blouse were too small. I always felt shabbily dressed even in my makeshift uniform, when all the other girls wore their nice, trim velvet jackets. Why did they make it so difficult for us? We constantly had problems in school because of the uniform. We were the only girls there without them.

"Margot, you sleep on the couch tonight. It's ready. Get a good rest. It may be quiet. Tomorrow will be a long day for you. I'm glad you're helping in the city." Mutter approved of what I was asked to do? That didn't happen often. Before drifting off I felt the clean, good smelling linens and saw the blackened faces.

"Wake up, Margot, you have to go to the city." Mutter shook my arm. Immediately I was wide-awake. Would we ride in open trucks? What would we be doing, with the city still burning? The area around the central railroad station was supposedly flattened out.

"Tell Frau Bartram, if she asks, that your uniform is dirty and has to be washed."

"Sure, as if I hadn't used that excuse a hundred times."

"Nobody's going to worry about your uniform today," Mutter said with finality. "Also tell her Erika has to work. And, listen, stay with the group, don't go off on your own. I don't want you wandering through burning houses, all right?"

I waved good-bye and ran all the way to the *Braune Haus.* Turning the last corner of the *Schlossallee* I saw a group of kids, all in uniform, milling in front of the three-story stone building. Some of them ran up to me.

"Margot, guess what? In the morning we have to make sandwiches and in the afternoon we help people get new clothes." I was glad to be included.

I told them, "My grandma and my aunts arrived from center city yesterday noon. They walked all the way. They lost everything." Somebody called, "*Achtung!*" Instantly we stood at attention in a long line on the sidewalk. I cringed knowing how I stuck out in civilian clothes. The *SA* official, shiny boots and all, walked up and down in front of us.

"We called you together to help in our city. You will be

told there what needs to be done. I expect everyone of you to do his full duty. *Heil Hitler.*" With outstretched arm and a sharp click, he dismissed us.

Two open army trucks pulled up. We swarmed onto the platform. How often I had wished to ride in an open truck. A soldier waited until we were all on board, then closed the back securely. "Hold on to the top and side rails so you don't fall out. Ready?"

"Ready!"

The soldiers drove fast, the streets were in poor conditions. Hard winters and lack of repairs had left their mark. We bounced around like pebbles on a washboard.

As we came closer to the city the smoke filled air turned into biting stench. The sun, so warm and clear in Benrath, disappeared behind a heavy smoke screen. It got darker and darker like before a heavy storm. The truck followed the streetcar tracks toward the central railroad station. Some streetcars still stood on their tracks, twisted, burned, windows blown out. Some lay beside the tracks as if a giant hand knocked them over and squashed them. Our joking and laughing subsided, we just stared.

Apartment buildings on both sides of the street, well known to most of us, were windowless, blackened, some still burning, some smoldering. Torn curtains flapped in the gusty wind. Through shattered windows we saw hanging ceilings, ready to collapse any moment.

The people looked just as blind, blackened, wandering around aimlessly, some searching in the rubble. One woman on hands and knees scraped away smoldering debris, looking for something. Street after street nothing but devastation. An eerie stillness lay over the city, occasionally interrupted by an ambulance siren, picking its way around holes and torn rails. The stenchy wind fanned smoldering heaps into flames.

Our truck lurched to a dead stop. Out of the inside of an apartment building that just collapsed, smoke, debris and fire shot like a fountain high into the air and onto the street. Two burning beams landed in front of our truck, barring the way. Our drivers kicked and pushed them aside with their boots. Slowly and more carefully we wound our way through the destruction.

On one main road a column of army trucks disgorged hundreds of prisoners and foreign laborers to start the cleanup and repair work.

Finally we arrived at our destination, the Exhibition Halls. In a spacious building with hastily set up long tables we formed a conveyer belt production to make sandwiches. The older boys tore open boxes with bread, butter, cold cuts and got the supply flowing. Nobody spoke. We were given terse instructions, we followed them, working rapidly. I unwrapped sliced, dark bread and fed it into the process for buttering and adding two slices of luncheon meat. At the end of the table the sandwiches were stacked into boxes.

A *SA* man stood at every table, watching. I was very hungry, but didn't dare to eat something. After I felt familiar with my task I looked around. Fifty to sixty youngsters between eleven and fifteen worked at the tables. That all wore uniforms was of no further concern to me. I was doing a job. I was helping and I was proud of it. Box after box was stacked into trucks and driving to different areas in the city for the thousands of homeless people.

What was the woman on hands and knees looking for? Some possessions? What if it was a child? At the thought a child might be trapped in the rubble my stomach twisted into a knot. No, don't think that, I told myself, you are getting yourself into trouble.

"Hey, you there, snap out of it, you are holding up the production." A sharp voice tore me out of my thoughts.

"Sorry." I hastened to make up the time. My back ached,

my feet were sore, my stomach empty. I felt a tap on my shoulder and looked into the round, concerned face of a heavy-set woman who kept things moving.

"Tired?"

"Yes, very," I said with a sigh.

"I'll get somebody to relieve you." Soon she had a group together to take our places. We slumped down along the wall to sit on the floor. The woman pushed a carton of sandwiches in front of us and handed us cups of coffee. "Here, you all have done a good job. Eat and relax."

The afternoon was spent as guides. In terse, minimal instructions we were told to lead the bombed-out through a maze of supply vans which was set up in a huge square. We needed to help them find the right clothing, keep track on a chart of what they received, and carry their new belongings for them until they were newly clothed, had money and temporary papers as well as food ration cards and could be released.

I was amazed at the organization. The bombed-out people, numb and silent, did not know why they had been trucked up here. I walked up to an elderly woman sitting on the grass, helped her up and explained the procedure.

"You mean you gonna help me get money and clothing?" she asked bewildered. A shy smile lit up her face, caked with soot and tears. The people gratefully accepted whatever we had for them. Their thankfulness spurred me on. Forgotten was my own gloom and tiredness.

After I led the elderly woman through the process I ran back to begin anew. A young mother, dazed and worn out, with two little girls sat next to the entrance. I took the oldest girl, I guessed her to be seven, by the hand, told the mother the sequence and showed them some of the new clothing for their size. I felt very grown up.

Suddenly I heard sirens. What was I doing in town? I should be home. What if anything happened to me out here?

Or if something happened at home? I felt panic creep in. The little girl squeezed my hand. "You're going to stay with us, aren't you?" she begged. Her smudged face showed she had cried.

"Yeah, of course."

My reply didn't convince her. "Are you afraid?"

"Of course I'm not afraid, silly," I lied. "But I would rather be home."

"I would too, but I don't have a home anymore." Tears welled up in her green eyes. "It's burned and so are my dolls."

I looked at her as if I saw her for the first time. "What's your name?"

"Hildegard."

"How nice. That's my oldest sister's name. And how old are you, Hildegard?"

"Six." She twisted and turned in her burned dress.

"And your little sister?"

"She's only four, that's why my mom has to take care of her. She doesn't have to do this with me."

The end siren sounded. With Hildegard's hand in mine I led them through the set-up until they were outfitted. Hildegard now wore a pretty green dress.

It was getting late. The trucks took us back to Benrath. Numb and exhausted we sat silently on the platform. The worst part of the day was the fifteen minutes walk home.

Crawling into bed I prayed, Please, God, don't let anything happen when I'm not home with everybody else.

The following morning Vater and Hilde walked to Düsseldorf. All day we waited. Was his business destroyed? In the late afternoon shuffling steps and knocks on the front door ended our waiting. Dirty faced and exhausted they carried in bags with charred papers.

"Is it burnt out completely?" Mutter asked anxiously, looking at Vater's red and teary eyes. He carefully placed the big leather bag into a corner of the living room. The burnt smell from their clothes and the bags saturated the air. We stood around, waiting for more information. After they washed and ate some soup, Papa cleared his throat.

"That's all that's left. Totally burnt out. We did manage to open the burned wooden safe. All papers," he pointed to the bags with the curled, blackened residues, "inside were charred, but in tact. We need to reconstruct the accounts." He wiped his face and head. "That's all. Burnt papers. Don't know if anything of the machinery can be salvaged." We sat in silence, there was nothing to say.

For days Papa stooped over the charred residues. The shiny, oxidized ink on the blackened surface made it possible to extract the needed information. Vater alone painstakingly copied and gently removed page after burned page of the various voluminous accounting books.

With six more people in the house we did a lot of improvising and sharing. While Vater started the search for an apartment in close vicinity, Erika and I slept on the floor. More difficult was the sharing of the available food. But, within days, they had ration cards and money.

"*Tante* Franziska, what did you mean when you said 'the breakthroughs saved your lives?'" I asked her the first chance I got. We all sat in the living room.

She took a deep breath as she reflected on that terrible night. "You see, our building was burning, all five floors. Our defense warden kicked in the breakthroughs of all other basements of our street. You know how long that street is, or, I should say, was. At the very end he found one house where the first floor was not yet burning, where we could escape. He lead us to it."

As she continued to recall the events of that night, I realized how important it was for her to talk about it. "We crawled on all fours through those breakthroughs." She chuckled. "Looking back, it must have been a funny sight, this endless row of crawling people. And I know some of them think of themselves as being dignified matrons. Nothing dignified about being on all fours."

Tante Franziska pulled her little daughter close to her and held her hand. "All I prayed for was not to lose Anneliese and for the basement ceilings to hold until we were through. We could hear the crashing of walls and the falling of debris above us. Thank God the ceilings held."

"And, what happened when you came out of the last house?" Papa asked.

Tante Grete picked up the story, her gentle voice almost inaudible. "The air was terribly smoky. The warden told us to hold a handkerchief over our nose and mouth and to run to the middle of the street, to get away from the burning buildings." She stopped and nodded. "I tell you, when we came out of that front door we stepped into an inferno. Flames everywhere, above and around us. Only the middle of the street was clear. And you know how wide our street is in addition to the streetcar tracks."

Hilde asked, "But didn't all these people clog up the streets? How did fire trucks or ambulances get through?"

"What fire trucks?" *Tante* Mia answered. "Firemen couldn't do a thing. Oh, they may have been somewhere, but if a whole city burns, there's nothing they can do. A few ambulances did get through."

"But how did you get out of that inferno?" Hilde wanted to know. I had the same question. "With thousands of people in the burning streets, where did they go?"

"Army trucks. After a while trucks took us to the *Hofgarten* ["castle garden"] and dumped us on the lawns," *Tante* Mia answered.

I remembered my recent experience with open trucks and looked at tiny Oma Brass. "You all climbed into army trucks, even you, Oma?"

She smiled and said in her quiet voice, "Of course. It's amazing what you can do if you have to. Besides, everybody was so helpful, so kind. Those soldiers, they just lifted me on and off."

"Then what?" Erika wanted to know.

Tante Franziska continued. "Of course, we didn't want to stay there, we wanted to come here. We heard Benrath was untouched. They told us, yes, to go ahead and walk to Benrath if we could. They told us to stick to major routes, not to get trapped in small, burning streets. So we walked along the tracks till we got here."

"Thank God you came," Mutter said with a relieved sigh. "It was terrible not to know how you were and what happened to you."

Oma nodded. "Yes, you are right, Trude, we do thank God. He protected us."

Within a few weeks Vater found an apartment on the *Benrode Strasse.* An evacuated family from our parish was glad to have the Brass family utilize their rooms until they would come back.

Some time later Mutter was reading a letter in the kitchen. "Who wrote?" I looked over her shoulder.

"A letter from your school."

"What do they want?" I recognized the artistic letterhead.

"They are encouraging parents to send their children out of the air raid zones. The children can either go alone or with a member of their family."

I shook my head. "Again? No thank you, not for me. By the way, didn't you say I should pick beans in Garrath?"

The Garrath farm asked people to come harvest their fields. As payment we could keep some of the vegetable. Mutter had learned that fields of beans were open.

The following days I bicycled to Garrath, received a container and picked with many others as long as there were beans. At the end of the week Mutter could fill ten glasses with green beans. I was glad I could contribute to our meager food supply and looked forward to enjoy them during the long winter months.

Each time I passed Papa's desk I saw the letter from my school. Did our parents really want me to go away again? Why? What if something did happen here while I was gone? What if they all got killed and I was left alone with Mutter? The fear of separation from Hilde and Erika haunted me.

FALL, 1943

CHAPTER 10

During supper a few nights later Mutter brought up the letter from school. "I heard the children are being sent to Thüringen; the school makes all the arrangements and pays for the expenses. I think we should seriously consider it." I shook my head. "I don't want to go." "We know that, Margot." Vater's eyebrow shot up. "However, there are important reasons why it would be good for you and Mutter to go." Horrified, I looked at him. The thought of again being sent away frightened me. "I really want to stay here with you all. Please, don't send me away again." I put knife and fork down, my appetite was gone, my stomach a knot. Why didn't anybody listen to me? Feeling tears welling up I ran to my room and sat on the bed crying.

Hilde came in and put her arms around me. "Margot, come on, it's not the end of the world."

"I can't leave you all here." It was difficult to speak between sobs. "What if something happens to you and I'm somewhere else?"

"That's exactly the reason why you and Mutter are going, so that nothing happens to the two of you. We can't leave, you can."

I freed myself and stared at Hilde. "Are you saying we are going? Is that decided?"

She nodded.

I got up, walked to the window. After a moment I turned

around. "So it's not a matter of considering it, but a matter of letting me know?"

"They didn't know how to tell you."

"That's why they sent you to bring the news 'gently' to me? Thanks, Hilde, I really appreciate that."

I stared out of the window. I was again being sent away with Mutter. The tears stopped. Anger welled up. Why did they make decisions about me without taking my feelings into consideration? I turned to Hilde. "When are we supposed to leave?"

"In about two weeks."

"And for how long may I ask?"

"Until the air raids are over, I guess."

"You mean till the end of the war?" I felt as if I were choking and took a deep breath. "But that can be years!" Panic welled up. I stuffed it down.

"I don't know, Margot," Hilde looked pained. "Don't you see? It's not easy for anyone of us, it's not easy for Mutter either."

"I don't care!" The moment I said it I was sorry. I had never said that before. I didn't mean to hurt anybody, but—I really did not care. "Well, I guess since it's decided, nothing I can do about it."

I ran past Hilde through the basement into the back yard behind the garage where nobody could find me.

Hilde betrayed me, she could have warned me. I knew I had no choice. If nobody cared about my feelings, why should I? From nowhere a verse came to my mind,

"...smiling in spite of hurts and a thousand pains,
but—what it looks like in here—
is nobody's business."

That was right, it was nobody's business what I really felt, how I was really hurting. I laughed bitterly, wiped the tears away, washed my face in the basement and went up to my room, encountering nobody.

The dreaded day came. Vater took us to the railroad station, the only structure still standing in the devastated area. I had said good-bye to Hilde and Erika as briefly and painlessly as I could. They had to work. It was a dismal looking morning. Low dark clouds moved rapidly across a gray sky. A special train, provided for the evacuation, stood way outside the main hall, all doors open as if ready to devour everything in its reach. Our tickets hung in celluloid envelopes around our necks with the destination clearly spelled out so railroad and other officials could easily spot and help us. From Erfurt our train section would take us to Heiligenstadt, where we would change in the late afternoon to a local train for Krokenburg, a little farm village.

The forlorn, sinking feeling in my stomach would not go away. The parents were quiet. Some kids close by sat on their suitcases like little heaps of misery. Nobody was with them. I wasn't sure if I envied or felt sorry for them. Red Cross ladies, the only ones chattering and laughing, poured coffee and hot chocolate. "How about finding the seats and loading our luggage?" I suggested. Papa welcomed the idea. We found our reserved seats in the assigned compartment in which we would stay till Heiligenstadt.

"Josef, why don't you go back to the shop, we're all right here. No need for you to wait with us." Papa agreed readily. We quickly said good-bye, waved, he was gone.

I slumped into my seat beside the window, opposite of Mutter. I was glad I could stare out of the window.

Mutter rummaged in her oversized travel bag, which usually held a great fascination for me. It always had surprises and goodies. The lump in my throat refused to go away. Slowly the train filled up with mothers, struggling with luggage and with children. Finally the whistle blew, doors slammed, we eased out of the station.

I shrank further into my corner. The whole force of my

loneliness engulfed me. No, you are not going to cry, I told myself. I opened my eyes and saw Mutter watching me.

"Anything you want to do?"

"No, not really. I'll read a bit." I took out my book, stared blindly at the pages.

In Köln, the only other stop, more mothers and children with tickets around their necks joined the train. Two mothers with three younger children piled into our compartment. Again ladies offered coffee and hot chocolate.

"Margot, take some hot chocolate. We won't stop until this afternoon in Erfurt." I took a cup, the ladies left the train, the whistle blew, we moved.

I settled back with my book. The dreariness and darkness outside had not changed. In spite of it being mid August it looked cold and wet.

I got up. "I'll go to the rest room, I'll be back."

"All right, but be careful and don't go too close to the doors."

The heavy door of the compartment slid open without a sound. In the narrow hallway I passed groups of women, some smoking, some talking quietly, and stepped over children playing on the floor. To make the time go by, I counted women and children in every compartment. The day seemed endless. At an empty window I watched the rain-drops float horizontally along the window pane.

"Margot, what're you doing out there? Why don't you come back?" Mutter poked her head out of the door.

"I'll be all right here. I like to stand a bit." I made my way to the toilets. Three women, each one with a child, stood silently in line. It seemed everybody was spreading gloom, nobody laughed or even smiled.

Back in our compartment I suggested, "Shall we play a game?" Mutter readily agreed. She was uncomfortable with me. In the meantime I knew what was wrong, but could do nothing about it.

After a short stop in Erfurt we reached Heiligenstadt from where the connecting local train took us to Krokenburg.

It was getting dark as the train came to a slow stop, the door opened and the stationmaster poked in his face. "Anybody from Düsseldorf?"

"Yes, yes, we are from Düsseldorf," Mutter answered.

"All right, this is your station. I'll help you." He took our luggage and helped us down. "Somebody will pick you up in a minute."

A boy, about my age, with a small hand cart ran up to us. "I'm Willie. You must be the people from Düsseldorf. I'll take you to my parents."

His open freckled face and reddish hair contrasted his dark farm clothing and sturdy shoes. Mutter introduced us. He loaded our two suitcases on the cart, we followed him into the road. In the subsiding light I could make out the silhouettes of farmhouses surrounded by high walls. It smelled of animals and dung heaps. From somewhere the pleasant smell of freshly baked bread drifted by.

At a large gate he stopped. "This is our farm." He opened a creaky door set into the huge gate in the brick wall and called out, "We are here."

The front door opened and a shaft of warm light lit up the cobblestoned inner courtyard. A woman with a round face and an easy smile stretched out her hand. "You are welcome here. I'm Frau Gestettner, this is my husband." Mutter introduced us, we shook hands.

Herr Gestettner's stern eyes in a leathery, tanned face studied us. "I'll show you where you'll be staying." He walked into the house, pointed out a lavatory at the bottom of a long staircase and climbed up the narrow steps. A heavy door at the top with squeaky hinges opened into a dark room. He flipped on the ceiling light. "Here you are."

The small room contained a large bed in the right-hand corner, a rough, handmade wooden wardrobe with a matching chest of drawers on the other side of the small window. A metal washstand behind the door completed the furnishings. The room smelled unused, musty.

"Please come down to eat when you are ready. You must be hungry." Mutter thanked him.

Willie laid our suitcases on the bed. "I'll bring you water in a moment." He disappeared with the water pitcher.

I was horrified. "We can't sleep in one bed. I won't be able to move."

The staircase creaked as Willie came up with the full pitcher. He set it into the bowl and carefully adjusted a dark shade over the window.

"Thank you, Willie."

I walked to the window and touched the heavy shade. "If they need black shades, they expect air raids. We could have stayed home."

Mutter sighed and poured water into the bowl. "Here, freshen up so we can go downstairs to eat. I'm sure you're hungry." Yes, I was, I had hardly eaten anything all day.

A few minutes later we walked carefully and slowly down the narrow, steep steps lit by a single bulb. Downstairs a door opened.

"Please do come in and sit down," Frau Gestettner invited us. "I hope you feel comfortable here. We cooked a special meal for you. Enjoy it."

Two plates had been set out on the square, large wooden table. I slipped behind the table onto a bench. Mutter sat on the side next to me.

Herr Gestettner pulled up a chair. "I killed two doves for you. My wife roasted them. I'm sure you'll like them."

I looked petrified from him to Mutter. Doves? "I didn't know doves could be eaten."

Mutter was embarrassed. "You may never have eaten one, but they are delicious."

Frau Gestettner set a plate with a scrawny roasted bird, some vegetable and potatoes with gravy in front of me. It smelled good but one look at that plucked dove, legs sticking up, turned my stomach upside down.

Mutter looked sharply at me. "Eat!"

I started with the vegetable and potatoes in a tasty gravy, didn't touch the bird.

"I can help you cut it," Mutter suggested, trying to cover up my problem.

"No, I can do it myself." But she firmly took the knife out of my hand with enough pressure to make me understand she had enough of my fuss. I did not dare to look up. She dismantled the poor bird. It was not stuffed, just skin and bones. After she handed the knife back to me I finished the vegetable and potatoes.

The farmer's wife said soothingly, "Don't worry. If you don't like it, you may push it aside." I felt miserable and sorry I made such a fuss but I knew one bite would make me sick. My stomach was a knot.

"She's tired," Mutter apologized. "We had a long train ride. She'll be fine tomorrow."

"That's all right. " Mercifully Frau Gestettner took the dismal looking bird away and gave me a tall glass of milk. We thanked them and walked upstairs to our room.

To avoid an outburst of Mutter's anger I quickly asked, "Are we supposed to stay in this tiny room all the time?" I felt the walls would fall down on me.

"I'm sure you can go outside. Whatever you want to do."

Sitting on the bed, I watched Mutter unpack and hang our clothes. The day had been awful. The people were friendly, but—I really wasn't sure what the but was. I also had to tell Mutter something I had realized during the train ride. Not only did I not know how to tell her, I didn't want to talk about it at all and yet I knew I had to. How could I say something important in a simple way?

I took a deep breath. "Oh, by the way, Mutter, I got my period today." There, it was out. I braced myself for what I knew was coming.

She stopped, turned around, stared at me. "Good heavens, why didn't you tell me."

I shrugged. "There's nothing to tell. I know all about it, I can handle it," I lied. I knew nothing about it. I knew it happened, that was all.

Her frown deepened, she glared at me. "Why didn't you tell me? That's why you're behaving so strangely."

"No, I just don't care to be here, that's all."

"Well, that's why you don't like it," she insisted.

"It has nothing to do with it."

"Do you have anything with you, are you prepared?"

"Of course not, but I'll make do."

She shook her head with a big sigh.

I was sure she tried to understand me, but I didn't want to be understood. I wanted to be left alone. If only Hilde or Erika were here, they would be able to help me.

"Margot, since you have come to this point in your life, why don't you try to tell me how you feel and what you are thinking?"

I cringed. How could I talk about my feelings when I was afraid she would use whatever I said against me? Besides, I was confused about them myself. "There's nothing to talk about." Silence. I ached inside, the black emptiness threatened to overtake me. I got up abruptly.

"I'm tired. I'm going to bed."

On the high, firm mattress I moved as far as I could against the wall. With my back to the room, I tried to sleep, only to feel tears trickle into the pillow.

I woke up to a bright and sunny morning. Mutter moved around quietly, getting dressed. I jumped out of bed and ran to the window overlooking the street. The little village had come to life. Farmers with horse and wagons drove noisily up and down the cobblestone road. Roosters, chickens, pigs, the sounds of a clucking and grunting barnyard drifted up. I was on a real farm. Forgotten was last night's misery and gloom, this was a new day. I quickly dressed in what Mutter selected, a dirndl skirt with white blouse and green sweater.

Downstairs, Frau Gestettner smiled at us. *"Guten Morgen.* I hope you slept well."

"Yes, thank you, very well," Mutter answered for both of us. "Can we help you with something?"

Frau Gestettner shook her head. "It's all on the table. Margot, I hope you feel better today, so you can eat something." The breakfast was delicious. Dark farm bread, butter in an earthen crock and a full plate of cold cuts and cheese. "Margot, I don't know what you like to do. You are welcome to stay around here." She made a sweeping gesture through the room, "or around the courtyard with the animals, or to go outside. The farm hands are all nice. They will be happy to take you with them to the fields, if that's something you like to do."

I didn't need another invitation. Chewing my last bite, I ran outside. Maybe I could find Willie. Looking for him I saw a farm hand hitching a horse to a tank wagon to spread manure. He grinned when he saw me coming.

"I'm Hans. Would you like to come out to the fields?"

"Sure, why not." He helped me on top of the driver's bench, then finished the hitching.

Soon we were on the road. We entered a side street and turned off into a field. He flipped a switch and opened the tank. I was glad we headed into the wind. When we did turn, it wasn't much worse than the whole village smelled anyhow.

About noon we were finished. He drove the empty tank wagon past other fields to check on them. The wheat and the oats were golden, almost ready to be harvested. The grass stood quite high.

"When are you going to mow the grass?"

"Don't know. Ask the farmer."

In the farmhouse Mutter stood beside the table. "Here you are. Did you have fun?" Under her scrutinizing look I blushed and turned away. Her eyes often stripped away my protection, leaving me feeling naked and angry.

"*Ja.* Frau Gestettner, are you going to mow the meadows soon?"

"My husband talked about it this morning. Maybe tomorrow. The weather has stabilized. Why do you ask?"

"I've helped with haying before. It's fun, especially riding the wagon into the barn."

"Where were you haying?"

"In Bavaria. We stayed there during a summer."

"How nice. When were you there?"

Mutter broke in. "Oh, it was in the summer of 1940." I was surprised I got in as many answers as I did. "Yes, my three daughters stayed there for seven months near Berchtesgaden," she said with importance. "Hilde, my oldest, was in charge. Margot went to an *Internat* ["boarding school"] in Bad Reichenhall, didn't you, Margot?"

I winced. Did she always have to make a fuss about everything? "Can I help with something?"

"No, thank you Margot, but you can get ready for our noon meal. I'll ring the bell in a moment." I left to get cleaned up in our room.

With a warm, low tone the bell soon called us to eat. We gathered around the table: our hosts, two farm hands, Hans and Günther; Willie, the son; two young girls, Brigitte and Maria who helped around the house and Mutter and I. The meal, served in heavy earthen dishes, was plentiful with vegetable, potatoes and gravy with meat in it. It tasted excellent. I was hungry from being out in the fresh air.

The conversation among the adults went from haying to the one poor horse that had to do all the work, because the other horses had been drafted by the military.

Mutter talked about Hilde having been in Thüringen in the RAD. The two young girls nodded eagerly. Yes, they were here as RAD work force. I was surprised, they looked much younger and did not wear uniforms. Then I remember-ed that the age had been lowered to sixteen.

After the meal Frau Gestettner asked if I wanted to help with baking in the afternoon or would I rather go out into the fields again.

"I would rather go out if that's all right."

Mutter shot me one of her disapproving glances.

Until supper I helped Willie in the barn. After supper everybody disappeared to their own quarters. That meant Mutter and I stayed for the remainder of the evening in our small, comfortless room. Mutter took out some embroidery. I sat on the bed, book in hand.

"How are you doing?"

"Fine."

"Do you feel all right?"

"Yes."

"No problems with the farm hands?"

The question annoyed me. "Of course not. They're friendly."

Silence. I wasn't sure, was I waiting for more or was the conversation finished. She cut a leftover thread, picked up a new color, threaded it. "Well, you know, you are now a young woman. And—you have to be careful with men."

My annoyance grew. "Why? They're all perfectly nice."

"That may be, but—men know what they want from a girl and after they get it, they don't care anymore."

Anger rose in me, cold anger. I wanted to shout, to shake

her and say, that's not true, that's absolutely not true. If you feel that way that's your problem, but it's not mine.

I had only the vaguest idea what "it" was, that it had something to do with sex. Even what sex was, I wasn't sure. It was another one of the many taboos in our family. But with her remark, that men only wanted "it" and then didn't care anymore, I felt "it" had been dirtied, cheapened.

I got up. With nowhere to go I picked up another book, opened it, stared blindly at the words. Something in me felt heavy, cold, like dying, as if I had been robbed of something before it had a chance to bloom. I took a few deep breaths; they did not lighten the heaviness.

I thought of Jürgen who was a wonderful friend, a brother to me. I thought of Willi. The picture she had painted in my mind did not fit them at all. They cared. I thought of Josef. No way did that description fit him. It certainly did not fit Vater. I was sure he was a difficult husband, but he was honest, trustworthy. No, I was not going to be robbed of trusting them.

"I'm going to bed." Behind her chair I quickly changed into my nightgown, crawled into bed and moved as close to the wall as I could.

It was not true! Why did she have to say that? Why did she always have to spoil everything? I moved around restlessly, but did not want to face the room.

"Are you all right, can I do something for you?"

Abruptly I sat up straight. "Mutter, for heaven's sake, leave me alone!" The last three words I said with all the heat I felt. I fell back on my pillow. If only Hilde were with me. Tears started to flow. Exhausted I fell asleep.

Loud noises, shouting, the rattling of an empty wagon in the courtyard woke me. Haying time! I jumped up and opened the window. A warm breeze flooded in. "I've to get downstairs to leave with them." After getting washed and dressed I ran down for breakfast. Mutter followed. *"Guten Morgen,* Frau Gestettner. Have they already left?"

"Yes, but you can find them easily. Take your time, eat something first." The table was still set. I waited for Mutter to sit down. As soon as I finished I looked at her. "Can I go?"

"First talk to Frau Gestettner."

I found her in the pantry. "Is it all right if I go to the meadow and help?"

"It certainly is, Margot. And you can bring them the food they forgot." She handed me a round basket and pointed across the road. With rhythmic strokes, five people swung long-handled sickles, cutting the grass in thick swaths.

I lugged the basket to the field. Herr Gestettner smiled when he saw me coming. "Yes, we forgot it this morning." He gave me a small sickle. "Here, but be careful, it's sharp. You can cut the grass along the fence posts and in the corners."

"Good, I've done it before." Like in Winkl. While it did not smell and look like the mountains, I was constantly reminded of it. How much fun we had. If only Hilde were here instead of Mutter.

No, I decided, I could not change that. I had to learn to cope with the situation.

Willie came running. "Dad wants you to rest with us."

I straightened up, my legs tired from crouching, and joined the mowers and the horse in the shade of the tall poplars. A jug of water made the round. Herr Gestettner poured for me a cup from the bottle and handed me a thick slice of dark bread and a slice of salami. I munched happily. Already a large area had been cut.

"Do you have to mow more meadows?" I asked Herr Gestettner.

Perched on a rough split rail fence, he took the long grass stem from his mouth and pointed with it toward the end of the village. "Two more over there. We'll finish this today, cut the others the next two days, then bring it in. Just hope the weather holds."

They worked hard and steady. By evening the meadow lay in long swaths. No wonder they all disappeared after supper. Gladly, I crawled into bed early.

"Margot, we need your help today," Frau Gestettner greeted us as we came down for breakfast. "Will you help Brigitte and Maria turn the hay in the first meadow? So the men can continue to mow?"

"Of course." After breakfast the three of us, armed with wooden rakes, walked to the meadow. Again the spicy, aromatic smell conjured up visions of snowcapped mountains.

Brigitte stopped my raking. "Hold your rake this way to avoid blisters. Otherwise your hands will be a bloody mess."

I tried to imitate her way of raking. It felt much better. I liked the two girls. They were only four years older and yet, here they worked on a strange farm, by themselves, while I was being chaperoned by Mutter.

"Let's take a rest, I'm thirsty," Maria suggested.

I dropped the rake, walked back with them into the shade. The sun was hot, sweat ran down my face. We passed the jug with water while Brigitte sliced dark bread and sausage for each of us.

"How come you are here, Margot?" Maria asked.

"Because my parents decided, against my will I must add, to participate in the sending-the-children-to-the-country program. The school made all arrangements. We didn't know where we would end up."

"Just like us, we didn't know we would be here either," Maria agreed.

"Do you like it, I mean here as well as in the RAD?" I asked them.

Brigitte tilted her pretty face with quiet green eyes and dark eyebrows thoughtfully. "My answer is 'yes' to both your questions." A bright orange ribbon held her bobbing blond ponytail high on her head.

I looked at Maria. "And you?"

"How I like it?" She gazed down the meadow. Her dark brown eyes, often sparkling with laughter, looked serious. Short, shiny brown hair stuck to her perspiring face. "I like it here, people are nice and considerate and it's clean. I don't care about being in the RAD."

"Really? I remember my sister Hilde liked it."

"Yes. It depends entirely on your leader and..." she continued with emphasis and feeling, "...our leader stinks!"

"Maria." With a soothing voice Brigitte tried to tone her down, but Maria was not about to be toned down.

"You know it, Brigitte. She is a bully, she is bossy, she is a fanatic. You name all the negatives you can think of, she is IT! And when she can, she sure as hell will get you in trouble. She's mean and nasty." Maria drew a deep breath and laughed. "Did I leave anything out?" She got up, carried an armful of hay into the shade and lay down, using the hay as pillow. "Hmm, smells good." She nestled her head into it and let out a sigh. "Oh, it's good to stretch out." I followed her example.

Brigitte, sitting on the fence, checked her watch. "A ten minute break. I'm going to time it." Maria dozed off. On the warm ground my tired body relaxed. A lazy breeze fanned my face.

"Ten minutes. Let's go." Brigitte jumped from the fence. "Maria, dear," she prodded her with her shoe, "remember, we are here to work."

Maria yawned, stretched, rolled over and raised herself on one elbow. "All right, you are bossy and mean too." We laughed. It was fun to work with them. Time flew. Soon the men stopped the wagon at the beginning of the field. "Time for our noon meal. Hop on." With dangling legs we sat at the end of the open wagon as it rumbled over dirt roads and cobblestones.

In the barn I washed up with the others, came into the house with them. Mutter, towel in hand, stood with Frau Gestettner in the kitchen. By now, I was convinced, Frau Gestettner knew all about our family.

"Did you have a good time?" Mutter looked more relaxed. She did not scrutinize me at all. I wondered if it had something to do with my working with girls today.

"How are your hands doing? No blisters?" Frau Gestettner examined them.

"No. Brigitte showed me how to hold the rake."

"Good, otherwise you are in trouble," Herr Gestettner agreed. "Because the hay has to come in."

After exactly thirty minutes we left the house again, carrying only water jugs. The men dropped us off. We worked steadily until Maria called a break and we plopped into the shade. My back started to hurt. I stretched out with a groan.

Brigitte was concerned. "Margot, you don't have to work the whole day with us, you are much younger. Stop if you get too tired."

By evening we had turned the whole field. I was so tired I could hardly stay awake during the meal and immediately dragged myself off to bed.

For two more days we turned hay. Then the fun part came, loading it onto the wagon and bringing it in. At sunrise the bell called us to breakfast. Afterwards pitchforks, rakes, food baskets and all available hands were piled into the hay wagon. It promised to be a bright and beautiful day.

We lifted fork after fork up to Willie and Hans on top of the wagon. Sweat ran down my face and neck. That the scratchy hay itched did not bother me. The sun was high and hot. Clouds popped up along the horizon. Over and over Herr Gestettner glanced at the sky. Would the weather hold?

At noontime the first load was ready for the barn. "Can I come up?" I called to Hans.

"Sure." He stretched down his hand. I climbed high on top of the load and used the heavy rope stretched across the hay to hang on. Willie stayed up, Hans moved to the driver's seat. I nestled into the hay.

"Make sure you hold onto the rope," Herr Gestettner called. On the uneven dirt road the top loaded wagon swayed with us sliding across the slippery hay. I tightened my grip.

"First load in!" I announced proudly in the farmhouse, while the others still unloaded the hay. "Do you think the weather will hold?" I asked Frau Gestettner.

"Don't know. It's awfully hot, always a sign of a thunderstorm. Also the flies are biting." That was true, the little creatures were a pest.

After the quick meal, Herr Gestettner got up. "We've got to get it in." Billowy thunderheads piled up on the horizon. The work on the second meadow took longer. In spite of the oppressive heat, Herr Gestettner pushed on. We moved to the last plot, working against time, against the menacing clouds. Halfway down the meadow Herr Gestettner called a five minute break to wipe off sweat, to replenish moisture. Finally, the last row.

"Hurrah, we did it!" Brigitte and Maria were jubilant. Again the rope was strapped across the load. I climbed up, my hands hurting badly. Hans spurred on the horse, we turned into the tree lined street. Willie and I lay almost at roof level in the fluffiness.

Somebody called from the front, "Watch out up there!" Not knowing what to look for I lifted my head as we passed under an old tree. Low hanging branches scraped over the hay. Willie flattened himself out in time, but a thick limb caught me unexpectedly, pushed me off the hay. I let go of the rope. The wagon passed under my legs as I grabbed for a branch above me. My feet plopped down, I dangled from the tree with nothing but ten feet of thin air beneath me. Frantically I screamed, "Help! Help!" when I realized my hair had got entangled in the bark. The hay wagon swayed down the road. With one hand I freed my hair, tearing out some of it, with the other I tried desperately to hang on. The bark scraped and cut into my blistered hand. Slowly I slipped. I looked down. UGH, what a drop. Then down I went. Somehow I managed to fall on both feet before the rest of me hit the cobblestones.

By that time Willie had stopped the wagon. Herr Gestettner and the girls reached me as I scrambled back on my feet. With their help I limped back to the wagon and rode beside Hans while the others walked rapidly. A gusty wind came up. If only Mutter would not hear about this, but I knew there was little chance of that. As we pulled into the barn, the first heavy drops of a brief but violent storm splashed on the hot pavement. But, as Herr Gestettner said, the hay had to get in, that was all that mattered.

During our stay at the farm, we realized the only school in Krokenburg was a farm school, the type we knew from Bischofswiesen. Mutter contacted the school authorities. I hoped fervently that would be a reason to let us go home. But they transferred me to a high school in Heiligenstadt. We said good-bye to the Gestettner family and the others, and left the friendly farm and village for the nearby city.

My first impression of Heiligenstadt was that of a wide, spacious avenue, Main Street. The school authorities assigned us a room over a store on Main Street. The tiny room was similar to the one on the farm. Again one bed.

We located the high school not far from us, a large,

utilitarian structure with a bland stucco facade and symmetrically distributed windows. Two more days, then school would start.

We had picked up a newspaper at the station. On the farm we got neither news nor a paper and felt out of touch with the rest of the world. We read Hamburg suffered a catastrophic air attack, which completely destroyed the historic city. The newspaper talked about "Piracy against innocent civilians". Another item was that Hitler had appointed Heinrich Himmler, who was head of the *Waffen SS*, as Minister of the Interior.

Mutter shook her head. "That makes him and the *SS* even more powerful. As if they weren't running the country anyway."

After our first meal, cooked on a tiny, two-burner portable stove, I leaned out of the window to watch people parade up and down Main street, enjoying the warm summer evening. The white sailor uniform could be seen everywhere. The next day we familiarized ourselves with the town and the stores. Now we had again to deal with ration card. On the farm Mutter had handed them over to Frau Gestettner.

In the afternoon Mutter realized we had no matches. It gave me an excuse to get out. Coming back up Main Street, a group of young sailors came towards me. I didn't pay any attention when suddenly I heard them whistle. Not being used to that sort of thing, I glanced up. They looked at me, grinned and whistled.

"Jerks!" flashed through my mind, "dumb jerks," when I happened to look down my front. My dress, a child's dress with a smocked yoke, was way too small. Good heavens, I had changed! And I hadn't noticed. The discovery hit me with such acute embarrassment that I ran up to the room, plopped down at the little table and cried.

"Margot, what's the matter, what happened?"

"Nothing, I don't feel well." I didn't want to talk about it.

"Did anything happen?"

"No, nothing, just those jerks of sailors grinning at me and whistling. I hate it."

"Well," Mutter smiled, relieved, "That's nothing terrible. You are growing into a woman."

"Oh, stop it." I didn't want to talk or hear about it. The whole idea of not being a little girl anymore, of being noticed, embarrassed me. If only Hilde or Erika were here, they could help me. The loneliness and the ache, having been pushed away for a while, crashed down on me. "I don't want to go to school tomorrow. I want to go home."

"You know we can't. We have signed up for this program, they paid for it and we have to stay down here. You know that."

"I didn't sign up for it." I pleaded, "Please, let's go home."

"Margot, for heaven's sake, we can't, *basta*! Tomorrow morning you start a new school and everything will be much better. You'll have more to do, you'll get to know some children."

"Sure. Just what I need. I hate it!"

Unfortunately the next morning came. We went to the ugly building with huge rooms, many children, many teachers. Frightened and desperate, I wanted to cry and run away. The principal led me into the classroom, introduced me as the girl from Düsseldorf, showed me my desk and left. Everybody stared at me. I could have crawled under the desk. The teacher smiled, continued her lecture and gradually the kids turned their attention back to her. My resolution not to cry evaporated, tears streamed down my face.

After a while the teacher realized my dilemma, put an arm around me and led me out of the class to the nurse. "Lie down until you feel better, then come back."

The elderly nurse felt my forehead. "No temperature. What's the matter?"

"I want to go home," was the only thing I could say through my sobbing. "I want to go home."

A short time later Mutter came in. The store below our room had relayed the nurse's message to pick me up. "What am I going to do with you?" she said, distressed.

I knew I was making it difficult for her, but I could do nothing about the terrible emptiness, the ache. This went on for a few days, I would go to school with the best intentions, could not stay in class and was sent home.

After a while I managed to stay in class. The students were all right, but they had their own friends, I was an outsider. I felt nobody cared about me.

One evening Mutter sent me to the store to buy milk. It was almost dark. She gave me the key to the room with the stern warning, "Don't lose it. It's the only one I have."

I put it in my pocket. Running back I heard a metallic sound and froze in my tracks. Good heavens, the key! I lost the key!

On hands and knees I fumbled in the fading light over every inch of the dirty road. All my desperation came back. "Please, God, let me find the key. And please let me go home". I took a deep breath, wiped my wet face with my sleeve and systematically searched the area when I heard Mutter's voice.

"Margot, Margot, where are you?" I got up and answered.

"What took you so long? What are you doing?"

I sobbed, "I lost the key and can't find it."

"I'll help you search, but I have good news for you."

"For me? Can we go home?"

"I think we're going home. I just got a phone call from

Düsseldorf." She stopped.

"What's the matter, Mutter? What happened?" All the anxiety that something could happen at home while we were away engulfed me. "Something wrong with Hilde or Erika or Papa? Is Josef all right?" The words tumbled out.

"No, they're all right. Oma Brass died."

"Oh, Mutter, I'm sorry. How come, when did she die?"

"I don't know much. Come on, let's find the key."

Mutter found it after I retraced my steps for her.

The next morning Mutter made the necessary arrangements to be very sure our papers were in order since we would take a regular train and would be subjected to all the train controls. We left the following day, finally going home!

After every station the train control, two military and one *Gestapo* officer, opened the sliding door and requested in precise military voices, "Your passports, please." Each time Mutter handed them over. Each time they checked them meticulously and handed them back with a crisp "Thank you."

At one station a young, dark haired woman entered our compartment. Without looking up she sat down quietly. Her hands moved restlessly in her lap. When the train control saw her, one of the officers raised his eyebrows.

"Your passport please, Fraulein." She handed him her papers. He checked them, gave them to his companion, who glanced at her and handed them to the *Gestapo* in the gangway. He shoved them into the fold of his sleeve. "Please follow us."

All color drained from her face. Without a sound she got up slowly, gathered her belongings and disappeared.

I glanced at Mutter, who made a move with her head, "Don't ask any questions," and looked out the window. I stared at the empty seat. What was going to happen to her?

The tall spires of the Cathedral of Köln came into view. Soon we would be home, only another hour. Then, without warning, the train came to a screeching halt. The three control officers shouted at us to leave the luggage and to get out. Mutter grabbed my hand. Channeling the military personnel into another area, they herded us civilians onto a narrow gangway with barbed wires on both sides. It ended at a control station with two officers behind a window and soldiers with mounted bayonets beside the door. Petrified but curious, I had never been that close, I glanced at the armed soldiers, who were staring straight ahead, and at the shiny deadly steel on their rifles. I shivered at the sight of the pointed blade. Would Josef ever carry that kind of weapon?

A few rows ahead of us an older couple stepped up to the window. The woman twisted her hands behind her back as her husband handed over their papers.

The Gestapo officer, after scrutinizing the couple, folded their papers, put them in his pocket. "Follow them," he pointed to the soldiers. Flanked by bayonets the couple was marched off.

I grabbed Mutter's hand. "What happened?" only to get a hissed, "Quiet!" Anxiety and panic swept over me. What if we would be marched off?

It was our turn to hand the papers through the window. Standing beside Mutter I did not dare to look afraid though I shook with fear.

The first officer asked sharply, "Why are you going back to Düsseldorf?"

Mutter replied quietly, "My mother died."

"When did she die?" he snapped back.

"Two days ago. We are going to the funeral."

He glared at Mutter, then at me, handed the papers back to us. "Proceed."

Still shaky we returned to our compartment. After more waiting and an agonizingly slow ride, we pulled hours later into the train hall in Düsseldorf.

Hilde, Papa and Erika saw us pass by and ran alongside

until we came to a stop. Tears streamed down my face, my knees almost buckled with relief. I was home again. I held tightly onto Hilde's and Erika's hand after they hugged and kissed me.

We carried our luggage to the streetcar platform and waited for number eighteen.

"Josef, what happened to her? How did she die?"

"She died the best way you could wish for, Trude. She got up from their breakfast table, turned around to get more coffee and simply collapsed. Dead. No pain, no lingering, like dying in your sleep."

Mutter nodded. "I guess so. It's just so sudden."

Oma Brass was dead. But, what would happen to us?

CHAPTER 11

Next day was Oma Brass' funeral. This was my first and I did not know what to expect. In a building at the cemetery, I found myself with the rest of the family slowly walking along a hallway when, at an opening in the draped-off glass wall, an open coffin, slightly raised at the head, came in sight. My heart just about stopped. A waxy yellowish face, deeply sunk closed eyes, white wispy hair blowing in the breeze of a fan, Oma's face looked as I remembered it, only it seemed like a mask. I shuddered and quickly looked away. A few more steps, we were out of the building.

Six pallbearers carried the coffin to the graveside. *Pfarrer* Antheck said the prayers, the coffin was lowered into the deep space. One person after the other, starting with the aunts, dropped a shovel of earth on the coffin. Hollow rumblings answered from the dark hole.

With Erika and Hilde beside me, I stepped up to the open grave. Hilde dropped earth into the grave and handed me the shovel. I peered down and imagined the mask with the wispy hair, the hollow eyes. I passed the shovel to Erika. "Here, I can't." She dug a full heap and scattered it lovingly over the coffin.

Mutter and I had been in Thüringen from mid August through September of 1943, but I felt I had been away for years. Papa had rebuilt his business with the help of the military. Erika still worked at Schuller's, Hilde in the finance department. I was glad to see Jürgen again. Many of my classmates were still in Thüringen. In addition to the nightly air raids, we now were constantly interrupted during our schooling.

Mutter decided it was time for us to be more self-sufficient. We acquired six chickens and a rabbit, a cute little furry thing that thumped its hind legs and made squeaky noises when hungry. To feed the chickens, Papa brought a sack of grain that had gotten wet and had started to sprout. It not only was sprouting, it also was fermenting. We had hours of fun watching six chickens reel like drunken sailors through their little makeshift barnyard behind the terrace. Feeding Twitchy was my responsibility.

"A letter from Josef." Jubilantly I held up the small envelope with his round handwriting. Mutter hastily slit it open, scanned it.

"He's going to get a leave, maybe even over Christmas." She smiled. "Josef's coming home."

"Josef's coming," I announced to everybody I saw. "He may be home for Christmas!"

The days flew by. Soon we got another note. Yes, he would be home before Christmas, planned arrival December 20, departure Jan. 5, 1944. What a long leave.

Mutter decided the whole house needed cleaning. We scrubbed and brushed and polished. To do some baking for Christmas and for his coming, we scraped together every bit of food and coupons available. Mutter wanted to wait with the actual baking till Josef was home. He always enjoyed it, especially cleaning out the dough dish.

Finally the day arrived. With so many soldiers at the station, would I recognize him since I had never seen him in uniform? On the platform the air was full of expectation.

"There he is, there is Josef!" Hilde shouted, pointing to an arm waving over the melee of people and luggage. We surged toward him, surrounded him. He looked terrific. He was a man. His angular face was lined, thinner, his dark heavy hair in military cut, but the same boyish grin. It flickered over his face when he gave me a hug, held me at arm's length and whistled.

"My little sister has grown into a young lady."

I shook my head. "I'm not a young lady at all."

He laughed. "I can hear that. Same old Margot."

Tears of joy ran down Papa's face. He grabbed Josef by the shoulder, "Good to have you home," and slapped his back.

Our tumultuous greeting surprised and delighted me. For a moment our family stepped out of its confinement, its seriousness and could be as loud and outgoing as others.

At home we extended the dinner table to accommodate our whole family, Oma included. For once we all were together.

Josef smiled. "Haven't sat at a festive table with a white tablecloth and napkins in a long, long time."

I marveled how Mutter got the feast together. We hadn't had a braised rump roast with potatoes and vegetable and a chocolate pudding as dessert, Josef's favorite, in years.

The next day we learned the reason for his long leave: dysentery. He saw a physician in Düsseldorf right away, who gave no promise he could effectively treat Josef in the short time available.

Christmas preparation started in earnest. Papa even got a little Christmas tree. We baked a small amount of cookies. The house took on the smell and look of the festive season with the tree standing on the table in the living room, waiting to be decorated.

Josef poked his head into the kitchen. "I smell something special. Anything I can do?"

"Of course," Mutter smiled, "You are in time. You can clean out the dish, we just emptied it. Here." She handed him a porcelain dish with lots of dough left. He relished it, smacking loudly, making an appreciative face, licking spoon and fingers.

Christmas Eve's day was cold but not blustery. "I need a few more things from the village, Margot." Mutter handed me a small shopping list. "The butcher on Main street is supposed to have *Gänseklein* ["small pieces of geese"]. Try there. I also heard drugstore Schreiber got some wine. See what you can get. And if you find anything else special, like coffee or chocolate, look into it, we have nothing. Check with Kaiser's. And don't hang around, come home."

I took the list. This kind of shopping was tiring and usually unproductive. I might stand in line for hours and get nothing. And no matter what I brought home, Mutter would not be satisfied.

"I'll come with you, Margot." Josef picked up his heavy army coat from the wardrobe. He wore his uniform because none of his clothes fit him any more. "Wanted to go to the village anyhow."

"Oh, wonderful." It was my first time alone with him. I tried to keep up with his big steps in his military boots. I glanced at him from the side. In his gray uniform, adorned with one silver V on his sleeve, his cap slightly askew, he looked dashing. I was proud of my big brother. He turned his head and grinned. I slipped my hand into his. For a while we said nothing walking down *Marbacher Strasse* toward the village. His strong hand enclosed mine completely, warming it.

"I'm so glad you're home. We've missed you," I broke the silence.

"I miss all of you too. How often I think of you when I stand on duty outside." He let go of my hand, put his arm around my shoulder, pulled me to him. My heart leaped. How wonderful, my big brother had his arm around me.

Again I lost step with his stride, skipped and hopped to get back into the rhythm.

He laughed. "Am I making it difficult for you? I'll slow down." He took smaller steps but soon forgot about it.

I was sorry we arrived so quickly in the village. The line at the butcher for *Gänseklein* snaked all the way up the road. Josef checked his watch. "While you stay here I'll look around and check back with you. If you're finished and I'm not back, don't wait, just go home. *Tschüs*."

I asked the woman in the last row, "Any chance that we get something?"

She shrugged. "Don't know." I decided to stay. The meat would be more important than chocolate or coffee.

I watched Josef walk down Main Street, stop at some of the festively decorated windows and disappear at the bend in the street. He had put his arm around my shoulder. I told him I missed him. That was all that mattered right now. Maybe I could get to know him better.

The line moved slowly. After hours of inching forward I finally made it into the store where the woman behind the counter handed me a package. I got a pound of *Gänseklein* and didn't get ice cold feet for nothing.

The drugstore was next on my list. Again a long line. It would be wonderful to have a bottle of wine with dinner. I knew Papa missed his wine. Would I be lucky twice?

At my turn the clerk pushed a bottle of *Rhein* wine across the counter. I was elated. Carefully I placed it into my shopping net. Satisfied with my bounty I walked up and down Maine street looking for Josef. Maybe we could walk home together. There was no sign of him.

At home Mutter thought I had taken too much time. As always before special days, she was irritable, fussed about everything, in spite of Josef being home. Each year we had a major blow-up before Christmas. It greatly diminished my joy and expectation of the holidays.

It was getting dark. Hilde and Papa decorated the little tree with Erika's help. She had Christmas Eve off. Josef came back late from a friend's house. I prepared one Christmas plate for all of us and counted out each cookie, each little piece of chocolate. After a brief rest I dressed in a skirt and sweater, the best I had. The living room door opened and the little bell send its silvery call up to us. I smiled. The old custom was still comforting, but did not have the same mystery and all absorbing meaning anymore. I looked at Erika. "Ready? Let's go." Once more she brushed her curly hair and pushed it back with curved tortoise combs. Her thick braids, my constant envy, had given way to a permanent. We knocked on Josef's and Oma's door, making sure they heard the bell's ringing.

Weeks before we decided not to exchange presents this year, because it was next to impossible to find anything. The little Christmas tree, standing on a table, shed its warm and friendly light. After wishing each other *Frohe Weihnachten* ["Merry Christmas"], Mutter set the Christmas plate in the center of the table. Hilde offered her guitar to Josef. He looked at his calloused hand, then shook ruefully his head. Hilde strummed, "*Stille Nacht, Heilige Nacht.*" I stared into the flickering light. What if this was the last Christmas for all of us to be together? Tears welled up. No, I could not cry. I did not dare to look at anybody, least of all at Josef. After two more carols Hilde set the guitar down.

Soon we exchanged the Christmas room for the shelter.

"Not even on Christmas Eve do they give us peace," Mutter mumbled, trudging down the steps.

"Of course not. It's war, remember?" I sounded as angry as I was. How senseless all of this was. While the others gathered in the kitchen after the alarm I went straight to bed. When Erika came I pretended to sleep. I was afraid, afraid for all of us, but especially for Josef.

For the Second Day of Christmas we planned a festive afternoon coffee time. Hilde wanted to introduce Wolfgang, her boy friend. She had shown us his picture before it became a permanent fixture on her dresser. The most attractive thing on him, in my opinion, was his spiffy white uniform with lots of gold. Josef invited Gisela, an old friend of his, for the first time to our house. We seldom brought our friends home.

Hilde baked two pies and even managed to get whipped cream from a girl friend whose parents owned a bakery.

At four o'clock sharp the doorbell rang. Hilde let Wolfgang in and brought him into the living room. Five pairs of eyes scrutinized him thoroughly, from his thin, dark hair to his highly polished shoes.

According to custom he arrived with two bunches of flowers. Skillfully he unwrapped the top of a large bouquet of yellow roses and, having wound the paper around the lower stems to avoid the danger of pricking for the recipient, handed them at the introduction to Mutter with a low bow. The rest of us got a solid handshake. Each easy smile in his friendly face exposed a line of rabbit teeth that protruded over a receding chin. His small frame looked even thinner in the spotless white tailored uniform. As an adjutant of the Merchant Marine, he wore lots of gold. Somehow I couldn't understand Hilde's attraction to him.

He unwrapped the top of the second bunch, a small arrangement of pink roses, and handed it to Hilde. Papa invited him to take the armchair opposite him.

One by one we left the room. The next thirty minutes would decide Wolfgang's future in our family. Vater would ask probing and very specific questions. If Hilde was nervous she didn't show it.

Gisela, a pleasant young woman, older than Josef, with a shock full of wavy blond short hair, arrived and Josef brought her into the kitchen. We kept the coffee warm under the cozy, the whipped cream cold in the refrigerator and stood around, laughing and joking—and waiting.

Finally Mutter came in with a noncommittal, "You can start bringing things to the table." We looked at each other and filed into the dining room.

The portiere, a heavy velvet drape separating the dining room from the living room, was open as always. Vater leaned back in his chair, enveloped in the aromatic blue smoke of an expensive cigar, a long missed pleasure. Wolfgang also enjoyed a cigar. Empty cognac glasses in front of the two spoke volumes. It seemed the Merchant Marine had plenty of resources. I knew Hilde would enjoy her cake.

Gisela stayed overnight with a friend to visit with Josef an additional day. They planned to spend time together with mutual friends from the youth group.

Josef's dysentery did not improve. He chose to ignore the strict diet he was supposed to observe. Slowly his time ticked away. Most of it he spent with Walter and Erich, also on leave.

"Josef, do you really think you can return to your unit while you are still sick?" Vater looked concerned at Josef at the supper table.

Mutter shook her head. "You can't possibly get better out there. Stay a few more weeks. Dr. Simon said he would certify if you couldn't return to your unit, didn't he. You told us. Why don't you take the opportunity?"

"It's no good to return sick," Hilde added.

Josef listened. "You're all correct. I don't disagree with your reasons. However, if I don't return now, my unit may have moved. And I don't want to be assigned to a different one. I want to be back with them, especially with Schmiernipple. I don't want to be anywhere else."

"Who is Schmiernipple?" I asked. What a funny name.

"He's a great guy, a wonderful friend. I can depend on him. No, I don't want to be assigned to a different outfit."

He got up.

Vater persisted. "You don't know that they will move. You don't know that you will be assigned to a different outfit. That may not happen. But what will happen is that you can't get better there with poor medical treatment." With his eyebrow raised to storm, Vater pushed back his chair and paced up and down.

A funny little proverb crossed my mind. *"Der Apfel fällt nicht weit vom Birnbaum"* ["the apple doesn't fall far from the pear tree"].

Josef picked up his plate, carried it into the kitchen and sat it down so hard I was surprised it didn't break. When he came back he looked straight at Vater. "Sorry, but I'm going back on the fifth." He swung his coat over his shoulders. "Going to see Erich off. He leaves tomorrow."

Mutter shook her head. Suddenly Vater's fist crashed on the table. The dishes clanked. "How idiotic can he be."

Erika and I cleared the table quickly, washed the dishes. The silence hung heavy over our family.

The next days were difficult. I took my cues from Erika. She was pleasant, helpful, made conversation. Josef said good-bye to his former buddies at the shop but did not wait to come home with Vater.

Without success I racked my brain to find a way to ease the tension in the house. I could not imagine Josef leaving under a cloud of disagreement.

I dreaded the last evening, but it came. As usual we sat together in the living room. Vater uncorked a bottle of *Rhein* wine, saved for the occasion. The clinking of the crystal glasses added a festive sound. Vater lifted his glass to Josef, we all followed. Even Erika and I got a small one for a sip.

"Here's to you, Josef, to your future. And while I don't always agree with you, it's your life. I appreciate your caring for your friend, that makes you who you are. *Zum Wohl.*" We toasted with each other. The tension was broken.

Josef drank his wine in one swig. "The train tomorrow leaves before six o'clock. It'll be best to say good-bye here shortly before five and I'll get to the station as quickly as I can." We all agreed, emptied our glasses. He got up.

"Do you need help with packing?" Hilde asked.

"No thanks, big sister," he smiled at her. I was glad he looked relaxed.

Early next morning we crowded into the center hall to kiss and hug him farewell. His face showed again the smiling expectation.

"Good-bye, little sister. Don't grow up too fast, all right?" He put his arms around me, his heavy uniform felt like a board between us, and kissed my cheek. I kissed him too. His smooth warm cheek smelled of shaving soap. I avoided looking at anybody. I wanted to say something clever, something light and funny so I would not cry, but as usual drew a blank. He gave me another one of his wonderful grins and turned to Erika. After he kissed and hugged us all, he had said good-bye to Oma the evening before, he consulted his watch.

"Gosh, it's late. I've to run." One more smile, one more wave, he disappeared into the dark early morning.

Slowly I walked upstairs, sat on my bed, stared at the pattern in the rug, aware of the aching emptiness. A moment later Erika sat beside me.

After a while she took a deep breath. "I just pray he comes back." With a big lump in my throat I nodded.

Hilde opened the door. "Come on, you two. You're not doing anybody any good commiserating here. It doesn't help you and it certainly doesn't help Josef. Right?"

Reluctantly I accepted her logic. "Cheer up. Life does go on, you know." Somehow I had heard that before. She pulled us up, gave us each a little slap. "Get going. It's time for you to get dressed. And if you come down soon I'll even make you some hot cocoa."

She was right. Worrying wouldn't do any good. And while I didn't enjoy hot water with thin cocoa powder without sugar, I appreciated her thoughtfulness. Getting dressed, a verse drifted through my mind, "…smile in spite of pains and a thousand hurts, but—what it looks like in here is nobody's business."

The news was filled with reports of the incessant bombing of Berlin. Could anything be left of the once beautiful city? Most major cities, like Düsseldorf, Köln and Hamburg were reduced to rubble. And still Hitler shouted in his New Year's message of 1944, "Germany is determined to continue its struggle against the Jewish-Bolshevist aggression and subversion." How long could this continue? Reluctantly the German leadership admitted that the Russians broke through the German defenses. Kiev was lost. I pushed the thought of Willi's senseless death in the battle of Kiev way down. How would this all end? Now, at the beginning of '44, after over four years of war, our army was losing on every front.

"Another few weeks and I'm done with my year of duty." Erika came into the little room upstairs, where I was doing my homework.

"What are you going to do then?"

"I don't know yet, I'd like to learn some more."

"Oh?"

"*Ja,* Josef said to me on the last day, 'Erika,' he said, 'learn as much as you can. A good education is terribly important.' I may go to business school."

I returned to the distasteful task of cramming my head with English vocabulary. Her practical business school skills might be more helpful than this. I could not see any use for me for English.

We did not have much snow in the winter of 43-44. I

waited for the first signs of spring to get fresh green for our rabbit. With good care during the winter little Twitchie had grown into a big rabbit. Which provided me with a huge problem. I knew the only reason we had the rabbit, the only reason Mutter would have an animal around, was to have additional food. But the thought of eating Twitchie was repulsive.

'*Aufruf zum Volkssturm*'! ["Appeal to the Peoples' Troops"] screamed the headlines. Every male from sixteen to sixty, regardless of infirmity, who was not serving already, was called to participate in the *Volkssturm*, to pick up a weapon and be ready to fight. "The total war needs you!" Dr. Göbbels said in one of his "inspiring" proclamations.

"What are you going to do?" I heard Mutter ask Vater that evening. "Do you have to report too?"

"Not that I know, my situation has not changed. The army needs me more than ever."

The following day Mutter and I returned home from the village. Suddenly Frau Leimbke walked beside us.

"*Heil Hitler*, Frau Füsser."

Mutter, having both hands full, nodded.

"Your husband has joined the *Volkssturm* I hope? Now he has no excuse anymore not to fight for our *Vaterland*, you know." She looked expectantly into Mutter's face, waiting for an answer, waiting to trap her. Her high pitched voice grated on my nerves.

"Just the contrary, Frau Leimbke," Mutter accentuated every word with relish. "The army needs him now more than ever. Good day." We happened to reach a side street, Mutter turned into it.

"You think that satisfied her, that snake?" I whispered. Mutter did not answer.

SPRING, 1944

CHAPTER 12

"We're supposed to have people live with us in our house?" Mutter asked irritated. "Who tells us what to do?" "That's what it looks like on here." Hilde read from a letter from the *Braune Haus*. "If you own more than 200 square foot per person, you have to house other people. And, we have more space than that in our house they tell us, wonder how they know, so we have to take in somebody. That somebody will be a Herr Mackenzie from Erkelenz. Isn't that interesting. They already selected somebody for us. We don't even have a choice. He'll arrive April 4. And that, I want you all to know, happens to be tomorrow."

Mutter looked horrified. "Tomorrow? Where is he supposed to sleep?"

"Why not under the steps in the basement," Erika threw in with a grin. "Obviously every little space needs to be utilized."

"You think every family is going to have some stranger living with them?" I wondered.

"That remains to be seen," Hilde snapped angrily. "I bet this is just another one of their chicaneries."

"But, where's he going to sleep?" Mutter asked again. "We haven't got an empty bed, certainly not an empty room."

Suitcase in hand, Herr Mackenzie showed up the next evening. He was a nervous type, skin and bones, about our parent's age. He worked for the EICOMAG, an immense industrial complex close to the *Rhein*. He apologized for inconveniencing us, assured us that it was not his choice to live with us, that he would only stay in the house to catch some sleep, otherwise would be at the company. Mutter offered him the couch upstairs in the little room or a temporary bed in the basement underneath the steps. Hastily he accepted the bed in the basement, followed Mutter downstairs, nodded absentmindedly to everything she said, pushed his suitcase under the bed and with keys to the house, departed for his company.

Hilde shook her head. "One gets to know all kinds of people. You can blow the 'Our Father' through his cheeks."

So far Vater had said nothing to this new development. He cleared his throat. We waited. "This Mackenzie may be perfectly innocent; however, absolutely no word, not one, when he is around."

Erika whistled through her teeth. We all understood.

"*Eintopf-Sonntag* again?" I asked Mutter, lifting the lid off the boiling pot.

She shrugged. "With no meat we have it three out of four Sundays anyhow." She browned chopped onions in a bit of lard to give the soup some flavor. I opened the kitchen window. It was cloudy, but pleasant outside.

From our walk home from church that morning, it was obvious spring had arrived. Over night the Redthorn had burst into fragrant blossoms and the birches showed off their shiny new leaves in spring green.

"You know the rabbit has gained a lot of weight," Mutter commented without forewarning.

"You mean Twitchie? So what?"

"Well, you know why we got it. We can't keep it forever."

"I know why we got it. But it was a rabbit then, it wasn't

Twitchie. I can't eat Twitchie."

"For heaven's sake stop calling it Twitchie. It's a rabbit and we got it for food. We could take it to the butcher and they could give us another rabbit instead."

"No, that wouldn't help. How would I know it was a different rabbit?" I had expected this conversation and knew I would lose this battle one way or another, but I didn't know how to deal with it. "If you get Twitchie killed I'll never feed another animal."

"All right." Mutter gave in for the time being.

I was about to leave the kitchen, angry and upset, when from the open kitchen window I heard a high pitched voice.

"*Heil Hitler*, Frau Füsser. I wanted to check if you are observing the *Eintopf-Sonntag* today. It smells like meat to me." Frau Leimbke poked her head into our kitchen window inside the terrace, scrutinizing counter and table.

"Sorry, Frau Leimbke, it's *Eintopf* soup." Mutter lifted the lid. Steam of the boiling soup rose up.

"I needed to make sure. You know there is a fine for non-observers. *Heil Hitler*, Frau Füsser."

"What on earth is that snake doing in our yard? The audacity to walk up to our window to spy on us! Why can't the Nazis leave us alone?"

Mutter hissed at me, "Margot, be quiet. Not another word. She might still be around." I shut the window with a bang.

"Margot!"

I resisted the urge to slam the door as I ran upstairs. If only I could kick or slam or break something. Yes, I could ride my bike. I ran downstairs again. Passing the kitchen I called, "I'm going to ride my bike."

"We are eating soon."

"I'm not hungry." I pushed the bike up the basement steps. Both tires were flat. Running back down I couldn't locate the foot pump but found the hand pump, rusty and dirty, hanging on a nail. I pumped and pumped until the tires were ready to explode, clamped the pump to the bike and took off.

The pumping siphoned off some of my anger and frustration. Standing on the pedals and bicycling as fast as I could did the rest. When I reached the *Rhein*, I was exhausted, ready to calm down.

Just as I leaned the bike against the rail to catch my breath and to enjoy the river, the sirens went off. On a Sunday afternoon? In an instant the busy *Rhein* promenade was deserted. People ran into the park to seek shelter.

Better get home or Mutter will be even more upset. Standing again in the pedals I raced back. Once I crossed the wide open *Schlossallee* with the streetcar tracks I felt somewhat protected by the trees lining the streets.

A burst from our flack. Good grief, they are here! Wheeling into our street I saw Mutter standing in the open door. I came to a screeching halt, jumped off, dragged the bike into the front yard and sprinted into the center hall just as our flack blasted one barrage after another.

"It's us. Hurry!" We herded into the shelter. The terrifying whistle of a bomb was followed by the earsplitting detonation that shook our house. I remembered somebody saying, "When you hear the whistling, don't worry, it's not for you."

Only then did I become aware of Herr Mackenzie. He kneeled in front of the chair we had pushed for him into our crowded quarters. His head buried between his elbows, he rattled one Our Father and Hail Mary after another. I nudged Erika, nodding in his direction.

"Poor guy, he's frightened out of his wits," she whispered. Just as his praying slowed, a sequence of explosions shattered the air. He whimpered. I felt sorry for him. Why was he so afraid?

Hilde got up, put a hand on his shoulder. Startled, he

looked up, his bulging eyes wide open with terror. "Our shelter is sturdy, you don't have to be afraid," she said gently. With that another explosion rocked us. He buried his face again, mumbling a new stream of prayers.

"He makes me nervous," I said to Hilde as she returned to our bed, shaking her head.

"*Ja*, me too. He may have claustrophobia."

Finally things calmed down. "Wonder if they tried to get the industry along the *Rhein*," Vater mumbled, leaving for inspection. Soon he was back. "There are huge black clouds toward the *Rhein* bend. That must have been the target."

"Oh God, I hope they didn't hit my office," Herr Mackenzie said in a whining tone.

I almost laughed. "I guess you'll have to find out."

As soon as the end of the raid siren sounded he ran out. It was an attack on the industry along the *Rhein*, but not much damage. Most of the bombs went into the river. Herr Mackenzie's office was not damaged. He never again stayed with us during an air raid. With the first sound of the sirens he dashed to his company, a ten minutes run.

It was a lovely May afternoon, mild, even somewhat sunny. Strolling through the village I looked for Jürgen. As I crossed the street by the movie theater, he walked rapidly from his house. I stopped and waited.

He smiled when he saw me. "Perfect timing. I wondered if I would see you." We shook hands. "You haven't been around recently. How are you?" He had to run some errands for his mother but was glad to walk with me through the Flower Garden and take care of the errands on his way back.

He asked, "No more grass cutting or do you rather do it by yourself?" He had helped me get fresh green in the park for Twitchie.

"No, soon there won't be a rabbit anymore."

"I see. It will meet its purpose, I assume?"

"*Ja.*" I kicked a few rocks out of the way. "And I don't know what to do about it. I didn't expect to get attached to a dumb rabbit, after all I knew why we got it. But...." I searched for the right words, "...I can't be part of anything they do with it."

He looked at me and grinned. "Sound as though you are in a fix. What are you planning to do?"

"Any suggestion?"

We turned into the quiet and peacefulness of the Flower Garden. I took a deep breath.

Jürgen shrugged. "As you said, you don't want to be part of it. Maybe your parents can deal with it without involving you."

I motioned to the bench along the little path, our bench. "Let's sit down. *Ja*, I guess that's the only way I can handle it. Have them get it butchered, just don't tell me and don't serve it to me." After a moment I added emphatically, "And don't ask me to feed another one."

"That's too bad. I enjoyed helping you."

I leaned back. That was off my mind. "Hmm, just smell." I took another deep breath. "I think whenever and wherever I shall smell azaleas, I'll think of this spot, of their sheer abundance and beauty."

"Will you think of me too?"

I kicked his foot gently. "I'm not talking about people. I'm talking of fragrance, of flowers, of the beauty of flowers."

"I know, but I asked you a question."

"I heard your question and I can't answer it. I don't know. But I do know sitting here I can forget for a moment this horrible war that goes on and on, that doesn't make any sense. Can we just sit quietly and absorb this, this stillness and tranquillity? It may have to go a long way."

Jürgen frowned. "What's that supposed to mean?"

"Pst." I put my finger on my lips. I wanted to wrap my soul into as many layers of this peacefulness as I could absorb, take with me.

Jürgen grew restless. "I've got to go. Mom will wonder what happened to me." We got up. "Are you still going to May vesper?"

"I haven't so far. Maybe tomorrow?"

"Good, I'll be there." He dashed off.

At home Mutter prepared supper. I sniffed. "Hmm, home fried potatoes. Anything else?"

"A sliced hot dog and cucumber salad."

"Sounds great. By the way, Mutter, I think I've come to a solution about the rabbit."

"Oh?" Mutter turned around, looked at me.

Strange, usually Mutter stood in front of a counter, her back to me. She seldom really looked at me.

"Well, what did you come up with?"

"You can take care of it whenever, whichever way, just don't involve me. And don't ask me to feed another one."

"All right, all right, don't make such a fuss about it. After all, these are necessities."

I shrugged. "*Ja*, I know." She really did not understand what made me feel this way. I wondered if she ever understood me.

The following day after school I mentioned to Mutter, "I'm going to May vesper tonight."

She nodded. "How was school?"

"Nothing special. We ended up again in the shelter. The only fun part is that it's in the basement of the castle, you know, with the many long and dark tunnels. Sometimes we try to get lost, but they put teachers at every turnoff just to spoil it. But it's difficult to concentrate there because it's so noisy. We were told that, besides having a Hitler *Jugend* meeting this Sunday—"

"Again?"

"—we'll be trucked next week to a farm for potato bug search."

"Potato bugs? Why are the schools involved in that?"

"It's a new campaign. It seems the bugs are plentiful and the chemicals are not. So, that's our task." Finished with our meager meal, we had sauerkraut with potatoes together, I went upstairs to do homework. Even though I just got up from the table, I was still hungry with hours to go before supper time. That happened often in recent months as the portions became smaller and smaller. And I couldn't ask for a second helping, there was none and I only got Mutter upset. Why couldn't I get used to being hungry? Even Hilde's advice to drink a lot of water didn't help, my stomach still hurt.

Supper was late. I ran to church. Jürgen stood outside with a friend when I arrived out of breath. He quickly excused himself and came to greet me.

"Can I persuade you to take a walk instead of going inside? I don't have much time."

"Oh sure. After all, it's a vesper and not a mass." We steered in direction of the park.

"My parents really keep my nose to the grindstone so I improve my grades. Right now they're very strict."

"Sure, you need them, you want to go to the university, don't you?"

"If I ever make it."

"Of course you will. In my case it seems nobody cares. Well, maybe Hilde."

Soon the cool stillness of the park surrounded us again. We slowed our harried pace. I looked at him. "Which way?"

"Let's go over to the Trumpet Pool." We talked easily, fell into silence. I picked up a leaf, kicked a stone. By the time we reached the Trumpet Pool, a small pond in the shape of a trumpet, it was getting dark rapidly. The air smelled musty under the tall, dense trees. The narrow path wound around the pond, disappeared in the lush green of the woods. "You think we might hear a nightingale sometime?" I had never heard one before.

"If we wait a month and stay longer. They'll be here, but they sing rather late."

We followed the spongy path. Every bench we passed was occupied. Often we could hear only the murmur of voices, hushed laughter.

I stopped and whispered, "By the amount of benches taken, it must be May."

"Why don't we sit down too?"

"Fine with me, if we find an empty one." Soon the small path emptied into a wide promenade, leading toward the river.

"Can we have a look at the *Rhein*?" I wanted to spend a few moments seeing it flow by. Each time I watched the majestic stream, it helped me to connect with myself, to anchor me.

Jürgen tried in vain to consult his watch." I don't have much time, we have to go back." We increased our steps, swung around the bend onto the *Rheinufer* ["Rhine bank"], stopped at the rail where the alarm had surprised me the other Sunday.

Still swollen from snow melts and spring floods the river spread like a wide silver ribbon before us. A bright moon rose above the dark mass of trees in the park.

"It's almost full moon. Perfect air raid weather."

"*Ja*, I know. Let's head back."

We took the straight, wide walkway back to the castle. I looked at Jürgen. "You are quiet tonight." He had hardly said a word.

He shrugged. "That's the way I feel. Let's take this short-cut." We wheeled around a corner, almost collided with a couple in tight embrace.

The clock of the *Evangelische Kirche* ["Lutheran

Church"] chimed twice. "Must be eight thirty. That's fine, I can make it home by nine."

"Is that your curfew?"

"Hmhm."

"Good. I would hate for your mother to think I waylaid you." He laughed. We reached our corner, stood for a moment in the shadow of the tall wall surrounding the *Rathaus* ["City Hall"] at the end of our street.

"You better get going."

Without warning Jürgen put his arm around my shoulders, pulled me to him and covered my lips with his. They were warm and soft. I was so surprised it took me a moment to struggle free.

"You kissed me. Why did you do that?"

Instead of an answer he said a cheerful, "Good night," and ran off.

Now what? I withdrew deeper into the shadow of the wall, leaned against it. He kissed me. Why did he do that? Before my eyes our friendship collapsed, came to a crashing end. Why did he have to kiss me? I didn't want to be a girl friend, I wanted to be his friend.

Disappointment and anger rose in me. Did everything have to be destroyed, was there nothing that could stay the way it was, beautiful, simple?

People walked past me. I had not realized how busy our corner was. I ran to our house, opened the little gate beside the garage and slipped into our yard. Moonlight bathed the garden. I withdrew into the shadow of the rambling roses and the garage, sat on the rough fieldstone step. How could he do this? Our beautiful friendship, the one thing that kept my life manageable, that gave me joy, was broken, gone.

After my face cooled down, I let myself into the house by reaching through the little window in the door and unlocking it, stopped at the downstairs bathroom for a quick look in the mirror.

In the kitchen Papa looked up from his paper. "That was a long vesper."

"No, the vesper wasn't that long. I met a friend. We just walked a bit and talked." I filled a glass of water, gulped it down completely. "But I'm tired." I said good night without further questions. Upstairs I leaned my head against the open window. My heart was heavy. Yes, I had lost the one beautiful thing in my life. Now what?

The door opened. In the light of the staircase I recognized Hilde.

"What's wrong, *Stöppchen*?" I shrugged, not daring to use my voice. "What happened? Are you all right?" Her love and concern crumbled my self-control.

I started to sob. "It's all over."

"What is all over?"

"My friendship with Jürgen."

"Why, what happened?"

"Because... because... he kissed me."

Hilde took her arm from my shoulder. She stood in front of me and lifted my face. "Now say that again."

The flicker of her smile infuriated me. I pushed her hand away. "You heard me. And it isn't funny either."

"Why are you so angry?"

"I don't want to be a girlfriend. I want to be a friend. We had such a beautiful friendship. Now it's gone. He ruined it."

"Because he kissed you? That can be the beginning of a more beautiful friendship." Hilde sat on the bed, pulled me beside her. The window was still wide open, the pale moonlight created a shaft of soft light across the floor. "You know, you're not a little girl anymore. You are almost fourteen. You may not want to grow up, but sooner or later you'll have to." She patted my hand. "Now get some sleep while it's still quiet." After a peck on my cheek she softly closed the door.

"A letter from Josef," I called through the house. It was a few days later, mid May of 1944. Erika came running from upstairs, Mutter from the basement. I slit it open, Mutter took it out of my hand, scanned it. "He's fine, the dysentery finally stopped. He's getting our mail." She sounded relieved. "I'm glad he's feeling better. He's in Romania and again together with Schmiernipple."

The *Düsseldorfer Nachrichten* lay on the kitchen table when I came down to go to school the next day. The headlines praised "our faithful ally Finland" for not signing a peace treaty under Russian pressure; they talked about solidifying defense lines west of Sevastopol which was lost; about the "treacheries of the Jews"; about the bitter fighting in Italy around Monte Casino.

From pictures I remembered the beautiful Benedictine Monastery high on a mountain. Would anything be left after this war? What had to happen to end this nightmare? The paper commended our Japanese allies for their brave resistance to the American and Australian "aggressors" in the Pacific as a whole and in New Guinea and Burma specifically. I was so totally absorbed in our own struggles I knew little about the war in the Pacific. It seemed, however, "the heroism and the courage of the Japanese" could not stem the advances of the Allied troops.

Mutter opened the kitchen door. "What? You are still here? Get going, it's late."

As I dashed out I heard the high pitched, sugary voice from next door. "*Heil Hitler*, Alice, do have a good day. See you tonight. *Heil Hitler*."

Alice, somewhat older than Erika, called back, "*Heil Hitler*, mother," and brusquely walked down the road. That must be the height of stupidity to use the Nazi greeting within a family setting. I swung around her and did not stop till I got to the Gymnasium. The school bell rang. Out of breath I slowed down.

Jürgen slipped out of his school. "Where have you been? I've been looking for you."

"I've no time. See you after school." I entered my classroom just ahead of Fraulein Wagner, our math teacher.

"It's a bit late to come in now, Margot, don't you think?" All other fifteen desks were occupied.

After school Jürgen waited in front of his school. "Can I walk you home?"

"Sure, let's go through the park." I had wondered what I should say to him. I didn't want to hurt his feeling, yet I knew mine. I came straight to the point.

"Jürgen, can we go on just being friends? You know I like you. Our friendship is terribly important to me. But, I don't think I'm ready to be a girlfriend."

He didn't look at me. "If that's the way you feel." His voice betrayed no emotion.

"Also, I think real friendships are much better and last longer than... than the other kind of relationships."

"I don't know about that. But, if you don't want to...."

"It's not that I don't want to. It's just... I'm not ready for that."

"All right, let's leave it the way it is."

"Oh yes, can we?" My heart soared, I could have skipped and jumped for joy. I would have loved to give him a kiss on the cheek, but decided against it.

The next day our school met for operation potato bug. Lined up along the *Schlossallee* army trucks waited to take us to Garrath where they deposited us beside an immense potato field, hoed in long, straight rows.

The farmer handed each of us a small paper bag, showed

us the potato beetle, about the size of his thumbnail, with dark stripes on the hard-shelled back which made it highly visible. "Collect them into the bag and, most importantly, keep it closed. The beetle damages the plant by eating the leaves. Without leaves the plant will die. Stick to your row. Don't trample any plants down. When you are finished at the other end, wait."

They assigned each one of us a row. Wearing gym clothes proved helpful in squatting beside the plants in the endless furrows, examining each one thoroughly, picking off the bugs. The weather was pleasant, the light cloud cover kept us from getting too warm.

Once we started it was fun. Some of the squeamish girls shrieked and giggled, each bug caused an exaggerated disgusted reaction. I shook my head. How typical of girls.

At the end of the row, we threw the bags with the crawling critters into a container filled with a chemical, got a new bag, moved to a new row and started again. By noon each of us thoroughly examined five long lines. The field was clean.

"You did a good job," the farmer smiled, "Come again."

At suppertime the radio announcer started the evening news with a report we hoped to hear. The *Wehrmacht* had withdrawn from Rome, saving the ancient city from destruction by keeping it an "open city".

"Thank God they didn't blow it up," Vater nodded with approval. "We have lost enough, how tragic and irreplaceable that devastation would have been."

Hilde agreed. "I didn't think Hitler had any sense left." After a moment she continued, "Did you hear the news about Walter?" Walter was Josef's and Jupp's best friend.

"What about him?" Erika asked. "Hilde, what happened to him?

Hilde shook her head sadly. "He got wounded. He lost both legs."

"Oh no!" Walter, with his laughter, his humor, now without legs. I could still see him in our center hall, smiling into Mutter's angry face that evening the boys crossed the *Rhein* over the ice. "This is history in the making, Frau Füsser." And afterwards, when he escorted me with his typical flair to the ice ice-skating. Walter without legs.

We fell silent. After a while Hilde said, "By the way, Wolfgang wrote yesterday. He is coming home for a few days before being sent on an extended tour of duty."

I didn't understand. "I thought he was in the Merchant Marine, not the Navy?"

She nodded sadly. "The Merchant Marine has lost as much tonnage as the Navy has, if not more. On the one hand they're always suspect on high sea for flying under false colors, on the other they are the vital link of support." Her voice was heavy with quiet resignation.

LATE SPRING, 1944

CHAPTER 13

Two days later at supper, we heard the announcer in his precise German begin his report, "American and British troops landed this morning in Normandy, the north coast of France."

With my mouth half full, I stared at the radio. We stopped eating. "They landed north of Caen with amphibious equipment as well as with paratroopers." He talked about the fearless and heroic German defense.

Vater pushed his chair from the table. "They landed in France? You know what that means? It's the beginning of the end! Once the Allies are on French soil, they will be coming from the west, not only from the south. They will be here in no time." He paced up and down.

Hilde thought for a moment. "Gosh, I wish we knew how many troops landed. The German defense line is heavily fortified. But we won't find out of course, it will be played down."

"You mean if the *Amis* ["a colloquial term for the American troops"] have enough men there? They will." Papa almost smiled. "They did not land at the Atlantic Wall, not even close to it. Caen is much further west."

I listened with ambivalent feelings. Maybe the end was in sight, but how would it come about? And when? What would happen in the course of it? How much would it cost in lives and destruction? Obviously Hitler was determined to fight to the last man. What if we became like Stalingrad a house-to-house fighting zone? I pushed the thought from my mind. I couldn't live with that fear.

Vater rubbed his head. "With the Russians coming from the east, I hope the Americans get here first."

"I sure hope so, too." Hilde spoke with emphasis. "I definitely would not want to be 'liberated' by the Russians. The stories from Poland and Prussia are gruesome."

"Remember, much of that may be propaganda," Vater cautioned.

"But our soldiers know it from the front. Before Josef left he said he would not fall into Russian hands alive."

"Josef said that?" I looked incredulously at Hilde. "He would rather kill himself than be taken prisoner?"

"That's exactly what he meant," Erika agreed. "He mentioned that to me too," she added quietly.

Vater's eyebrow shot up. "What a person says and what a person does when it come to that are two different things entirely!" He left the room abruptly.

When I opened the front door the next morning, I was stunned. The yard and the street were littered with paper, single white sheets with black printing. I ran out, picked some up, brought them in. "Mutter, look! What are they?"

"Where did you find them?"

"They're all over." I pointed out the kitchen window. "See, the back yard is full of them too."

They were addressed in German to the German Civilian Population, signed by the Allied High Command and stated that about one million troops landed in Normandy, that we could learn about troop movements, get the real facts and not Nazi propaganda, by listening to BBC, London on short wave. They gave specific wavelengths for different areas.

I examined the sheet. "What are they? Where do the come from?"

Hilde took it from me. "Must be *Flugblätter* ["fly sheets"], dropped by enemy planes." She waved the white sheet in her hand. "I hope you all are aware that those listening to BBC are called *Feindhörer* ["enemy listener"], a crime of treason and punishable by being shot on the spot as traitor."

"Well, you'll have to make sure nobody finds out." Mutter glanced at our large Grundig radio with short wave on a side table in the kitchen.

We were still up that night when the sirens wailed. "Josef, I'd like to have the radio in the basement. Can you carry it downstairs?" We all looked at Mutter, knowing exactly what she was up to.

"Trude, are you sure you want it there all the time?"

"Absolutely." She looked innocently at him. "I wouldn't want anything to happen to our good radio. We can exchange it for the small one that's now down there."

In the shelter Mutter situated herself in front of the box, started to tune in on short wave. Hilde looked pained and pale. She shook her head.

"Shhh," we implored Mutter to tune it down.

"Bong, bong, bong booooong," boomed loud and clear over the air. "Bong, bong, bong, booooong." My heart thumped in my throat, my mouth was dry. What if anybody heard this? What if Herr Mackenzie decided to come here in-stead of sleeping in the office? "Bong, bong, bong, booooong."

"Trude, for heavens sake, tune the darn thing down. It's too strong, too obvious." Mutter adjusted the sound, pressed her ear to the fabric-covered loudspeaker.

"Bring a few pillows," she whispered without moving her head. Hilde ran upstairs, came back with three pillows from the couch. Mutter stuffed the silk covered one between the wall and radio and stacked the others on either side. She motioned impatiently, "I need more." Hilde ran up again, brought two more. Those Mutter piled on top of the radio. Then she poked her head between them, halfway disappearing underneath her fluffy mountain.

Vater crouched beside her. We could not understand a word. I saw Mutter nod, Vater nod, they looked at each other, nodded meaningfully with raised eyebrows, then pressed their ears back to the box.

Erika beside me watched them and whispered, "If I can't hear anything in here, how could anybody on the outside detect a sound, let alone understand?" After a moment she laughed out loud, but her laugh sounded forced. "Why am I whispering?"

"Shhh," came from the two heads glued to the speaker.

Hilde shook her head. "Just look at them. It would be comical if it weren't so deadly. Wonder if they know what they're doing." She was silent, then turned to us. "Please, don't breathe a word of this. Forget what you have heard once you leave this room."

Finally, with a sigh Mutter straightened up. Vater stood up from his crouched position, stretched.

"So what's going on? What did they say?" Erika wanted to know. "By the way, we couldn't understand a word."

"Good," Mutter smiled with satisfaction. "The Allies are still landing more troops. They plan to occupy Caen and Cherbourg in a few days. After the initial surprise the Germans are giving stiff resistance."

"How about losses?" Hilde asked.

"Great losses on both sides."

"You know, you two are quite a sight," Erika grinned.

"That's all right," Mutter said. "At least now we know what's going on."

Vater cleared his throat. I knew what was coming. "Remember not to say one word of this or of what you have heard. You don't even know this station exists."

I nodded. "We got that sermon already from Hilde."

"So you get it again from me. Not a word."

"*Ja*, Papa, we got the message." I was getting tired of the same old song. "By the way, the end of the alarm has long been sounded. We can go to bed if that's all right with you." I was upset and angry about what our parents were doing. Yet I agreed it was helpful.

Mutter glared at me. "Margot, don't be nasty. This is important."

"*Ja*, I know."

A few hours later we stumbled again into the shelter, sleepy and groggy. This was the start of three or four interruptions at night, every night. Soon Vater decided it would be better if we slept all night in the shelter. He arranged for two more bunk beds for himself and Mutter, and built a sleeping bench for Oma. Within a few days we were equipped to sleep all night in the basement.

Hilde looked nice in her cream colored suit with a pink blouse. I remembered her sewing the outfit a few years ago.

"Picking up Wolfgang at the station? How long will he stay?"

"Till next week. He probably wants all of us to get together at his parent's house this Sunday."

"Oh? Why?" I grinned at her. "Could there be, maybe, an occasion, a specific reason for that?"

She looked at me with sisterly contempt. "Stop being a brat. It is unbecoming to you."

I burst with laughter. "But it's so much fun. By the way, remember, we are sleeping in the basement."

"*Ja*, I know. What a pain."

Just as Hilde came back home, the sirens went off. Erika and I stayed in our beds, didn't bother to get dressed.

"Did you have a good afternoon?" I asked Hilde.

"Hmhm." A few minutes later she turned to our parents. "Wolfgang and his family have invited us this Sunday afternoon at four o'clock for coffee."

From my bunk I coughed importantly. Hilde ignored me. Vater glanced at her. "For a special reason?"

"Well, yes."

"Good. We'll be there."

I was straightening the kitchen a few days later, listening to the radio, when the Lehar music was interrupted and replaced by the triumphant *Sondermeldung* music. A *Sondermeldung?* We had not heard one in such a long time, I had almost forgotten about it.

The OKW announced the successful firing of the V1 into the city of London where it created great destruction. The announcer explained the V1 was a jet propelled, pilotless air-craft carrying a large load of explosives.

The headlines the following day shouted that we had "THE weapon to crush the enemy, to break down the aggressor, to retaliate for the outrage of the desecrations that ravished innocent civilians, that victimized mothers and children."

"Rubbish!" Hilde tossed the newspaper down. "What idiotic statements. Göbbels must have had a heyday." He was the Minister for Propaganda.

That Sunday afternoon I found myself seated in Bruck's apartment between Wolfgang's sister, who was much older than us, and Erika. After the usual pleasantries and the consumption of a *Rodonkuchen* ["pound cake baked in a fluted cast"] with whipped cream and a fruit torte, Wolfgang got up. With a glass of wine in his hand, he announced that he and Hilde planned to get married as soon as the war was over. We toasted to their health, the *Verlobungsfest* ["engagement partei"] was over.

Strange, I reflected on our short walk home, I felt very different about Wolfgang than I had felt about Willi. Wolfgang part of our family? It was difficult to imagine. Sure, I had known Willi, did not know Wolfgang at all, but that was not it. Hilde looked happy. I hoped she was.

Every evening in the shelter Mutter tuned into BBC, waited patiently for their bong, bong, bong, booooong, and filled us in afterwards. Sometimes Papa listened with her. The Allied troops made slow but steady progress. The resistance of the German army under General Feldmarschall Rommel was fierce. Soon Cherbourg fell, then Caen was lost to the Allies. Our papers mentioned these losses only briefly. Yet from BBC we knew of their strategic importance for military reasons as well as for the demoralization of the German soldiers. The German troops were reshuffled, pulled out of the east to be applied in the west. There were no further resources available, no more manpower to draw on.

Yet, it soon became clear that every soldier was desperately needed in the east. The thrust of the Russian offensive from Finland to Romania was relentless. Finally they achieved their objective, they broke through the German defenses.

Where was Josef? We had not heard from him for almost a month. As far as we knew he was still in Jassy, Romania.

"Mutter, today is my names day. And I'm already fourteen." I announced a few days later in the kitchen.

Mutter looked at me with a blank expression. "Oh, today is the twentieth of July. That's right. Well," she thought for a moment, "with all that's going on I just can't keep up with it. After all, I can't keep track of everything."

"That's all right. I only wanted to say today is my names day, that's all. Don't worry about it." I was sorry I mentioned it. She was so easily defensive.

Food was also a sore point. I knew it was difficult to feed us. I was always hungry, yet I knew I could not ask for more. She took it personally that she could not give us more.

On the evening of my names day, Mutter as usual listened to BBC. Suddenly she waved her hand excitedly.

"Shhh." She motioned for us to listen with her. "They tried to kill Hitler!" she hastily whispered at a break in the news. "What? Tried to kill Hitler? Why didn't they succeed?" We looked at each other. What an opportunity. Unfortunately, they obviously failed, whoever "they" were. We hung in suspense till the next break. Finally she straightened up, reset the dial, as she did religiously after each listening and turned off the radio.

"What happened?" we beleaguered her. Vater came in.

"Josef, they tried to kill Hitler! Imagine!"

Vater looked at her aghast. "And?"

"Hitler was hardly wounded, but many others are dead.

"Where?"

"In his headquarters in East Prussia."

"Who did it?"

"They don't know. Nothing else is known."

Vater sat down with a heavy thud, leaned his face into his hands. "They dared it and they failed." He stared ahead. "In his headquarters? Must have been the military around him." After a moment he added in deep distress, "May God have mercy on those they find guilty." He turned to us. "Remember, you don't know anything about this."

It took days for the news to be released. The headlines blasted, "A cowardly attempt on the life of our great leader and hero failed." Göbbels said in a statement, "Only God Almighty could have saved Hitler's life." "The traitors and conspirators of this dastardly deed will be and some have already been brought to justice!"

Slowly information emerged. Colonel von Stauffenberg smuggled the bomb in a briefcase into the headquarters, placed it underneath the table beside Hitler. Stauffenberg, who sat at the right of Hitler, left the room a few minutes before the timed explosion. A general moved over and happened to push the briefcase further away from Hitler. That saved his life.

The assassination attempt caught us all by surprise. I had expected the military and *SS* surrounding Hitler to be loyal to him. I wished, we all wished it had been successful. With Hitler dead the war would be over. The consequence of this failure could only be an even greater determination to fight to the bitter end; a more brutal clamping down on all opposition. What would happen to those found guilty? Would there be a trial? Would they even make it to a trial? Nobody knew the extent and proportion of the conspiracy.

"*Heil Hitler*, Frau Füsser. What do you say about this hideous crime committed against our beloved *Führer*?" The sugary, high-pitched voice from next door overtook us again on our way shopping. I swore she was waiting to harass us and to catch Mutter off guard.

"You must agree that obviously God, in whom you so ardently believe, has protected him," she added sarcastically. She stared into Mutter's face, waiting for an answer. I held my breath.

Mutter smiled sweetly at her. "Frau Leimbke, I'm not in the habit of second-guessing God Almighty, of trying to find out what he thinks. I leave that to others. Good day."

"That snake!" I hissed at a safe distance.

"Margot, I don't want to hear that expression again. I don't like her either, but she is an adult to whom you have to show proper respect."

I couldn't believe my ears. "You want me to have respect for her?" I almost added "that snake". I rather liked that apt expression.

Mutter nodded. "Not for her opinions or beliefs but because she is a grownup and you are a child."

"Some grownup," I muttered under my breath.

"Margot! You heard what I said!" We continued the rest of the way in silence.

Frau Leimbke's remark stuck in my mind. While helping Mutter in the kitchen, I got back to it. "Why did Frau

Leimbke make that nasty remark about us believing 'so ardently in God'? In what does she believe?"

"She is *gottgläubig* ["believer in God"]."

"So? If *gottgläubig* means believe in God, she sure doesn't sound like it."

Mutter looked for help at Hilde who had come in and listened to the last exchange.

Hilde hung her purse on the wardrobe and closed the kitchen door. "You asked what *gottgläubig* means? It doesn't mean what it says, Margot. Those that say they are *gottgläubig* belong to the *Deutsche Glaubensbewegung* ["German Faith Movement"], a spiritual offshoot of the Nazi movement. It's really designed to replace Christianity." Hilde leaned against the doorpost, trying to stay out of Mutter's way, who was cooking.

"For instance: they try to change Christmas into a pagan solstice festival; they try to change our beliefs and rituals about birth, death and certainly about marriage. That's why they have banned prayers in schools in addition to banning all religious instructions in schools."

"Is that how we got this new Christmas carol, *Stille Nacht der Hohen Sterne* ["Quiet Night of the High Stars"]?"

Hilde laughed. "*Ja.* That's where it comes from."

I tried to remember. "How does it go?

'Stille Nacht der hohen Sterne,
die wie eine Brücke ziehn
über eine tiefe Ferne,
über unsre Herzen hin'.
["Quiet night of the high stars
that move like a bridge
over a deep remoteness
across our hearts".]

I thought for a moment. "It has a lovely melody, but what does it mean?"

Hilde chuckled. "You tell me. I don't know."

Pondering all this while helping Mutter I came back to it
after a while. "A few of my classmates are *gottgläubig*. I
always thought it meant what it said. Yes, their fathers are
all members in the partei. The girls have made snide remarks
about my going to 'that old fashioned church'. The You-
don't-really-believe-what-they-tell-you type of remarks. You
know," I said to Hilde, who still leaned against the doorpost,
listening, "now I understand where they are coming from,
why they say this."
I mused about this some more. "Now I understand why
in *Deutschkunde* Fraulein Dr. Schulte talked about the 'pure
German nordic race' and the 'restoration of the old Nordic
values'. I think she called it 'positive Christianity'. Is that
part of the *Deutsche Glaubensbewegung*?"
Hilde nodded emphatically. "It certainly is."
"Fraulein Dr. Schulte said it combines belief in Christ
with the 'laws of blood and soil'. It substitutes the—what
did she call it—'the spirit of the hero for that of the
Crucifixion'. I really don't understand all of this. How can
the spirit of a hero substitute for the crucifixion? I wonder
which hero they are talking about?"
Hilde grinned. "That's not difficult to figure out."
Mutter, who had been working around us, broke in. "I
wouldn't worry about it, Margot. You can set the table."
I was still mulling this over. "Hilde, let me think this
through, this is fascinating. Because Hitler doesn't like
Christianity, he wants to do away with it and give us a new
religion, the Nordic pagan religion. He doesn't like the Jews
and other 'inferior races' and those opposed to his ideas, so
he does away with them to 'purify our race', to establish a
Herrenrasse ["master race"], the Aryan race. To that end he
forbids interracial marriages and establishes bordellos for
the *SS* with German Nordic looking girls." Satisfied with my
logic I nodded. "I'm starting to understand."
"Margot, you don't know what you are talking about,"

Mutter heatedly interrupted me. "I don't want to hear you talk this way."

"Mutter, it's true! Ask Frau Schmidt. She knows."

Mutter stared at me aghast. "Frau Schmidt, what does she have to do with that? What does she know?"

"Frau Schmidt's relative was part of the 'breeding experi-ment'. Remember the blue eyed, blond haired kid?"

Mutter nodded defiantly. "So? What about him?"

"He is the result of his mother's stay in the house the *SS* has in Berchtesgaden. They invite young Aryan looking ladies and... get them pregnant."

"That's enough!" Mutter's face was beet red. She turned around so agitated and angry she toppled over the chair beside the table. It crashed to the floor. "I don't want to hear this kind of talk in my house. *Basta!* You should be ashamed of yourself."

"Good heavens, Mutter, Margot is only relating facts, not her opinion." Hilde stepped in to soothe Mutter's feeling and to defend me.

"And you should not let her talk this way either," Mutter snapped. "But of course you were there with her. She probably knows all of this from you." Furious, Mutter picked up the chair, slammed it back under the table.

Hilde took a deep breath. "I don't happen to go blindly through life, you know." I looked at Hilde. She waved her hand, saying "forget it" and went upstairs.

After setting the table I ran up to her room. "Tell me more about this new religion the Nazis have established. I didn't realize the connection."

Hilde chuckled. "And get into more trouble than I'm in already? No thank you. Maybe another time. Now you better run down, so you don't make things worse."

The next day Vater came home with the news the army

wanted to relocate his business to Marburg.

"Why Marburg?" I wanted to know.

"They think it's safer there, away from industry, bombing and probably artillery."

"Artillery?"

"Sooner or later the *Amis* will be on the other side of the *Rhein* and we here in Benrath with all the industry along the *Rhein*, especially the chemical industry, we'll be in the target zone."

Mutter was alarmed. "You mean you are leaving us? Now, that we are getting to the worst part of the war?"

"Let's hope it does not come to that. I'll do my best to procrastinate. Let's hope the *Amis* will be here before I have to leave."

The invasion changed our lives slowly but dramatically.

The next day rumors had it the elementary school would become a *Lazarett* ["field hospital"]. The rumors were confirmed when Red Cross cars and trucks arrived. We were notified, an *SA* man from the *Braune Haus* handed Mutter the papers, we had to house one or two *Unterärzte* ["assistant medical doctors"].

The following afternoon a pleasant looking young officer stood in front of the door. "I'm Ferdinand Kahle, *Unterarzt*. I have been assigned to a room in your house."

Mutter greeted him, introduced me, showed him the little room upstairs. She explained that we slept in the shelter at night.

An hour later he returned with his belongings, told us that his duty was at night and that he would catch some sleep during the morning. That suited Mutter well. She was anxious not to have her "evening activities" restricted or interfered with.

Air raids increased drastically, especially during the day.

It was difficult to get our few potatoes, margarine, some vegetable and bread from the store to the house. But regular work life continued. Hilde and Erika left every morning for their company. Whole departments had been moved to the basement. In late July we received another letter from Josef. They were still in Jassy, Romania. The Russians were in hot pursuit. It did not look good, but he hoped they would get out of the area in time. Otherwise he was all right. Vater exploded when he read this. His fist hit the table. "Hitler never gives permission for withdrawal. He refused it in every case, be it Leningrad or Stalingrad or Sevastopol. Whenever our boys are encircled they have to fight to the last man. *Was ein Wahnsinn!*" ["What an insanity".]

At least we knew he was still alive at the end of July.

In August the newspapers reported on the actions of the *Volksgericht* ["Peoples Court"], consisting of two judges and three *SS* Officers, that dealt with the "enemies of the Third Reich" in a court-martial fashion. The headlines blasted the "conspirators" of the twentieth July *Putsch* ["uprising"] and assassination attempt. They were getting their "just reward," as Dr. Göbbels promised earlier. Many high-ranking officers and senior diplomats were sentenced to death, some by hanging, some were shot. Some, like the Theologian Dietrich Bornhöffer, were sentenced to death by the *Volksgericht*, but executed much later.

Angry and frustrated, Papa crumpled up the newspaper in his big hands. "They kill the best people, the only ones that see what's going on. And they don't just hang them, they hang them with wire or on meat hooks," he mumbled.

"With wire or on meat hooks? Why?" Shocked, I looked up from the section I was reading.

"To prolong the agony and pain of dying, that's why.

Von Stauffenberg, who smuggled in the bomb, was lucky. They shot him the same evening. By now they have executed almost five thousand people in connection with the Putsch. Five thousand of the best." He stalked from the kitchen.

"Hang people by wire or on meat hooks to prolong the agony and pain of dying?" Their own people. I shuddered. "...enemies of the country...." Obviously it did not matter if they were Germans or not, or maybe because they were Germans were they treated more brutally. "Who doesn't agree gets eliminated."

Some months earlier the Brass sisters moved into an apartment in the village. Mutter was concerned about them. We had not heard from them in weeks and she wanted me to check on them. I left the house the moment the alarm was over to be back before the next one.

The quickest way was past the *Evangelische Kirche* and the field hospital, the former elementary school. What a different picture. Red Cross cars zipped in and out, medical personnel, soldiers and officers swarmed around. But something bothered me, something was different. Then I realized what it was. The uniformed men did not greet with the customary smart military salute to the head but with the outstretched arm of the Nazi greeting.

Then I remembered that last year Himmler as *Reichsfuehrer* of the *SS* and the *Gestapo* was appointed Minister of the Interior, which strengthened his position greatly. This change in saluting showed the influence and power Himmler had achieved over the traditional army. The *SS* and *Gestapo* were stronger than the army. Did that mean that the Nazis could get at Vater, that the *Wehrmacht* might not be able to protect him?

I found the Brass sisters well and worried. "What do you hear from Josef?"

I told them about his latest letter. They had heard that Hermann, my cousin, was killed on the Westfront. Heinz, the middle son, was with the Navy on one of the destroyers and Josef, the youngest, had just been drafted.

Tante Grete glanced at me with a mischievous smile. "How is your boyfriend?"

I protested. "I don't have a boyfriend, *Tante* Grete."

"Don't lie, Margot, you know that's a sin. I have seen you walking with a nice young man."

"He is not a boyfriend, he's my friend."

"As I said, he's a nice young man."

I put my arm around her shoulder and squeezed her. "Thank you, I agree. But now I have to run. Take care. *Tschüs*."

"Wait." She pushed something into my hand.

"A candy bar! How wonderful. Haven't had one in years. Thank you." I planted another kiss on her cheek and ran home.

A few days later Erika came in, slumped into the chair at the kitchen table. "Gosh, was I scared!"

"What happened?" Startled I sat down with her. Her face was white as a sheet. Her hands shook, her mouth was dry. I got a glass of water, she gulped it down. Finally, with a deep sigh, she leaned back.

"What happened?"

"I went to the cemetery to check on Oma Brass' grave."

"You walked?" I knew it was a long hike.

"No, I took the bike. After working at the grave I heard this absolutely terrifying noise coming towards me out of nowhere. I looked up and here came this plane so low I could see the pilot. An American plane. And, can you believe that, he suddenly opened fire with his machine gun on the people in the road, on the cemetery, on me. I saw him coming, he skimmed over the tree tops, that's how low he was. He was in direct approach, as if he aimed at me, shooting all the time." She still looked terror-stricken. She took another sip, her hands still shaking.

"Good heavens, Erika, what did you do?"

"The first time I just ducked, I was so bewildered. And, would you believe, he turned around and came back, strafing us again. When I saw him coming the second time I crouched behind Oma's tombstone. As he went over I could see the marking underneath his plane. Gosh, did he frighten me!" She took another gulp.

"Would scare me to death. I'm glad you weren't hit. Anybody wounded?"

"I wasn't hit, but the tombstone was. No, I don't think anybody was wounded."

"You mean Oma's tombstone was hit while you crouched behind it?"

Erika nodded slowly. "Yes. Granite splinters flew everywhere. Once he was gone, I gathered my stuff and pedaled as furiously as I could. It's just good there are trees all along the road for cover." She let her arms hang down, relaxed her shoulders. "I sure hope I never experience that again!"

Next day the paper confirmed a low flying American plane "committed the hideous atrocity of shooting on innocent people in cold blood". Nobody was injured.

Lieutenant Kahle knocked on the kitchen door the next evening to let us know he would be gone for a few days but would be back. Would we hold his place for him?

"We have nothing to do with that," Hilde assured him. She asked him what he thought of the military situation.

He shrugged his shoulders. "Not good. The Allied troops are advancing rapidly. They have all the reserves they need. We're drafting fifteen year old kids."

"Have you seen the *Volkssturm* in action anywhere?"

"I know they are only supposed to be used for local

defense, but I saw some groups in France two months ago."
He looked around. "Is Erika not home?"

I was surprised at his direct question. "No, she's with her girl friend. Why do you want to know?"

"I was just wondering. Haven't seen her recently."

The next day another *Unterarzt*, Lieutenant Strauss, appeared with a billet. He took the bed. When a tired looking Kahle returned, he found Strauss in his bed. From the kitchen below their room, we heard their angry voices. They con-tinued their quarrel in the front yard. With apprehension Erika and I watched from behind the living room curtains, when a pale and angry Kahle slapped Strauss across the face in response to a remark. Kahle stormed upstairs and moments later thrust clothes and belongings into the face of the dumbfounded Strauss. "Get out!" Kahle came back in, Strauss, more vexed than furious, clutched his things and trudged in his pajamas to the *Lazarett* ["field hospital"].

A few minutes later Kahle, still tense and pained, politely apologized for the unnecessary conflict. He seemed to be speaking more to Erika than to us.

To our surprise the same evening Kahle showed up with Strauss. This time Strauss apologized and asked if they could both utilize the room since they had different shifts. Kahle would sleep during the day, Strauss during the night. Mutter was not happy with the arrangement, but Strauss still had his billet. It had not been withdrawn.

The evening news began as we finished supper. The OKW glowingly reported about a counter-offensive in Lithuania and Estonia, about the brave and courageous spirit of our soldiers despite the predominance of the Russian army. We listened intently. "In Romania," the announcer continued, "the German army withdrew in an orderly fashion from Jassy and Budapest." He stated further the Romanian government gave in to the Russian demands for an unconditional surrender.

Vater buried his face in his hands and broke into racking sobs. His whole body shook. I was stunned. I had never seen him cry this way. Nobody knew what to do. I stared at the tablecloth, helpless. The silence, only interrupted by his sobbing that seemed to come out of the deepest cavities of his chest, was painful and heavy. I fought back my tears. Abruptly he got up and left the room.

What happened to Josef? Was he dead? Was there any hope? "Orderly withdrawal" meant retreat, surrender or wiped out. He did not want to fall alive into Russian hands.

The announcer continued with the statement that Paris was taken over by the provisional French government.

"If we only knew, if there was a way to find out." Hilde spoke more to herself than to us. Mutter sat motionless, no tears, her face a mask of stone.

Vater came back, in complete control, as if nothing happened. "Any other news?"

"Paris has been liberated," Hilde filled him in.

Later that evening the BBC spokesman confirmed the elimination of the pocket at Jassy. 130,000 German soldiers were "wiped out".

The days dragged on. No news, no formal "killed in action" or "missing in action" notice. Nothing. I was sure Josef was on everybody's mind but nobody mentioned his name or talked about him. On the surface life continued.

The arrangement with Kahle and Strauss worked out. Herr Mackenzie picked up his suitcase from under the bed and settled in the basement of his company.

The American troops steamrollered through France. After consolidating along the Seine, their next obvious goal was the *Rhein*. Coming from the southwest the French Army liberated their own cities Toulon and Marseilles. In Italy the

Germans retreated into the mountains. In the north Finland agreed to the Russian offer of an armistice. And in the east the Russian colossus pressed on through Bulgaria, Poland, Prussia, driving whatever was left of the German troops, ahead of them. The enemy was coming closer, the net was being pulled tighter around us.

But were they the enemy? We all feverishly hoped the Allied troops would come, come soon, to avoid further bloodshed, to end this senseless war, to keep Germany from being totally destroyed either by bombs or from being blown up by our own retreating army. Who was the enemy? After hearing what happened to those involved in the *Putsch* I wasn't at all sure.

Hilde came home later than usual one evening. She often stopped at Wolfgang's parents on her way from work. Her steps dragged as she sat at the kitchen table. Her shoulders sagged, she leaned her face into her hands.

"Hilde, what's wrong?" I sat down with her. She looked up, struggling to speak. Her eyes were puffy and red. With a despairing shrug she shook her head, buried her face again.

"Hilde, something happened to Wolfgang?" Almost imperceptibly she nodded. With my arms around her, I laid my head on hers. Poor Hilde. First Willi, now Wolfgang. I could feel her pain, could sense her agony. Her hopes, her future, her love—destroyed. Again.

I felt her struggle for control, not to be overwhelmed by this new tragedy, not to be suffocated by pain, not to give up and give in. Slowly her body, her breathing calmed. She lifted her face, wiped her eyes. I waited.

Facts became incidental, did not matter anymore. When she finally spoke her voice sounded lifeless, resigned.

"His ship. His ship was blown up. He was part of a convoy. No survivors." She took a deep breath. We sat in silence.

The *Wehrmacht* was adamant. Vater's business was to be evacuated. The date was set for October 1944.

"Josef, you can't leave us!" Mutter insisted angrily. "Not now!"

"Trude, don't you think I know that? How do you think I feel? But I can do only so much. In the end they have the say. Let's be grateful it's the *Wehrmacht* and not the *SS*. Then I wouldn't be here at all anymore."

I was ready to leave for school. "I'm gone, *tschüs*." On my way to school Vater's words, "Let's be grateful it's the *Wehrmacht* and not the *SS*," haunted me. What if the *SS* controlled the *Wehrmacht*? Papa knew he was on the Nazi's black list. How long would they wait?

The Allied troops continued to sweep through Western Europe while the Russian army advanced rapidly. How long till we were overrun by the enemy? Would it be the Russians or the Allied troops? These were the two questions on everybody's mind. How long and who.

We heard horror stories about the brutality of the Russians, of rapes and killings. Were they all propaganda? Vater made it clear he was not taking any chances with us three girls. He would hide us however long it took if the Russians would come first.

"Hide us? Where?" I looked puzzled at Vater, who stood in the kitchen talking about it. I couldn't think of a place in the house where we three could hide for weeks, maybe months.

"Under the coal chute."

Hilde looked at him in disbelief. "Under the coal chute? You can't be serious."

"Absolutely!" Vater looked and sounded angry and determined. "I will build a hide-out underneath the coals in the chute where you can be concealed. All three of you. Nobody will find you."

I saw myself all crunched up into a tiny space, black with coal dust, with little or no fresh air. "That's impossible. We can't hide there." I shook my head.

Vater's fist hit the closest surface he could find, which happened to be a small space on the table between two saucers. Both saucers somersaulted through the air, followed by the empty cups, and shattered on the floor.

He turned to me with fury. "You will do what I say when it comes to that," and walked out.

Without a word Hilde got the broom. Bending down to help her, I felt an irrepressible giggle come up, as it had happened a few times before.

"Two cups and two saucers broken. Soon we have no china left," Mutter lamented. Hastily I dumped the debris into the trashcan and ran to my room to vent my laughter.

The situation had been too comical. But, at the picture of us being buried under the coals for an indefinite time, panic rose from the pit of my stomach. Heat penetrated my body, every nerve tingled. I felt the waves of the fear would so engulf and cover me that I would scream. I stepped to the open window and breathed deeply to fight the panic down. Maybe it wouldn't come to that, maybe the Allied troops would liberate us first. "Please, God, let the Americans be here first, before the Russians."

Our lecture plan since the beginning of school in August of '44 called for two hours of twenty minutes mini-lectures every morning. However, more and more of the two hours were taken up by Fraulein Dr. Schulte. In "Germanistic," a new subject, she reiterated what we heard before in *Deutschkunde*: about the Teutonic blood and it's superiority, about *Blutschande* ["blood shame"], where the word "incest" was interpreted as intermarriage between Jews and Germans. We heard about the "leadership principle", that the

Grossdeutsche Reich ["Great German Nation"] was an authoritarian state with the leadership coming from the *Führer*, that democracy was wrong and unworkable. She extolled the virtues of the *Führer* and reminded us that Dr. Göbbels challenged every family to place a picture of Hitler in a quiet place in the house with candles beside it.

In the following week all Hitler *Jugend* groups started the *Winterhilfe* ["Winter collection"] of clothes and shoes. I had the same district as last year. But this time not only indivi-dual givers were monitored but collectors had quotas to fill. Companies and businesses could be publicly branded if they didn't fulfill their quota, established by the Nazis.

In the same week the OKW proudly reported the success-ful launching of the V2 rocket, a more accurate and more deadly weapon than V1. The announcer went on to say that this sophisticated and destructive weapon will strike terror in the enemy, crush him and help us achieve victory.

A few days later Mutter went through her evening ritual of hiding under the pillows, listening to the latest news. "The *Amis* crossed the German border. Can you believe that?" We all breathed a sigh of relief.

"Where?" Vater whispered back.

"By Aachen."

"Maybe the war will be over by Christmas," Erika speculated hopefully. Maybe the Russians would not be the first ones to reach us? Within days Allied troops occupied the German border between Aachen and Luxembourg.

Lying on my bunk bed I let this reality carefully sink in. The American army was in Aachen, only a few hours drive from us, while the Russians were not even close to Berlin, hundreds of kilometers away. With that the nightmare of being buried under the coal chute lost some of its terror.

During Fall of 1944 the Western Allies and the Russians

were closing in from all sides. The net around the retreating German army was being pulled closer and closer. All Germany was one huge pocket.

We waited for news about Josef which did not come.

The preparations for the relocation of Vater's business continued slowly. We still hoped it would not happen.

Food and sleep were scarce and that took its toll. One Sunday morning on the way to church, I happened to look clearly at Vater for the first time in months. The frayed collar of his white shirt gaped by a finger's width on either side of his neck. He looked so frail it scared me. "Vater" and "frail" were two mutually exclusive concepts. Until now. Also Mutter had lost a lot of weight and had aged. Some of her resoluteness, her determination was gone. The burdens and sufferings had left their mark.

Every day brought more disastrous news. Because German troops did not surrender Aachen, the city was pounded with bombs and artillery. Feldmarschall Rommel, the 'Desert Fox' died, was buried with full military honors "as the most glorious and best loved soldier". (Much later, rumors had it he was forced by Hitler to commit suicide.)

By the end of October the German army finally relinquished Aachen, now totally demolished, even though it had no strategic importance.

A new expression appeared in the news, "Kamikaze," the Japanese suicide pilots. They were lauded as the "ultimate in bravery and heroism". The news talked about the gigantic battle the Japanese fought in the Gulf of Elite where the Kamikaze pilots first scored their "noble victories" against the superior force of the American Navy.

A low gray sky hung over the village as I stepped into

the empty church. All I wanted was a moment's rest in the coolness of the sanctuary after wasting two hours standing in line at the butcher and not having any luck at the bakery either. With deep breaths I took in the peacefulness and quiet. "God, if Josef is still alive, please protect him. If he's dead, let us know." It was the uncertainty that hung like a black cloud over us.

The heavy church door creaked, somebody entered, disturbing my solitude. Steps came up behind me, stopped at my pew. I looked up into Jürgen's face, full of concern and love.

"Are you all right?" he whispered. I nodded and moved over. "I saw you go in. Haven't seen you recently."

"*Ja*, I know. It's just... so much is going on." How could I explain the turmoil of my feelings, the fear, the sorrow, the pain?

"Any news about Josef?" I shook my head, felt a lump growing in my throat and choked it down.

"Do you have some time for a walk?"

"I guess. Tomorrow?" He nodded.

"Four o'clock at the entrance of the Flower Garden?"

He nodded again and got up. "Don't want to disturb you." I gave him my hand to say good-bye, he lifted it up, kissed it gently and left.

Poor Jürgen. I was making it difficult for him. I saw the love in his eyes and knew I loved him too. But, obviously, there was a difference in our feelings. That difference I only vaguely perceived, but right now that was not an overriding concern for me. I stayed a moment longer. Slowly I walked home, carrying the peace and stillness with me, and the determination to stay alive.

WINTER, 1944-45

CHAPTER 14

The week before Christmas in 1944 was bitter cold. The icy wind whistled through the street as we walked rapidly home after the late Sunday service. Papa quickly lit the stove in the little room to give us some warmth and comfort. After a quick *Eintopf* from the day before, I curled up in my corner on the sofa with my book, *The Weaver* by Gerhard Hauptmann. Our parents took a nap, Erika was writing a letter. I assumed it was to Jupp, her friend on the *Ostfront*. Hilde was absorbed in her book.

All of a sudden she cocked her head, listened. "Is that *Sondermeldung* music?" So as not to disturb the parent's nap the radio was tuned low. She jumped up, turned the volume higher. "*Ja*, it is. Wonder what that means?"

"The OKW announces: This morning the German *Wehrmacht* successfully launched a counter offensive in the Ardennes. We will keep you informed."

Erika groaned. "Good God, how many more lives do we have to lose?" A counter offensive in the Ardennes, the hilly, wooded area west of Aachen? I remembered it well from my stay in the Convent. Why? We could not roll back the enemy troops from our borders. Even if we won a battle, how long could our soldiers hold out before running out of supplies, or the vastly outnumbering enemy crushed them?

When Papa got up we told him. His only comment was *"Was eine irrsinnige Verblendung."* ["What an insane delusion".]

The surprise element was favorable for the German army. Our propaganda tried to make us believe every inch of soil our soldiers gained was worth being drenched in blood. On Christmas Eve we went to the six o'clock Christmas Mass. Vater could not get a Christmas tree, not even a few branches. Three paraffin candles, carefully saved by Hilde, were the only reminders of former celebrations. There was no Christmas plate. Each of us got a baked *Nikolaus* ["St. Nicholaus-Santa Claus"] made of sweet dough, (like an oversized gingerbread man).

"Why do we get a *Nikolaus* at Christmas?" I wondered aloud, sitting in the little room after the service. "*Nikolaus* has nothing to do with Christmas."

"Because the Nazis want to get away from the real meaning of Christmas," Hilde answered as she tuned her guitar. Oma came in, Erika lit the candles.

"*Stille Nacht, Heilige Nacht*," Hilde started. I stared into the flickering light. The much loved Christmas carol had lost its magic. Where it had spread warmth and love before, it now could only reflect the agonizing emptiness of weary, hurting hearts. Hilde was the only one who finished the third verse. "Well, let's see how *St. Nikolaus* tastes at Christmas," she said with painful cheerfulness, setting her guitar aside.

"I bet the bakers got an extra allotment of ingredients and forms from the *Propaganda Ministerium*," Erika remarked sarcastically, holding her *Nikolaus* in front of her. "I've seen these in every bakery window in town." With relish she bit off the head. "Hmm, doesn't taste bad."

All evening the lump stuck in my throat. Lying on my bunk bed in the basement that night the tears finally flowed. Would Christmas ever again be as beautiful as I once knew it?

The first days of January of 1945 brought more dropping

temperatures, ice and snow. Schools had been shut down since the beginning of December due to lack of coal. Vater bartered two *Zentner* ["approximately 110 pounds each"] of anthracite coal, which we shared with Oma. The ration cards provided only a small amount of poor burning briquettes.

The Army transferred the heavy equipment of Vater's business to Marburg, where his partner and most of their workers set it up and began their work. Vater remained in Düsseldorf with two of his people to wrap up things for the final phase of their evacuation.

Every morning at eight o'clock I trudged to school to return my homework and get new assignments. We sat in the classroom with coat, hat and gloves. The school was so cold I could see my breath. My feet were always frozen, most of my toes had the beginnings of frost bite. Into the school papers I put little effort, but I did enjoy the reading assignments.

The one book I did not know and was supposed to have read was *Mein Kampf* ["My Fight"] by Adolf Hitler. Our parents refused to buy it or have it in the house. Vater had made that abundantly clear years ago and I decided never to bring the subject up again.

I liked reading Gerhard Hauptmann. Somehow his mystical writings spoke to me. From his works I distilled the feeling that for every good hour one has to pay with a bad hour; for every positive with a negative. Instinctively I knew this was not right, but it started to affect me. Why bother to do anything, strive for anything if you had to pay dearly for it later? I needed somebody to help me sort these things out, somebody I could talk with.

One Sunday afternoon I was reading while Hilde sewed. "Hilde, what do you think of Gerhard Hauptmann? I have to read him as an assignment. I like his books, but his negative attitude bothers me."

Hilde stopped treadling the sewing machine, leaned back

in her chair, pushed the hair from her face.

"I don't know about Hauptmann, haven't read him. However," she paused for a moment to reflect, "however, the fact that you have him as an assignment means he bought into the Nazi's thinking. Otherwise he wouldn't be around, would have left with the others."

"Which others?"

"Most of the well known writers have left, really the best. You know them, you've read them: Thomas Mann, Franz Werfel, Erich Maria Remarque, Emil Ludwig.... I can go on and on. Arnold Zweig. And of course, Albert Einstein who writes as a scientist."

"Why did they leave? Couldn't they have stayed and fought the regime? Why did Germany buckle down under Hitler, under the Nazis anyhow? I've never understood that."

"Whew, what a question, Margot." Hilde took a deep breath. "Let's see. Hitler became powerful in the early thirties through shrewd politics and ruthlessness. Germany was totally demoralized after the lost war of 1914-18. The French occupied the *Rheinland* here, remember? We had high unemployment. Hitler changed all that. He got rid of the French. He practically wiped out unemployment. He surrounded himself with hand picked troops, the *SS* and the *SA*, and quickly became very powerful. And he restored the German pride."

"Pride in what?"

"Pride in being German. We were a nation known for its thinkers, its music, its art. He built on that pride. Besides, he used tactics of brutality and terror. Those who did not agree with him were eliminated, are eliminated."

She took a deep breath before she continued. "When people finally realized what was going on, when we woke up, it was much too late. He was entrenched. That's why so many have left: poets, writers, scientists, artists. If they spoke up, they disappeared. You know about the

Konzentration camps. They were built for the enemies of the country, for Germans that did not agree with them. They got rid of the best." She got up, walked to the window.

"Hilde, this is fascinating. It answers so many of my questions."

She nodded. "What happened to the Baumann's has happened to thousands of Germans. Remember, the family with four children from the *Ruhrtal Strasse*, who opposed the Nazis? He lost job, housing, ration cards, probably life. What happened to the Bible researcher, Dr. Hartmann. We know what happens to Vater if he isn't careful. Or anyone of us for that matter. We'll all pay for it through *Sippenhaftung* ["clan imprisonment"]. They'll pick up all of us. Vater is walking a very fine line. The principle of tyranny, either you agree with me or you are eliminated, the principle of fear in this type of regime works. It's that simple and it's very effective."

I listened carefully. "I still don't understand how he could inspire the fanatic loyalty and dedication that I see in the *SS* and *SA*?"

Hilde thought for a moment, staring out the window. "Probably because he appealed to the lowest human traits like fear, hate, greed and, not the least, power."

"I see." I got up, couldn't sit still any longer. "It's amazing that this can happen in a nation like ours."

With a deep sigh Hilde nodded. "Yes, it's frightening." She returned to her sewing.

It had gotten cold in the room. Stoking the stove, I watched a flickering shower of embers rise in the heat of the crumbling coals and disappear in the black sooty circle of the flue. Carefully I placed a handful of fresh coal nuggets in the center of the glowing remains, opened the lower door for air and, kneeling in front of it, blew gently through the grate into the embers. Soon flames leaped up, radiating renewed heat.

One night a few days later Papa told us, "Next Monday we leave for Marburg."

Mutter sat down, looked at him with apprehension. "That's it? No further delay possible?"

"No". Vater sounded fatigued. "Pitter will stay with me to load the final truck. Hermann leaves tomorrow by train." Mutter dished out the food. Vater got the remaining sauerkraut mixed with potatoes and a little hamburger, we shared a large pancake with molasses.

As usual we listened to the news. Several cities in Brandenburg had fallen into Russian hands. We knew that by now millions of civilians were fleeing before the onslaught of the Russian troops. They were coming closer.

"If only the Americans were here," Erika blurted out what I was thinking. "I'm so afraid they wait somewhere and the Russians use that opportunity to rush in."

"We'll have to wait and hope," Vater tried to calm us.

"And you won't even be here." Mutter angrily pushed her plate back and got up.

"Trude, before that happens, believe me, I'll be back, I'll be here."

Two days later we waited for Vater with supper. He always was home on time unless we had an air raid in the late afternoon. We had an air attack that morning by a small group of planes, but nothing serious in our area happened.

As time went by Mutter became concerned. What could have happened? Without a phone we had no way of finding out. She told us to eat and left Vater's portion on the stove. We waited. Mutter got up, pushed some pots around, sat down again. Hilde told a story from her RAD-time, Mutter didn't seem to listen. Erika read aloud an article from the *Düsseldorfer Nachrichten* about the "degenerated art" of modern artists like Picasso, Klee and Feininger. Mutter nodded a few times, stared at the clock. We looked at each other. Fear crept up in me.

"I can call the shop from Maria's house to see if he's still there," Erika suggested.

"No, you stay here. He's not in the shop. He doesn't work that late." Vater did not work outside his regular working hours from 7:30 to 6 o'clock, Saturdays 'till 1. He flatly refused to work on Sundays.

Hilde wondered, "Maybe with the battle in the Ardennes the *Wehrmacht* had special work for him?"

Mutter was adamant. "To be home for supper is very important for him."

Time crept by agonizingly slow. Mutter got up, went again to the front door to look down the street.

Erika whispered, "I don't dare to think what might have happened."

"Shhh," Hilde put the finger on her lips. Mutter came back, her face tense and pale, anxiety in her restless eyes. Hilde went to the stove, filled the kettle with water. "I'll make some tea."

"I don't want any," Mutter shook her head. Undisturbed, Hilde continued her preparation. It gave me something to focus on. Something was being done.

"I'll bet Papa got an urgent repair, could not refuse it," Hilde said with a consoling voice, pouring peppermint tea into cups for us three. "Are you sure, Mutter, you don't want one?"

"*Ja*, you can give me one since you have it ready," Mutter conceded. Just then we heard a noise at the front door. We jumped up, piled through the kitchen door into the center hall. The doorbell rang up a storm. Mutter tore open the door. In the light stood Vater, white as a sheet, being steadied by Pitter, his workman. Vater had a thick, white bandage around his neck.

"*Oh mein Gott* ["oh my God"], what happened?" Mutter rushed back into the kitchen, followed slowly by Vater. With faltering steps he made it to the chair, sank down heavily, leaned back and carefully took a deep breath.

Mutter set her cup of tea before him. "Here, we just made it." Papa's hands shook, he was too weak to pick up the cup. Hilde held it to his lips. He sipped it slowly. We still did not know what happened but seeing him my fear and anxiety ebbed away. Mutter poured a cup of tea for Pitter who sat down, haggard and exhausted. While Hilde helped Papa drink, Pitter related in his low German dialect what happened.

During the air attack in the early noon hours, a splinter penetrated the thick glass roof over the workshop and hit Vater in the neck, directly beside the main artery. Vater insisted on leaving the splinter where it hit, held it steady with a towel and asked Pitter to walk with him to the hospital. It took them over half an hour.

"How big was the splinter?" Hilde asked as Pitter sipped his hot tea. Vater motioned to his coat pocket. Hilde searched, held up a ragged piece of iron twice the length and thickness of her finger. "That stuck in the side of your neck?" Papa closed his eyes in agreement.

In the emergency room the doctor took one look at the site of the impact and ordered him transferred to the operating room. Some hours afterwards Pitter was notified that Vater was all right, but needed to stay in bed. Pitter found Vater in a room, agitated and upset, insisting on going home. He got dressed with Pitter's help and proceeded to walk out of the hospital.

The doctor, called by the nurse, told him he would never make it home, that he was too weak. "Of course," Pitter grinned with a look at Vater, "he ignored the doctor." When the doctor told him that he came within a millimeter of death, Vater stopped. Had he taken the splinter out he would have died.

"And what does he do?" Pitter concluded his story, "he still walked out. It took us all this time to get here."

After eating a toasted slice of bread with beet syrup, Pitter insisted on walking home, not staying over night. He would check on Vater in a few days. Papa rested in the kitchen and was able to go to bed in the shelter.

"Thank you, God, for protecting Papa today," I prayed that evening. I knew we expected the worst waiting for him. If "they" had taken him away what would have happened to him and to us? I banished the thought from my mind. How quickly a life is snuffed out, how fragile it is. Vater was very weak, he had lost a lot of blood. It was the first time I could remember him ever staying in bed. The plans for the final relocation were postponed again.

A few days later the OKW from Berlin admitted that the Russians crossed the Oder. They were coming closer, while we knew from BBC that American troops were fighting around Emmerich, a German city northwest of us. Hearing a familiar name in the news brought the advance of the Allied troops closer to home. We were excited and yet I dreaded it, not knowing what would happen.

When the doctor was satisfied with Vater's healing and recuperation, the new date for the relocation was set for the first week in March.

Air attacks increased. Historic Dresden, teeming with refugees fleeing before the Russians, was mercilessly blanketed with bombs and incendiary bombs for two nights and one day. Later estimates placed the death toll at 120-130,000 civilians.

By the end of February, Allied forces were closing in on Köln, Mönchen Gladbach and Neuss.

"They'll be here soon. What's going to happen?" Hilde's voice showed fear mixed with relief. I felt the same way. What was going to happen? Would they just walk into a vacuum or would there be fighting? Street fighting? And once the *Amis* were established, then what? After all, we were their enemies. How would they treat us? Because of us they had lost a lot of their men.

Listening with Mutter to BBC, the announcer reported more troop landings in Iwo Jima. We were so focused on our struggle, it was difficult to imagine that halfway around the globe the same fighting went on.

Erika needed to go to the Post Office in the village for Mutter. She also wanted to stop at a drugstore. "You want to come with me?" she asked me.

"Sure." We had not had an alarm for the last hour.

"Let's go around the *Schlossweiher* ["castle pond"]," she suggested. The ice and snow of December and January had given way to a wet grayness. For February it was a mild Saturday afternoon with a low hanging, fluffy sky.

I smelled the air. "It still looks wintry, but can't you feel the spring behind this?"

Erika took a deep breath. "Not only can I feel it, I can taste it, I'm waiting for it that desperately." We had not shared much time together recently.

"What do you hear from Jupp?"

"Nothing. His parents think he is a prisoner in Russia."

"Are you worried?"

She shrugged. "Wouldn't do any good. I'm concerned, I hope he's all right. It's not as if we were engaged or anything. When he comes back we may not pick up our relationship. We are just friends."

"*Ja*, I know."

We passed the castle and our school, walked along the Itterbach, a little stream running along the periphery of the park. The railroad station was straight ahead.

Suddenly Erika gripped my arm. "Oh my God, a plane!" With a wide-open intersection in front of us, no protection to our right but the railing along the stream, our only cover was the building on the other side of the wide *Schlossallee*. We both glanced over.

"Run." Holding hands we dashed across the road and the streetcar tracks into the entrance of the restaurant. The terrifying noise of the low, fast approaching plane was blood-curdling. We ducked deep into the corner of the door. I covered my ears, felt like crawling into myself to get away from the howling sound. The plane flew so low over the street we had just crossed, I was sure the pilot could see us huddled in the doorway. The machine gun fired up the street toward the railroad station, past Jürgen's house, I realized with a startled gasp.

Over the railroad station the plane turned, shooting in direction of the tracks, obviously targeting a train.

"You think he'll come back?" I whispered to Erika.

She glanced down the road, then pointed ahead. "You bet he is." The plane made a U-turn, strafing the tracks again. Alongside us, a streetcar screeched to a halt. The train engineer sensed the danger, stopped and waited. Nothing. He poked out his head and listened. After a few minutes he decided to continue. We got up from our cramped position.

"Whew, that was close." Slowly people emerged from the protection of doorways. "What do you need from the drugstore?"

Erika looked at me, grinned. "A lipstick."

"A lipstick? Are you crazy? What do you think Vater will say to that?"

"He may just have to get used to it. After all I am seventeen years old." Knowing Erika he would have to.

I laughed. "Let me know when you plan to use it. I may decide to be somewhere else."

"No, I don't think he'll make a fuss. But we'll see."

I looked at her curly, full hair. "You got your permanent half a year ago?" She nodded. "I'd like to get one too. After all," I mimicked her, "I'm going to be fifteen soon."

The rumbling of artillery, which we had heard for days, came closer. German military convoys crowded every street, especially thoroughfares like the *Schlossallee*. Soldiers were everywhere, many with bandages and crutches. Of our phantom houseguests, the two young doctors, we saw less and less. They worked longs shifts in the Lazarett, slept little, moved quietly in and out. Vater looked thin and worn, but he was recuperated. The inevitable was going to happen, his truck stood packed. He planned to leave the next morning. Sitting in the kitchen, he rubbed his bald head as he often did when in thought. "I wonder how far we'll get. The *Amis* may be in Marburg before us."

"Then why don't you stay here?" I asked him.

"I can't. I have orders."

The next morning Mutter handed him two heavy packages with our good silver. "Here, take them with you. They may be safer with you than with us here in the house."

"But Trude, I don't know if we'll get through, or what may become of the truck."

"Take them."

We said good-bye quickly. "I'll be back as soon as I can," he called and climbed into the cab of his military truck. Pitter had arrived with the vehicle an hour earlier.

The shelter looked strange and empty without Vater. BBC announced the Allied troops reached the *Rhein* at Krefeld, Neuss, and opposite Düsseldorf; that all bridges had been destroyed by the retreating German army.

"The Americans are on the other side of the *Rhein*? Right across from us here?" I couldn't believe it. It had been relatively quiet.

Suddenly the house shook from an explosion. Startled, Mutter asked, "What was that? Did we miss the siren?" Another explosion.

"No, that's artillery," Hilde shrugged. "May be with us

for a while."

"And now Vater has to be gone." Mutter was annoyed and irritated.

"Let's just hope the Allies don't sit opposite us for a long time. Let's hope they move on, get this over with." Erika was her practical self. I had to concur with her.

Another explosion rocked us. "That was close. I hope they don't keep this up all night." Mutter made sure she returned the radio dial to the innocent state of patriotic listening. With this shelling going on, Lieutenant Strauss could come down any minute.

He didn't, he probably didn't even hear it. Heavy shelling continued through the night. At first with each whistling I pulled in my head, after a few hours I dozed off.

Early next morning the yard was again covered with paper. I brought a few leaflets in.

"Here, a message for us, in German." I read out loud, "To the civilian population on the East side of the Rhine river. We have reached the Rhine River opposite your town. We are not interested in destroying civilian lives or properties. You will be under artillery fire twenty-two hours a day. For two hours each morning, between eight and ten o'clock, you can move around without endangering your lives. Signed, Allied Supreme Command."

"So we are under curfew," Hilde observed. "Actually it's rather decent to let us know when we are safe. Of course, our work continues, shelling or no shelling."

"You can't walk along the *Rhein* in view of the American troops," Mutter said in disbelief.

"*Ja*, the company told us already, in case of artillery the work continues."

"But you can't—" Incessant ringing of the doorbell interrupted Mutter's argument. She ran to open the door.

"Frau Füsser, quick, we need you. The Leimbke's, they're trying to flee. In a Red Cross truck. Quick! We have to force them out of it." Frau Niermann, her flushed face angry, her blond hair disheveled, pointed to a Red Cross truck with driver, standing next door. Other neighbors, already alerted, came running from their houses. We all slowly converged on the truck. Frau Niermann planted herself in front of the white vehicle. "You bastard! You aren't going to leave, not in this truck," she shouted at Herr Leimbke, spreading her arms. I hardly recognized him in civilian clothes. He looked deflated, scared. Why were we ever afraid of him? "You hid while my husband got killed. You and your damn Nazi friends. Your time is over! Get your loot out! You're not gonna leave with it."

Frau Hartmann joined her. "Coward," she shouted angrily, spitting with excitement, "move your stuff."

Herr Leimbke's face was red with fury. He shook his fist. "You'll be sorry. You'll pay for this."

"Shut up! You're through with threatening us. We don't have to be afraid of you peacocks any more."

Other neighbors chimed in. "You, you have made our lives miserable. Now we get even. Now's our turn. You'll pay for it." Threateningly, they came closer.

The young driver looked terrified. Frantically, Frau Leimbke tore an oil painting in an elaborate gold frame from the platform and dragged it back into the house. Her husband pulled out other pictures, lamps and suitcases.

"My husband died so you fat cats could sit in the *Braune Haus*, do nothing," Frau Niermann screamed as they unloaded.

Frau Hartmann shouted, "Move it! Move it! Go faster! You don't know what work is anymore, do you?"

Frau Leimbke looked terrified at the group that encircled them and still came closer.

"Out, everything out!" Frau Niermann ran around the truck to make sure nothing was left. "All right driver, off you go." He gunned the motor, people jumped out of the way. With spinning wheels he took off.

Swearing and shaking their fists at us, the Leimbke's dragged their stuff into their house and slammed the door.

Frau Niermann took a deep breath, brushed her curly hair back and rubbed her hands gleefully, her blue eyes sparkling. "I've watched them, I knew this would happen. Now, with the *Amis* across from us, this was their moment." She turned to us. "Thanks for coming out. I couldn't have done it alone. Now I feel much better." Her eyes filled with tears. "I'm just sorry Frank couldn't see this."

We walked back into the house. I shook my head. "Strange, how the tables turn." Vividly I recalled my terror, when a group of Leimbke's *SA* friends blocked our way home from Midnight Mass.

Mutter, who had always a little saying at hand, nodded. "*Ja*, I've always said, *Bäume wachsen nicht in den Himmel* ["trees don't grow into heaven"]."

In the hall Hilde snatched her coat from the wardrobe. "Erika, we better run, it's late."

"Be careful," Mutter called after them.

The American troops were across the *Rhein* from us. That reality sunk in as at ten o'clock sharp the artillery blasted away. Some of the shelling came close, some shots whistled over the house to targets further inland. Most of the shooting was directed either at the companies along the river or at the troop movements along the main arteries. Long convoys of military vehicles and soldiers were being pushed inland by the Allied troops. Through pincers north of Düsseldorf and Duisburg and south of Köln they started to form a huge pocket, the *Ruhrkessel*, forcing the retreating German army into it.

"Do we have to stay down there all day? In addition to sleeping there?" I asked Mutter in the kitchen after another barrage whistled over us.

"*Ja*, here, hurry up. Take the pot with soup, get down. I'll bring a few dishes." Another whining, another explosion. The windows shook. I ran down with the watery soup precariously sloshing in the pot. On the already overcrowded little table, we made space for an electric plate and some dishes. Oma moved some of her belongings.

I started to arrange things for our new circumstance. "Might as well get comfortable if we spend twenty-four hours down here. You know, Mama, between eight and ten we can cook upstairs, then have the food down here for the rest of the day."

Mutter nodded absentmindedly. "Wonder if Vater made it all right? BBC said last night the Americans are moving rapidly toward Marburg."

I didn't know what to say. How would we know? Better not think about it. The shelling continued all day, let up somewhat in the late afternoon. Would Hilde and Erika make it home safely? Just then the front door opened upstairs, they came running into the shelter, out of breath.

Relieved, I asked, "How was it?"

"Not too bad, really." Erika threw her coat on top of a chair, so did Hilde. "The company was not the target and in that basement we are safe."

Mutter looked worried. "Any problem coming home?"

"No, but we ran most of the way. Especially where we are unprotected by buildings and in plain view of the *Amis*. You know the spot I mean?" Hilde asked me. I nodded. "We dashed across that space."

"Any news of what's going on otherwise?"

Hilde sat down, took off her shoes that were frayed at the seams. "*Ja*, roads are pretty bad. They're choked, with only a trickle getting through."

"What about civilians? Do they get through at all?"

"Haven't heard anything else."

For supper we warmed up the soup on the little hot plate. The shelling increased. We heard from BBC that the Americans found the bridge at Remagen in tact, seized this unexpected opportunity and poured troops and heavy equipment across the *Rhein*. In the middle of the night, having dozed off with artillery pounding and the siren sounding another alarm, I woke up hearing heavy steps enter the center hall. I sat straight up in bed, so did Mutter and Hilde. Hilde hastily slipped into her housecoat and opened the airtight door to listen. The steps stopped at the wardrobe.

"It's Vater!" Mutter cried. Vater opened the basement door, came slowly down. "What happened? Are you all right?"

Papa waved at us, slumped exhausted in the chair Hilde hastily emptied by dumping the stuff on her bed. He rubbed his ashen face, his bloodshot eyes, his head.

"What happened?" Mutter prompted him after a while as she warmed the remaining soup.

He took a deep breath. "We couldn't get any further. Our soldiers let nobody enter the main highways. Even having a military truck didn't help." His voice sounded dead tired, lifeless.

"What happened to the truck?" I remembered Mutter having urged him to take all our good silver.

"Don't know. Had to leave it in a side street. Pitter wanted to stay with it, see if he might find a way. I wanted to get back home, wanted to be here."

"How did you get here?" Hilde asked. Vater grinned in spite of his exhaustion.

"Plain luck. Pitter and I, we were still debating what to do. Suddenly there is this other truck, the driver wants to know how to get to Düsseldorf. I told him if he took us along we would show him. He agreed, but we had to hurry. So, we pulled our truck into the next empty driveway. It's locked, but I doubt we'll find anything left. That was all we could do. We took back roads, retracing our steps. The driver dumped us east of Düsseldorf, the rest we walked."

Mutter set the dish of warmed soup before him. "Here. Have you eaten anything at all?"

"Not since yesterday." He washed in the wash basement, sat down again. Mutter added two slices of bread, spread thin with lard. Papa, who usually demanded his coffee and soup scalding hot, ate without comment.

A few days later, artillery had been pounding all day, Hilde came home from work agitated. "I can't believe it!" She slapped her often-mended gloves on the little table in the shelter. "What a stupidity!"

"What's the matter?" I looked up from my book. I was sitting beside the bunk beds, where a small lamp gave me the best light to read.

Her eyes blazed with anger, her face was tense. "They plan to install a command post in Leimbke's house!"

"A command post? How do you know?"

Hilde sat down on her bunk, got up again. "On my way home from the company, an army officer overtook me, asked if I didn't know the Americans were shelling us. That alone was an insult. I told him I had to get home. He asked me how far I had to walk, where I lived. When I told him, he said he also lived on the *Erlanger Strasse* number twenty two. I knew Leimbke's had left overnight for good. I said I didn't know that soldiers were living in that house. And he said, get this, 'No, we are not living there, we have orders to start a command post there, a transmitter station.' A transmitter station in our street!" Hilde slapped her flat hand against her forehead. "What a stupidity!"

I seldom saw her that furious.

"Here the *Amis* are standing in front of our door, minutes

away and this bird wants to start a transmitter station. When they zero in on them they'll flatten us all."

"Did you say something to him?" I asked.

"Yes, I did. I told him exactly what I thought."

"Hilde! How could you! What did he say?" Mutter asked, aghast.

"Nothing. He listened. I told him it was only a matter of time till the Allies would be here, that organized resistance was suicide and would only cost more unnecessary bloodshed, that we had lost enough men as it was, not to mention civilian lives."

"Good heavens!" Mutter sat down on her bed, her hand in front of her face.

"And he said nothing?" Erika, who had listened while standing in the door, sounded surprised.

"Not a word. Oh, it won't do any good. I'm sure he will do exactly as he has been ordered." Hilde shook her head, mumbled, "Stupidity."

Papa, who was home since there was nothing for him to do in the empty shop, had listened silently. "Doesn't surprise me. They are not ready to give in, to surrender. What's his name?"

"Something like Hauptmann Horn or so."

Hauptmann Horn stood in front of our door the next day. "*Heil Hitler*. My name is Hauptmann Horn. I am in charge of the command post next door."

Vater shook his hand. "Josef Füsser. Pleased to meet you. Would you like to come in, Herr Hauptmann?"

"Certainly." Hauptmann Horn, pleasant looking, blondish, with a ruddy complexion, somewhat younger than Vater, came in. We sat in the living room after Vater introduced Mutter and me.

"You are in charge of the command post next door?"

Hauptmann Horn nodded. "Correct."

"Do you feel that is still a worthwhile undertaking with

the Americans standing on the other side of the *Rhein*?"
Vater asked, looking at him directly.

"Those are my orders."

"Where do you come from, Herr Hauptmann?" He came
from Osnabruck, had been in the war from the beginning,
had not been home to his wife and two daughters in over a
year. The conversation drifted to Vater's abandoned relocation, to war experiences until the Hauptmann got up.

"Have to get back. I am glad to have met all of you." He
shook Vater's hand, bowed to us, "Good day," and left. We
looked at each other, wondering. Good day?

The worst shelling was at night since most of the troop
movements were after dark. During the day, in addition to
regular air raid and artillery, low flying planes screamed
from the sky, fired into streets, strafing everything that
moved. They especially frightened me going shopping in the
two hours allotted time. I tried to stay close to house walls
and door openings, never knowing when a plane might drop
out of the sky. In the basement I was afraid a direct hit might
penetrate the window opposite my bunk bed, even though
the window was covered with a one and a half-inch wooden
door.

Only basic food was available and only in small quan-
tities, potatoes, lard, sometimes margarine, ground meat or
sausages, *Kommissbrot*, ["a dark, solid military ration
bread"], milk for families with young children and cabbage,
that grew on the local farms. We often preserved the cabbage
and made sauerkraut, which needed no canning or other pre-
servation but lots of work and salt and time. Our ration cards
for clothing were useless, the stores were empty. We learned
to be creative with dyes. Many a bed sheet ended up as skirt
or dress.

Our doorbell rang incessantly one morning. Margaret, a

friend of Hilde, stood in the door. "Hilde, imagine, a barge loaded with detergent has been opened to the population. It's beached along the *Rheinufer* ["bank of the Rhine"]. If you want to get some, bring a cart or whatever you have."

"In the river? That's in front of the *Amis*."

"*Ja*, they don't seem to mind."

"Thanks, Margaret." Detergent! Hilde and I hurried into the basement and pulled out a rusty and dirty cart, threw a tarp on it and ran to the *Rhein*. What a sight! A huge, half sunken barge lay on its side close to the shore. A long two-by-ten plank was propped against the rail, just clearing the water's edge. A woman walked carefully up the shaky slope, disappeared in the immense hull and minutes later emerged loaded with boxes. Somebody had already stacked up on the grass boxes of Persil, Sil, Imi, Henko, all products of Henkel & Cie, a local chemical company.

Running down the steep embankment with our cart we stood in front of the huge vessel, sizing up the situation.

"What do you think, Hilde? Shall we try to get up there? We can't get more than wet if we fall down."

"*Ja*. Let's try. You stay here. I'll go up and see what can be done." A woman emerged from the hull with a heavy box under each arm, stepped onto the plank and inched her way down the swaying and vibrating board. I looked at Hilde.

"Sure," she grinned. "Nothing risked, nothing gained." As soon as the woman stepped down and the plank stopped vibrating, Hilde walked up carefully. I held my breath. She grabbed the rail, swung herself over, disappeared.

"Excuse me, can you watch my packages while I go again?" With a perspiring face the woman anxiously eyed me. "Such an unexpected opportunity. Just don't know how to get it all home."

"Of course." She was already up the board. Way down the boat Hilde reappeared with two large packages. I ran to the bottom of the plank, ready to scoop the detergent from the water. Carefully, she climbed over the rail, steadied herself with her load, came slowly and calmly down the steeply declining plank. I lifted the load from her.

"Those hulls are full of boxes. Each one has a different type, it seems. Unfortunately Persil, the most important one, is way down."

"Can I go next?"

"No, I'll go once more, that plank is steep. Then you can try." Walking more swiftly this time, she soon came back with two more packages of Persil. At the rail she eased herself onto the plank. Four large boxes of Persil!

"All right, your turn. Just go slow." I moved up carefully. The steep wood vibrated only a little. Catching myself at the rail I took a deep breath. That wasn't bad.

"Get some Henko," Hilde called up. The tilt of the barge made it impossible to stand straight as I peeked into the deep holes stacked with boxes. With no way of getting down there, I had to rely on cartons close to the upper rim. Lying flat on my stomach I reached for box after box, stacking them up beside me on the gangway. With more than I could reasonably carry, I scrambled back to my feet, moved to the plank. How small Hilde looked!

"Go slow," She called up. It was awkward to climb over the railing loaded down. "You have too much. Leave some."

I didn't intend to leave anything back. At the upper edge of the plank, I took another deep breath, moved gingerly but steadily down.

"Well done!" Hilde took the packages from me. "One more trip, then we have to run home. Otherwise we'll get caught in the shelling. I'll go." That was right, I forgot American troops stood some five hundred yards across the water. The tilted barge blocked the view of the other side. Hilde appeared with more. She moved down faster than before, the plank under her weight started to vibrate. I tried to steady it at the bottom but with no effect. Hilde stood still in mid air, clinging to her boxes, waiting. For a moment I saw her swaying until the swinging subsided, then she inched forward.

"Whew! That was close. I'd hate to get wet in this cold weather," she laughed, piling the new packages up. She glanced at her watch. "We've got to get back." The other woman must have somehow been able to carry all of her detergent, she and her boxes were gone.

Hilde pulled, I pushed the cart up the bank. Once up we both pulled. The small metal wheels rattled and crunched over the cobblestone. I stopped to look across the water. In the flat meadow a long convoy of dark green military vehicles stood in line, poised. American soldiers walked around, climbed into small square cars and roared off.

"Margot, come on, only ten minutes," Hilde urged. So, that was the enemy. In plain view. We pushed and pulled, hoping not to get stalled by military traffic on the *Schlossallee*. We were lucky, rattled across between two convoys.

Mutter stood in the door. "It's about time!"

We pulled the cart to the front door, flung back the tarp. "Look, six big Persil, some Henko and Sil."

"That's a good load," she nodded approvingly. I was proud, Mutter seldom acknowledged our efforts.

A heavy barrage split the air. End of curfew. A few minutes later Hilde was dressed for work.

"Hilde, you can't leave. They've just started."

"Don't worry, Mutter. I'll zigzag along the *Rhein*. See you tonight."

In the evening Hilde and I planned our excursion to the boat carefully. Now we knew what to expect. We collected cord to tie packages together, old leather bags with handles to carry them more easily down the plank. The old cart was helpful, but was there another way to transport the heavy load? My dusty doll carriage was rejected as too flimsy, the bike did not offer enough carrying capabilities. Next morning at eight o'clock sharp we ran off with the cart. Erika and Vater had left for work early. Word had gotten around, a steady procession of people flocked to the barge. A second two-by-ten leaned against the boat rail. Like busy ants, women balanced boxes up and down the two precarious bridges. Soon piles of detergent surrounded the barge. Hilde and I worked fast, alternating the running on the plank and the piling. With not a minute to spare we reached our house.

In the basement we stacked the detergent against the wall, took inventory and found that more soaking powder Henko and Sil was needed to balance out our treasure.

With more and more people hearing about it, by the end of the week the huge barge was empty. Our elderly neighbor, Frau Schmitz, watched as we pulled the last loaded cart off the street.

"You are so lucky, Frau Füsser, you have two young daughters to help you. I can't do this." Her only daughter, unmarried, lived in South Germany. Mutter looked at us. We took a few packages of Persil with the needed soaking materials and carried them over to her door. She was over-joyed and thankful. We felt good, we had something to share.

In the basement we inspected our impressive gain. "We may be starving to death but we'll be clean," Hilde grinned.

"What are we doing with all of this?" Mutter wondered.

"Let's wait and see. I have the feeling this will come in handy. Who knows what happens," Hilde mused, running her hand lovingly along the boxes. "Who knows?"

On one of the next evenings, we learned from BBC that Allied troops crossed the *Rhein* at many points, accelerating their drive into Germany; that fresh troops had been dropped into North Germany. Why only in our area they remained west of the river, we didn't understand.

"Frau Füsser, have you heard they opened another beached barge? This time it's coal." Frau Schmitz called across the back fence to our kitchen window.

"No, I didn't know. Thank you. I'll tell my husband." Again the cart was brought out, buckets and shovels collected. Next morning at eight sharp, we marched out in search of precious coal. This time Vater went with us. These sunken barges proved to be quite a treasure. At the *Rhein* I glanced over to the other side. The long convoys had disappeared. Only an occasional square car roared by.

The huge coal barge lay below the *Rhein* promenade. People were letting buckets with coal by a rope into the water, where another person dumped it into a wagon.

"Why don't I go up and dig out the coal," Hilde suggested, "you two empty it into the cart."

Papa thought for a moment. "No, I'll go up with you, help you with a second bucket. Margot, you stay here and unload them." Hilde walked up steadily, quickly. Vater followed with heavy, unsure steps. The board vibrated violently. I held my breath. Halfway up he stopped, hesitated. I wanted to close my eyes, not to see him crash down. In midair he slowly turned, a maneuver I would not have dared to do. Gingerly he came back down and laughed.

"Getting old. That's too risky for me."

"Sure, Papa, I'll help Hilde with the second bucket." When I took it from him, his hand was shaking. "Are you all right?"

"*Ja, ja,* just go up." I walked up briskly. Hilde had scooped her bucket full. I lowered it to Vater who waded into the water with bare feet, pants rolled up to his knees. Soon we got a system worked out and quickly filled our cart.

"Come down, we've got to get back," Vater called.

At that moment a voice boomed over a megaphone from the other bank. "*Geht nach hause, wir schiessen um zehn Uhr.*" ["Go home, we start shelling at ten o'clock".]

I was startled, couldn't believe it. The Americans warned us to go home, not to get hit when they would start shelling!

We shoved and pushed the heavily loaded cart with wobbling wheels, which was never made for this weight, up the bank. Hilde looked at them. "Hope they hold."

In front Vater pulled, his face getting red. Hilde ran forward, grabbed the other side of the handle. He didn't want her help but she persisted, pulling alongside him while I pushed. The cart crunched and wobbled along. At the *Schlossallee* with three minutes left, we stopped.

"Let's go!" Papa shouted the moment a path cleared. We rumbled across. Halfway down *Kapeller Strasse* it was ten. We listened above the racket of the cart for the shelling. All was quiet. Only a few more streets. Papa's red face was dripping. The wobbly wheels crunched. Just as we turned into our street the first explosions shook the air. Mutter at the door was furious with Vater for not getting us home in time.

"Mutter, don't worry. Look what we got." But the sight of the cart heaped with coal did not mollify her.

In the garage, where the old Olympia stood on blocks, dreaming of the day it again could be useful, I helped Papa unload while Hilde scrubbed off the black dust to go to work. We had gotten used to the unpredictable shelling. It was something to be endured. All during that day Vater tried to strengthen the wheels and axles of the rusty cart.

The next three mornings we pulled home heavy loads. Our coal cellar filled up as the barge was emptied of its treasure.

Each day I had to tell myself we were working in plain view of the enemy, that the Allied troops watched us as they did when we unloaded the detergent vessel. Often, at nine thirty, they warned us through a megaphone to leave the boat. The bank would be deserted in an instant.

When would they come across? What would happen?

SPRING, 1945

CHAPTER 15

The Allied troops still remained on the West bank of the *Rhein* at the end of March 1945, while south and north of Düsseldorf they deeply penetrated into German territory, continuing to form a pocket to trap the German army.

Mild air and a gentle breeze brought the promise of spring. I ventured into the yard carefully, listening to the barrages of artillery, when on the walkway in front of the raspberry hedge, something shiny caught my eye. A large splinter had halfway buried itself into the ground. The ragged piece of torn metal would make a suitable addition to my collection of splinters, started the previous year with the one that almost took Vater's life.

Further down the walkway a patch of crocuses poked their pointed leaves through the earth, protecting the tender yellow flower. How lovely. Spring finally did come, regardless of the war. Nature still functioned according to its own laws. We could not tamper with it, could not alter it. It did not depend on us.

Erika came slowly out of the basement, sat on the steps to the terrace, close to the basement door.

I pointed to my discovery. "Look, Erika. Spring!"

A ghost of a smile crossed her face. "We really do have spring?" She sounded as if she had doubts about it. "And the war's still going on. How much longer? Will it ever end?" Her eyes looked hollow, tired. The emptiness of her expression, her almost lifeless voice frightened me.

"Erika, what's the matter? Of course this stupid war will end. For many it has already ended."

"*Ja*, I know. For too many of our men it has ended."

"That's not what I meant. Yes, for those who died the war is over. But also for those that are occupied by now, the war is over. I just wish the *Amis* would cross the river and end it for us too."

She shrugged, shook her head. "You really think it will end? I've almost given up hope."

I nudged her, put my arms around her. I had never seen her that way. "Come on, Erika, you are the one who is always optimistic. Don't give up now. It's only a matter of time." I was desperate. I had to get her out of this.

She pushed a black strand of hair from her face with a slow, tired movement. "We said that six months ago and we're still waiting. In the meantime how many thousands more have been killed? How many more will lose their lives? I can't face it anymore. I just can't face it." Her thin face showed a deadly resignation, mixed with deep anxiety. Red blotches spread over her high cheekbones.

She went on in a monotonous tone, "Artillery day and night. Bombings. Planes with machine guns any time, anywhere. Josef, Jupp. Willi. The fear of them coming in the middle of the night to pick up Vater. The fear something will happen to us. And my hunger. I'm so hungry I could scream." She slumped over, her shoulders sagged. "Sometimes I don't know how to get the strength to get up in the morning. I just don't know how to cope with it any more." Exhausted, her head sank into her arms.

Yes, the hunger was the worst. It undermined our ability to deal with the rest. "Erika, come on." I squeezed her shoulders. "It can't take much longer. Look at the crocus. After the cold, snowy winter, it comes up regardless. That's its nature. And it's our nature to survive, to live, regardless. Believe me, only another few weeks and this will be over.

The Americans are making great progress." I wished I felt as confident as I sounded, but I had to get her out of this. She lifted her head and bravely tried a smile. "I'm glad you feel that way. And you are probably right. I'm just so tired of all of this." She got up, walked down the steps and disappeared into the darkness of the basement.

The doorbell rang. Mutter opened. "*Guten Morgen,* Frau Füsser." Hauptmann Horn stood in the door. Mutter greeted him, invited him in.

"Is your husband home?"

"Yes. Have a seat. Some coffee?"

"Delighted." We had gotten used to the command post next door. Around the clock guards marched four houses above and four houses below the post. Even in the shelter we heard the sharp clicking of their boots, up and down, up and down.

"*Guten Morgen,* Herr Hauptmann." Vater greeted him heartily with a handshake. Mutter set two cups of coffee in front of them.

"How are things going?" I heard Vater ask as Mutter closed the door to the living room.

Hauptmann Horn often stopped by, talked with Vater. He knew Vater's position on the war, as he knew Hilde's. But he never said anything, neither did he use the military or the Nazi greeting in our house.

After a while the two men left the house. The garage door was being opened.

"Good heavens, the car!" Mutter held her hand in front of her mouth. "What if he confiscates it?" I strained to listen, heard nothing. He could take anything he wanted, we could not prevent it. But would he do it? A short time later Vater came back, alone.

"What happened? What did he say?"

Papa sat down, rubbed his shiny head. "He asked me to open the garage. He wanted to see the car."

"And?" Mutter prodded him.

"He looked at the dusty Olympia on blocks and said, 'Herr Füsser, you know I can confiscate your car?' 'But it has no wheels, Herr Hauptmann,' I said. 'That's no problem for me, I can get those,' he said. I kept quiet, said nothing. After a while, he looked all around the garage, he said, 'Don't let it be known that I saw your car. Close the door,' and left."

Papa studied his large hands which he kept meticulously clean in spite of his greasy work. "That was decent of him. He didn't have to do that. And, under the circumstances, it would take us a long time to replace that car." He shook his head. "Wonder why he wanted to see it now?"

In the shelter that night we heard from BBC that the encircling Allied armies closed the *Ruhrkessel*, trapping an estimated two hundred thousand German soldiers. We listened silently. With a tense face Vater motioned to Mutter to tune the volume down even further. With the measured clicking of military boots on the pavement in front of our house, the bong, bong, bong, booooong sounded alarmingly loud. It pulsated in my ears. In his British accent, the announcer informed us further that Allied Forces crossed the *Rhein* on many other places, that the swiftly advancing Russian troops 'eliminated' pockets of German soldiers not fleeing quickly enough. The strangling fingers of the massive thrust of enemy troops reaching through Germany from east to west, would soon link up, crushing everybody and everything within their reach. How much longer?

"I'm going to sit in the sun," Hilde announced. "It's lovely outside." She carried a chair up the basement steps. We hadn't heard much artillery in the last few days.

Sitting at the wobbly little table in the shelter I worked on my school assignment, a German composition based on the ballad *Die Bürgschaft* by Friedrich von Schiller. "I come with you." I left the papers and ran after her. The blinding brightness of the sunny afternoon made me squint. Chirping birds flitted through the thickening blue spruce beside the basin in the rock garden. The crocus, their little heads hanging down, had spent themselves reaching for the sunlight, while a few delicate white narcissus and buttery daffodils swayed in the gentle breeze. The tulips took their time to unfold, waiting for more assurance of warmth.

I stretched out my arms and filled my lungs with fresh, warm air. Spring! In a few days it would be Easter. And we were alive to celebrate it.

Hilde and I looked at each other and smiled. She opened her manicure set of satiny black leather, a present from Josef before he left, and soon was absorbed in polishing her nails.

I leaned my head against the rail of the basement steps to look at the blue sky. Instead of raining death, puffy clouds sailed across, spurred on by the breeze. It carried a butterfly, with orange and brown wings still crinkly from being furled up in a cocoon for so long, to a buttery yellow trumpet with its sweet treasure. Holding onto the fluted rim, the airy creature probed into the flower and pumped the sweetness into its hungry little body. With supply momentarily exhausted, it sailed on to the narcissus, continuing its breakfast. We need more spring flowers for our hungry little friends, I thought, cherishing the sunny air a moment longer. I loathed going back into the dark basement, but, with a deep sigh, I submitted to the inevitable.

Hilde looked up, blowing at her nails. "Come back when you're finished."

The air in the shelter was staler than before, damp and cold. Forcing myself to focus on the intricacies of the poem's theme of trust and responsibility, revenge and cynicism, I was startled when Hilde burst into the room, white as a sheet. "Good grief, that was close!"

"What happened?" I hadn't heard anything.

She took a deep breath. "I'm sitting there, doing my nails, listening. All was quiet, when I hear this strange sound, not a whistling but a kind of swishing, like something on a wobbly course. And suddenly this thing hits the embankment right beside me. I mean, right beside me, showering me with dirt. Look!" she brushed loose earth off her blouse. "Now it's halfway sticking out."

"You mean a dud sticks out beside our basement steps?"

"Exactly."

"Imagine if it hadn't been a dud?"

Papa had been working in the coal cellar. When he came in, he rubbed his head. "I'll ask Hauptmann Horn what to do about it."

An hour later Hauptmann Horn inspected the dud carefully. "I think it can be safely removed by my people. I'll take care of it, Herr Füsser, don't worry. Just stay inside, stay away from it." He looked at Hilde. "You were lucky, Fraulein Hilde." We were relieved and thanked him. By next morning a sizable hole in the protecting earth wall at the back of the house was the only reminder of Hilde's narrow escape.

On Easter Sunday we went to Mass at eight o'clock. Easter to me meant spring, flowers, new life. The very thought of Easter was a happy thought. Walking home between Hilde and Erika I felt good. The air was light and aromatic.

I had set the table beforehand in the dining room. One single daffodil adorned the white linen tablecloth. I didn't have the heart to cut more. No eggs, no Stuten, one slice of dark *Kommissbrot* for each of us, margarine, some syrup. It still looked like a feast.

We just finished breakfast when the doorbell rang. Hilde

opened. "*Guten Morgen,* Herr Hauptmann," I heard her say. Vater joined her.

"Did you have your Easter coffee already?" Hauptmann Horn wanted to know.

Hilde sounded puzzled. "Yes. Would you like to share a cup with us?" I got up, greeted him.

Hauptmann Horn shook his head. "Only wanted to know if you had your Easter coffee with eggs from the Easter bunny?"

I shook my head. "No Easter bunny this year, unfortunately. Maybe some day again."

"Why? Didn't you look in the yard to see if the Easter bunny left something?" We glanced at each other. "Well, it's about time you checked, otherwise he will think you don't want them and take them back again."

"Oh, *ja,* of course," I stuttered. I dashed out the door, past the garage through the little gate into the yard, closely followed by Hilde and Erika. I jumped into the rock garden and searched underneath the clumps of moss and leaves. "I found one!" I cradled a blue egg in my hands.

"Well, look some more," Hauptmann Horn encouraged me.

"I got one too," Erika called out, holding up a yellow egg she found in the raspberry hedge.

"Here's another one," Hilde found a red one in the same hedge. We ran back and forth, carefully carrying our treasures.

"Mama, please hold mine so I don't drop them." I handed her three brightly colored eggs. Hauptmann Horn, standing with our parents in front of the basement steps, seemed silently to be counting.

"You are not tired already? Or do you give up so easily?" he teased us. "Either you are slow or you had a very clever bunny." I searched some more.

Hilde ran past him, peeked into the hole left by the dud.

"Got one more." We looked at the Hauptmann expectantly. "Don't look at me. I don't know what the Easter bunny did." His kind face beamed, his eyes that could be so stern sparkled with delight. He winked at Papa, who smiled back. "All right, this requires a systematic search," Erika called. I took the rock garden, Hilde the side beds, Erika the raspberry hedge. We examined every inch. "Oh, what's that?" A piece of white paper stuck out of a bed of leaves. Carefully I lifted out a bag. "Bonbons, real to goodness bonbons." I held one up, a brown candy shell with chocolate filling, popped it into my mouth. "Hmmm, haven't had a bonbon in years." The others found two more bags with sweets. What a treat!

"Thank you so much, Herr Hauptmann. What a wonderful surprise!" I carried my treasures inside, four colored eggs and a bag of bonbons. At the dining room table we emptied our treats into a dish. While Mutter got a cup of coffee for Hauptmann Horn, he smuggled two chocolate bars from his pockets underneath Vater's and Mutter's cups. He winked at us with a secretive face. Obviously he cherished our surprise and joy.

"You should have seen the fun Hans, my orderly, had yesterday coloring the eggs, once he understood what I wanted him to do. How he grinned and ran around hiding them this morning, while you were in church. Like a little boy." He sipped his coffee silently, then added, "I'm glad there are some things we don't outgrow." He rose. "I have to go." We thanked him again for his kindness.

Next morning he stopped in full uniform, his chest adorned with little ribbons. "We are moving out. I have come to say good-bye."

"Into... you mean into the *Ruhrkessel*, Herr Hauptmann?" Hilde asked with a shaky voice.

He shrugged. "Not much choice, is there?" He looked at his boot, searching for words. "You will be interested to know, the reason it has been so quiet is that we did not establish a transmitter." He looked directly at Hilde. "You were correct, Fraulein Hilde, it served no purpose. Thank you for having the courage to be honest."

Hilde's eyes filled with tears. "Thank you, Herr Hauptmann."

He turned, climbed beside his driver. After fiddling with his gloves for a moment, he called back, "See you after the war." They roared off.

We stood at the door. Will he make it? He had a good chance to be taken prisoner by the Allies and to return after a while. Quietly we walked back into the house.

Hilde still had tears in her eyes. "What a nice guy. Hope he makes it, for his wife's sake."

Without the soldiers next door, without the guards, without the military vehicles roaring back and forth, our street was empty and quiet. The following day Kahle and Strauss knocked at the kitchen door to say good-bye.

"Where are you being sent?" Hilde asked Kahle.

"The *Lazarett* has been moved fifty kilometers into the *Ruhrkessel* to be closer to the fighting. We may be the only facility left."

"Let us know after the war that you made it, will you?" she asked him.

He smiled, looked at Erika who leaned quietly against the kitchen sink. "You'll hear from me." We shook hands.

All the soldiers were gone. We felt like being deserted. What will happen to them? What will happen to us in the next few days? We could only hope and pray they were being permitted to surrender to the Allies.

Then came an unexpected news flash: The American president Franklin D. Roosevelt died. Harry S. Truman as Vice President became his successor. We were not sure what impact the change in leadership had. If Hitler died now the war would be over. Radio Berlin stated over and over that

Hitler would stay in Berlin, that the Germans were determined to defend their *Vaterland* under his leadership to the
last breath.

The next few days went by agonizingly slow. It was
quiet. Was it the stillness before the storm? Not even gun
fire could be heard. The *Amis* still held their position across
the *Rhein*, while the *kessel* slowly was "eliminated". When
would they come?

Then, one evening the BBC announcer reported that the
Allied troops linked up with the Russians along the Elbe. He
went on to say that the following day the Americans would
sweep up the East side of the *Rhein* from Köln through
Leverkusen, Garrath, Benrath to Düsseldorf.

Benrath! They would be coming tomorrow? They were
finally moving through? All next day we waited. Nothing.
Many times we opened the front door to listen for tanks, for
troops, for any kind of movement. Nothing. An occasional
gunshot punctured the stillness. Otherwise nothing.

It was a warm and somewhat sunny afternoon. I ran out
of the basement into the backyard, sat on the veranda steps,
took a deep breath. Soon the war would be over for us. Already I felt great relief and peace. It did not matter any more
how the takeover was accomplished, soon all danger would
be passed. It was difficult to imagine, we had lived with it
for so long, five and a half long years. No more fears! For
Vater, for our lives, for tomorrow.

Erika came slowly up the steps, sat quietly beside me,
leaning her head against the rail. Hilde joined us, sat on the
step below. We waited and listened. By evening still nothing
had happened.

Frau Schmitz saw us sitting outside and came out. "Is
anything going on?"

Hilde shook her head. "No. Did you hear anything?
Where are they? Didn't they plan to be here today?" She did
not realize her slip, that she had given herself away. Or

maybe it did not matter anymore.

Frau Schmitz nodded eagerly. "I heard they came with their tanks and trucks as far as the railroad station earlier tonight and retreated to Garrath. By tomorrow they should be here." Usually a reserved person, she had become much more talkative since we shared some of our detergent with her. "Finally this war will be over! I just worry what happens to our soldiers in the *Ruhr* pocket." She had no direct family members in the war. She looked sympathetically at us. "Any news about Josef?"

A shadow flew over Hilde's face. "No. Nothing."

Soon Mutter joined us outside, Papa came out too. It was a pleasant evening. Here we sat, alive, to enjoy the spring air. No more listening to bombs, to shelling or to planes. Just peace and quietness.

"Mama, can we sleep upstairs in our beds tonight?" Erika asked at the dinner table. "It would be wonderful." Mutter glanced at Vater.

He thought for a moment. "I guess you can."

After supper Erika and I climbed up to the second floor to our bedroom. The room felt strange, unused. Silently we got into our pajamas. I slipped between the smooth, cool sheets. How wonderful to feel the softness of a mattress again.

"Erika, we are sleeping in our own beds! Not on thin paper sacks over wooden slats. In our own beds!"

I heard a deep sigh. After a moment she said quietly, "It's really happening, isn't it? I still don't dare to believe it."

By about ten o'clock next morning, we had only heard sporadic shots, Hilde called in a subdued voice, "Quickly, come here!" We rushed to the bathroom window where we peeked through the wooden slats of the closed shutters into the street below. My stomach tightened into a knot. This was it. This was the moment we had been waiting for so long!

There, in single file on both sides of our narrow street, a long line of American soldiers crept slowly, noiselessly along, guns pointed. In lightweight jackets, pants tucked into strange, soft boots that were laced all the way up, they moved cautiously forward. A sudden gunshot sent them flying over the privet hedges of the front yards, leaving the road instantly deserted. When nothing happened, flat helmets began to reappear. They climbed back onto the sidewalks, continued their advance. At the end of the street they fanned out into the field, checked it carefully, then returned, scanning the houses.

We looked at each other. That was it! We were in American hands! For us the war was finally ended!

With knees like jelly I sat on the rim of the bathtub, such relief swept over me. Erika let out a long, deep sigh. Nobody spoke.

Finally Hilde broke the silence. "Wonder what happens next?" We had no answer.

That night I slept in the luxury of my soft bed peacefully through the whole night. No more sirens, no more air raids. For us it was all over.

The following morning we found out what was going to happen next. Through leaflets we learned that our curfew was from seven o'clock in the evening to six o'clock in the morning, that every German male above age fifteen without discharge papers would be taken prisoner, that any guns, pistols and ammunition had to be delivered to the *Rathaus* or would be confiscated, that houses would be searched for compliance to the order, that noncompliance was punishable with imprisonment. Signed: The Allied Supreme Command.

Papa dug out his discharge papers from 1918 as well as his papers deferring him from military duty for reason of previous injury.

POSTWAR, 1945

CHAPTER 16

The following morning on our search for food, Erika and I passed our *Rathaus*. On the opposite side we stopped under the cover of a large chestnut tree to watch with apprehension a long line of people waiting to surrender guns and pistols. American soldiers, highly visible in their white helmets, white covers over their soft boots and white arm bands with M.P. in block letters, guarded the large, square building. More M.P.'s checked the papers of every male passing by. Two soldiers, guns slung over their shoulders, marched a young man in civilian clothing to a truck already half filled with German men. Somehow the absence of the mounted bayonets, the soft boots, the relaxed demeanor of the Americans made the scene less oppressive, less frightening. The following day we learned the *Rhein* meadows south of Düsseldorf had been turned into provisional POW camps to collect the thousands of German soldiers.

When we arrived at the bakery, Frau Zinsheim shook her head. "Sorry, Erika, I sold the last bread an hour ago. You have to be here before nine. We're only permitted to use a certain amount of flour per day and whatever we bake will be sold. How long our reserves hold out I don't know. Nothing new is coming in."

At the butcher we heard the same story. Nothing was coming in. As we came close to the grocery store two women emerged with packages in their shopping nets. We ran across the road, stood in line and left an hour later with five pounds of potatoes and a quarter pound of lard, grateful to bring home something.

In the evening Vater placed the large Grundig radio back on top of the side table in the kitchen. Now BBC was our official station.

The *Ruhr* pocket was eliminated with 320,000 German soldiers captured. Heavy fighting still raged in the unoccupied part of Germany, especially in Berlin.

To our surprise Heinrich Himmler, the leader of the *SS*, offered surrender through the Red Cross to the Allied Forces. They rejected the offer and demanded unconditional surren-der.

Then, finally, the end came. From BBC we heard that Hitler committed suicide.

Hitler was dead! His suicide came as no surprise, there was no other way for him. Either victory or death. Nothing specific was known. And it did not matter, for us what mattered was his death. The person most responsible for the death of uncounted millions had finally met his own death.

Dead also was Dr. Göbbels with wife and their six children. The German headquarters conceded the end of the struggle. Admiral Donitz became Hitler's successor.

On May 7, 1945, in Rheims, General Jodl as representative of Germany signed the unconditional surrender of all German troops, effective as of May 9, 1945.

The 'thousand year nation' lasted twelve years.

That evening, quietly, with great relief that the nightmare was over and a heavy heart when I thought about the devastation, I helped rip the black paper from every window in the house.

However, a new nightmare unfolded as the indescribable atrocities of the concentration camps surfaced. The Allies discovered *Dachau* and *Buchenwald*, where thousands of inmates starved, most of them Jews. Every day more abhorrent crimes came to light as one camp after the other was liberated.

Numb and hungry we listened to these reports with horror. Was that what happened to the trainloads of people, to those marched off at bayonet point who didn't have the correct papers, to those threatened with 'being taken care of'; what the *Gestapo* and the *SS* under Himmler did, what Hitler ordered? It sounded unbelievable, but we did not doubt the reports. This was not propaganda, these were horrible facts.

Remembering the terrible fate of those thousands found guilty in the July '44 *Putsch*, I was shocked but not surprised. And yet, my mind refused to believe, revolted against these abominable facts, that Germans could have been that cruel, that degenerate. The deep ache returned.

One day Mutter came in from the yard. "We have new neighbors in Leimbke's house. I saw a girl your age."

"Oh?" My curiosity was mildly stirred. I glanced out the window but saw nobody. I knew Mutter would learn more before long.

Next morning she told me, "Just talked to our new neighbor. Imagine, they are Jewish."

"Jewish?" I had never seen or talked to a Jewish person. What an irony! The first people to live in the former Nazi's house were Jewish. "Where do they come from?"

"They're just coming out of hiding. She said they lost their whole clan in concentration camps. Only three survived —the young girl, her name is Ruth, her father and the woman I talked with. She's the girl's cousin."

"How awful!" For a moment I fought a surge of emotions welling up. "Who hid them? Where were they?"

"That's the strange thing," Mutter continued. "A merchant in the village, one I always thought of as a terrible loudmouth and a Nazi, hid them. The girl's mother worked in the merchant's house and when the Nazis threw out all Jews, this merchant concealed the girl and her father."

"They were hidden all these years? Where?"

"Underground in some cave in Grafenberg, you know, north of Düsseldorf. The merchant's wife fed them."

"A girl my age lived in an underground cave for four years? That's impossible!"

"Yes, with her father. They're both very frail. The dampness and cold must have been especially difficult for the father. He has arthritis now and many other problems. But the rest of the family is dead."

Silently I continued washing dishes. Four years in a cave! No sun, no fresh breeze. In damp darkness. I shuddered.

Later in the afternoon from my bedroom window I saw the slender figure of Ruth in a white flowing dress walk slowly through the yard. Gently her hand moved over bushes, over leaves, touched the bark of a fruit tree. Her shoulder-length hair fell forward, concealing her face. With a slow and soft movement she pushed it back.

Four long years in a cave, without sun, without warmth! Watching her, tears streamed down my face. Ruth stopped, sat in the grass, held her face up to the sun. She looked like a delicate flower. I stepped back from the window and sat on my bed. She didn't need to feel observed.

What was she thinking, what was she feeling? Did she hate us? Did she think all Germans were the same?

I never found out. I saw her a few more times in the backyard, then they were gone. Would I have been able to talk to her had she stayed?

As spring moved into summer in 1945, my fifteenth

birthday passed unnoticed. Every morning I left, with a gnawing, empty feeling in my stomach, on my search for food. Sometimes I was lucky to get a small loaf of bread, a pound of onions or a pound of potatoes, but most times I came home empty-handed. I rode my bike to Himmelgeist, a little farm village at the *Rhein*, to scout for some vegetables from farmers. Whatever we got Mutter doled out in small portions to stretch it.

One day Mutter looked at me expectantly as I came home. Seeing my empty hands she sat down at the table, tears in her eyes. "I have nothing for you to eat, nothing at all." Her voice sounded desperate. "What are we going to do?"

As much as my empty stomach ached, I tried to console her. "Don't worry, Mama, we'll find something." But where? Women cooked soups from old potato peels. I saw respect-able housewives rummaging through trashcans for scraps of food.

That evening, Vater brought home a small sack of potatoes hidden in a big leather bag. The Occupation Forces strictly prohibited hoarding, and any food obtained outside the regular channels, the stores, was seen as hoarding and punished with imprisonment.

Farmers were prohibited to sell to the population directly. At night they guarded their vegetable fields with dogs, clubs and pitchforks and still people stole whatever was available.

A few days later, the potatoes were used up, Hilde came home from her work in the shipping department. "I made arrangements with one of our truckers to take me to the *Weserbergland* ["hill country at the Weser"] to get food."

"But you can't, it's not permitted, you know that," Vater said sternly.

"*Ja*, I know. But it seems to be permitted to starve to death." She shook her head. "Not if I can help it. Anneliese from the clubhouse is coming with me." Vater wanted to say something, but changed his mind.

Mutter looked anxiously at her. "Hilde, you can't do that. What if they catch you? With curfew and all. There are controls everywhere."

"I guess I'll have to take that chance," she said calmly. "I depend in part on the wits of the driver and he's good. He doesn't want to lose his truck and end up in jail, either."

"When are you leaving?"

"Tomorrow morning at six, right after curfew. They'll pick me up at the end of our alley before it gets light. He can't drive into our narrow street, besides, we don't want to arouse any suspicion. For bartering I'll use our detergent." She turned to me and grinned. "Didn't I say that would come in handy some day? Some of it is for the driver. And we'll take our bikes. The driver thinks we'll make it back in four days, but it will be around midnight." She looked at Vater. "You'll have to come down with the cart to pick me up and, we hope, some food."

"But we don't have a gate in the fence to the alley," Mutter said.

Hilde shrugged. "Then we'll heave things over it."

The following morning, in the quiet grayness before dawn, we carried in a silent procession package after package from the basement. Vater and Hilde lifted the cart across the fence, loaded it with boxes of Persil, Sil, Henko, Imi and Atta and covered them with a tarp. The cart rattled and ground over the stony alley. Mutter, Erika and I stayed back, watching from the basement steps.

"If only nobody hears them," Mutter whispered. We all were afraid neighbors might find out and report us to the Occupation Force. Also recently people broke into houses when it became known there was food available.

Papa returned with the empty cart before it was light. "The driver makes a good impression. He says he'll be careful, he'll bring them home all right." He shook his head. "But I have to do something about this cart, it's way too noisy." In the evening he wrapped old bicycle inner tubes around the iron wheels. Next evening he constructed a provisional gate for the fence.

On the fourth day after supper, Erika and I took turns to listen for the sound of the truck in the backyard. Our parents tried to pass the time reading, watching the handle of the clock creep along. After eleven o'clock the tension became unbearable. What if something happened? My imagination played tricks on me. I saw her being led away at bayonet point.

Mutter jumped up. "There's the truck!"

We strained to listen, but the sound faded away. Vater paced up and down in the small kitchen, up and down. Finally I could not endure it any longer and ran out again. Erika crouched in the back of the yard beside the raspberry hedge, keeping watch. I squatted beside her. My heart hammered. Would Hilde make it? Would she bring something to eat? If only nobody heard us. Time ticked away, minute by agonizing minute.

"Erika! Look!"

At the end of the alley a truck pulled up slowly, stopped. Its lights went dark.

I raced up the basement steps. "She's here! She's here!" On tiptoes we ran down the alley, followed by Vater dragging the almost noiseless cart.

The driver climbed down, tipped his cap and gently opened the back while Hilde and Anneliese emerged from the cabin. They waved and started to separate their belongings. From the loading platform Hilde first handed me her bike, and then packages of different sizes to Vater who stacked them into the cart, covering them as they piled up.

I looked around. It was curfew. What if an M.P. patrol saw us?

302   *Margot Füsser Blewett*

Finally Hilde whispered, "I think that's it." Without a sound she climbed down, thanked the driver, shook hands with Anneliese. The truck left as unobtrusively as it arrived. In the cloudy night our little group moved silently through the alley. Hilde nodded approvingly at the makeshift gate that Erika carefully closed behind us.

In the kitchen Hilde plopped down on a chair. With bloodshot eyes from lack of sleep and a dirty face, she grinned happily. "Look what I got!" She unwrapped the first package, a big chunk of bacon.

Mutter grabbed it. "Bacon! This is half a side! Hmmm, smell it!" She sucked in the smoky aroma. "Haven't seen this in years." Next was a tub of butter.

"Real butter?"

"*Ja*, the real thing, churned on the farm." Hilde weighed it in her hand. "Maybe two pounds." Pushing the hair from her tired face, she proudly displayed three dozen eggs, three big round loaves of dark bread, a large sack of potatoes, a small sack of unbroken wheat. We examined each piece, smelled it, especially the butter and the bread. How lucky we were. It felt like Christmas.

"Where did you get all of this?" Vater asked.

"The owner of a big farm, and I mean big," Hilde opened her tired eyes wide for emphasis, "his name is Kerst, he invited me to come back in a few weeks to bring more detergent for more food. Next time I'll get sugar and flour and other things." That was good news. "The farmer also needs tools and other rare commodities like tar."

Papa listened carefully. "Might be a possibility."

Hilde cut a thick slice of the dark, aromatic bread, covered it with a slice of bacon (a sandwich with "raw" bacon and Düsseldorfer Mustard is a delicacy!) and bit into it. "Haven't eaten anything all day," she apologized with full cheeks. Vater followed with a piece of bread, opened the butter tub and sniffed it.

"Wait, wait, let me do it." Expertly Mutter cut thin slices of bread, thin slices of bacon.

"Mustard anybody?" I opened my latest acquisition, a jar of Düsseldorfer Mustard, our hometown brand and spread it on my bacon. I took as big a bite as I could to feel what it was like to chew with a full mouth. Mmmm, I savored the flavor of the salty bacon with the pungent mustard. What a feast!

"Eat slowly, your stomach is not used to this heavy food," Mutter warned us. Carefully she wrapped up the bread, closed the butter tub.

I gave Hilde a hug and a kiss. "Thank you." She wrinkled her nose at me.

We heard the Occupation Forces took over the East Wing of the castle, the one that had housed the *Heimatmuseum* ["local museum"] and the fire department and police. The following Saturday afternoon, out of curiosity, Erika and I decided to have a look.

Clustered around the entrance door sat the new inhabitants, leaning back in their chairs, their feet propped up on other chairs, smoking, laughing, chewing gum, watching the traffic and the people. And—they were all black. The only thing I could see of their faces were the white in their eyes and their white teeth, exposed in big grins.

Just a few weeks before, for the first time in my life, had I seen a black man, a soldier. I had been so surprised I stopped in the middle of the sidewalk and stared at him. My only other exposure to a different skin color had been "Othello", the Moor, in Verdi's opera. And, I was convinced, his blackness could be washed off.

"Good grief, Erika, do we have to pass them?" I whispered.

"Of course, why not?" Erika walked straight ahead.

"Let's just talk." We talked animatedly to each other, ignoring the grins, the calls, "Hello Frauleins," the holding out of cigarettes, the whistling.

Once past I took a deep breath. "I'm not going by that twice a day when school starts. I'll rather take the long way and get to school from the other side."

Erika laughed. "I don't think they mean any harm. They're soldiers. You'll get used to it, and so will they."

A few days later I picked an official looking envelope off the floor in the entrance hall.

"Mail for you, Mutter." I handed her the letter. She slit it open, glanced at it, sat down abruptly. She read the two pages again, slowly. I started washing the dishes when I heard a deep groan behind me, a moaning sob.

Her face was pale, full of pain. My heart pounded. "Something about Josef?" I picked up the pages she dropped on the table. One was a form letter from the Allied Supreme Command informing us that checking through the Nazi files in Benrath, they found the enclosed undelivered notice. The second page, another form letter, stated that Josef Füsser was missing in action since August 24, 1944 in Jassy, Romania. The letter was dated September 10, 1944, nine months ago.

"Why didn't they let us know?" The wound was torn open again and still, we knew nothing.

Mutter lifted her face from her hands. "Pure spitefulness."

In the evening Vater was silent for a long time after reading it. Then he nodded. "Does not surprise me. In their callousness they would have withheld a death notice just to hurt us even more." He looked at Mutter. "Trude, when our soldiers return from Russia we'll find out what happened to Josef. We'll get the answers we need."

Later in bed I realized with a shock Vater had lost hope

that Josef was still alive. How could he give up so easily? We didn't know, but we could still hope.

It took months for the schools to reopen. The major reason was the "denazification" of Germany, including teachers and study material. Every person over eighteen received a *Fragebogen* ["Questionnaire"] with over one hundred questions as to activities—membership of which organizations, financial status and holdings, employment history and many other. They were designed to identify former Partei members. No teacher was permitted to teach, no person was permitted to work without clearance from the Occupation Forces.

There was limited opportunity to work. Factories in working conditions were dismantled and shipped to the United States according to surrender terms. The remaining industry was in shambles.

The few newspapers permitted to circulate stated another factor for the slow start of schooling: the undernourished status of the children and the lack of clothing, especially shoes. Available clothing went first to the Foreign Labor Force still in German territory. Most of the rest found its way to the black market.

Papa received permission to open his business because of his clean background, but with no civilian cars allowed he had no work. The Allied Occupation Forces used their own repair shops. Under Army regulations soldiers were not permitted to "fraternize" with Germans. They were strictly forbidden to give food or anything else to us.

And we were hungry. I thought I had gotten used to the constant gnawing pain, but it only became worse. Our watery soup with little taste and less substance was our main fare. We were fortunate when we had a dry slice of bread with it. Hilde's bartering trips brought less and less and had to be discontinued when they became too dangerous.

Mutter decided Vater should have his meager noon meal fresh, at least on some days. So, before eleven I straddled my bike for the fifteen mile ride through Düsseldorf to be there by noon sharp, carrying the soup and a bit of vegetable with a potato in a basket.

I picked my way around bomb craters, twisted and torn street car rails and burnt-out military vehicles. According to official estimate Düsseldorf was ninety two percent destroyed. I pedaled through street after street of mountains of rubble, rubble with iron beams sticking out.

These mountains were populated by women who, like ants on giant anthills, crawled to the top and hunched down to knock old cement off pieces of bricks. With kerchiefs tied around their hair and knotted in front, with dirty faces and dusty, torn clothing, some wearing rags wrapped around their feet, these women picked up bricks one by one, sorted them, cleaned them from cement, tossed the usable ones into buckets handed down a human chain to the street level, where they were piled on carts and pulled away by women.

The first time I saw this, I stopped and watched in disbelief. It reminded me of children trying to empty the ocean with toy buckets. Only this was no play. Anybody working in rubble removal received a ration card number one, giving the owner the privilege of seven hundred extra calories a day, if the food was available in stores.

When in the beginning I saw the destruction, felt the eerie stillness of the city, smelled the stench of the decaying bodies in the rubble, I was horrified. The desolated feeling stayed with me for days. Gradually, seeing it daily, I became numb to it. When somewhat later I passed a rubble removal group as the women with kerchiefs around nose and mouth, pulled a half decayed body from the debris it hardly touched me. I could not absorb any more, felt a remoteness to the devastation, the loss. We all knew bodies were still buried under the heaps. How long would it take to level these mountains, the work being done by hand? Years? How long until all the bodies would be buried?

On days I didn't bring food to Vater, I searched for food. Our cupboards were empty. I was the only one available, the others had to work. Each time I neared a farmer's barnyard with my bike, I entered slowly, carefully, ready to jump back on to avoid the dog or dogs. When the front door slammed shut, my heart sank. I forced myself to walk up anyhow and to knock. But nobody answered. After having knocked on as many doors as I could, with no result, I dragged myself home. I went from one farm community to the next.

At one place, I was dead tired and at the end of my strength, a farmer's wife took pity on me. With a little smile she handed me half a glass of milk. Milk had never tasted that sweet and smooth. Then she walked back to her kitchen table, took the loaf of bread already started and handed it to me. Gratefully I wrapped it in the flower sack I carried on the stand and raced home. I had gotten food.

One evening Hilde came home with the exciting news that a farmer in Monheim sold sugar beets. The following noon Hilde bicycled, I perched on the rear carrier. After a forty-five minutes ride we arrived in Monheim. Hilde was exhausted. How would we get the beets home without being caught by the M.P.'s?

We found the farmer, filled two roomy shopping bags to hang on the handlebars and two potato sacks with the fleshy, purplish roots. The farmer ask for only ten marks, we would have gladly paid five times that much. We tied one sack to the rear carrier, one to the fork of the bike.

Hilde eyed the overloaded bike with almost flat tires with apprehension. "Hope it makes it. Let's go!" She took the handlebar, I pushed.

"We've got to go faster, we have to be home by curfew!" she urged. The tree-lined road between acres and acres of open field stretched endlessly. My arms and back ached. The bag on the handlebar was open, the fleshy beets visible. "What do they taste like?" With Hilde's pocketknife I sliced off thick chunks, scraped off the dirt, stuck one into Hilde's open mouth. They tasted like raw potatoes, but with more fiber and sweeter. It was something to chew on, to give me new strength.

As we entered Benrath, the cloudy afternoon took on an evening hue. We pushed our heavy load through side streets, stayed close to houses. At the *Evangelische Kirche* the clock struck seven times.

"Good heavens! Curfew time! Mutter will be furious." I imagined her standing in the door, getting more upset by the minute. "What happens if we get caught?"

Hilde shrugged. "Go to jail! At least we can keep each other company. Cut us another slice, would you please?" She continued her rapid walk, scanning the road. Suddenly she froze. Way down Marbacher Strasse a jeep with two M.P.'s came slowly toward us. Gently we inched to the house wall, stood motionless, watched them. At the *Rathaus* they turned the corner and disappeared.

We had to get off the deserted street. Only another hundred yards. I started to perspire from weakness, my knees felt like jelly. We strained to listen for a patrol car. At the alley, we swung off the street. Coming up to the level of our house I saw Mutter standing in the doorway. I squeaked. Her head jerked around, we waved, she spotted us. I felt faint and lightheaded. After what seemed an eternity we stumbled into our yard. Mutter came running to the gate, red faced and angry. When she saw my exhaustion, that I was close to tears, she pressed her lips together, said nothing.

The beets were our only food for the following weeks. The peeled skin made an awful tasting, bitter soup. Some of the roots we boiled to make molasses. The rest we used for our daily meal.

One evening at supper, as we ate that night's fried beets

we listened to the news. Now instead of reports from the war zones, we heard about the gruesome discoveries the Allies made sifting through the legacy of Nazi crimes. The death toll collected from records of extermination centers and concentration camps rose daily. So did the numbers of former Nazi partei members being imprisoned and tried. Plans for an International Tribunal in Nurnberg to bring to justice those responsible for the crimes were being publicized.

Each time I heard about the atrocities, the horror, my stomach turned into a knot, the deep ache came back. By now it was estimated that eighteen to twenty six million people had been killed, shot, gassed or starved—six million of them Jews, the other twelve to twenty millions were foreigners and Germans. Murdered by Germans.

The question of "collective guilt" of the German people became a main theme in the news. Were we all guilty by the fact of being German? How could we be guilty if we did not know what happened? And even if we had known, could we have changed anything? We, too, would have ended up statistics. Our family had lived with that danger for over five years.

Was this horror, this guilt, ever going to end? Would we as a nation ever overcome this? These questions weighed heavily on me, but nobody talked about them at home.

While the world debated our guilt, our all-consuming task was to stay alive, to find food for the next meal. If we could afford it we could buy it on the black market at exorbitant prices.

Our cities were destroyed, roads and railroads unusable, industry non-existent, and there was no manpower. The economic situation came close to a complete breakdown. Some people were lucky enough to receive CARE packages from the USA, but they were a drop in the vast bucket of hunger.

In addition another problem arrived in the form of

thousands of refugees from Eastern Europe. They fled before the Russians, poured into the already ravaged western zones.

We listened to the news during supper one evening when the reporter talked about the deportations of thousands of Jews, of foreigners, of Germans; he talked of gas chambers, of crematories, of annihilation of the feebleminded and those unsuited for work, especially women and children; of extermination centers. I had long stopped eating. I wanted to cover my ears to shut out the voice and the pictures of children being led to slaughter houses. My whole being revolted against this barbarism. Finally I could no longer sit at the table and ran to my room.

Hilde followed me. "Margot, what's wrong?"

"I don't want to hear this. I can't stand it." I cried. "How could they do that?"

She put her arms around me. "*Ja*, I know, it's difficult to believe people can be such beasts. But you don't have to listen to this."

"Hilde, these were Germans who did this," I wept bitterly. She stayed with me for another moment, then went downstairs. Finally, exhausted, I fell asleep.

A few nights later I washed the dishes, still having this hollow, gnawing feeling of hunger in my stomach. Our suppertime had been moved up. The parents listened in the dining room to the news. In the previous week Vater had brought home a small sack of unbroken wheat which Mutter guarded like a treasure. Now I stole into the basement, got a handful of the wheat kernels, hid them in the corner beside the sink and chewed them slowly, savoring the somewhat nutty flavor of each hard little kernel. With plenty of water I hoped they would reduce the pain.

Just as I finished my cleaning chores, Vater came in, leaving the door to the dining room open. For a moment I listened. The reporter, with his trained unemotional voice talked about a specific camp and described the atrocities committed there. I heard him say "...conducted an experiment on young female inmates by pumping cement into their vaginas. They all died." I shuddered and fled upstairs to the bathroom, nauseated, my whole body in turmoil. When my stomach finally calmed down, I walked slowly, in a daze, up to my room, sat on my bed.

"...pumped cement into...." I had only a vague idea what he was talking about. Germans did that to innocent people. A feeling of deep shame came over me, rose up from the pit of my sore stomach, engulfed me. I felt I could never again be proud of my country, proud of my heritage. And I knew at that moment that I would not be able to live in my homeland.

To the Nazis, I realized, what mattered was not the difference in race, nor the difference in nationality because Germans had been victims as well. It was the fanaticism of believing they alone knew what was right and eliminating every opposition. Their mind-set said, "My way or none." No, I could not live with that mind-set.

After a long time I got up, washed my face and deeply buried the shame, the silent vow for many, many years.

It was a lovely, warm spring day. White veils shrouded the sky. I stopped across from Jürgen's house with my bike and whistled our tune. He stepped onto his balcony, waved and came out with his bike. I had not seen much of him in recent weeks.

"Let's go somewhere. I've to get out of the house."

"Sure. How about the *Rhein* meadow?"

As we crossed an intersection in Urdenbach, two M.P. stopped us. Even after almost a year of occupation, they still checked the papers of every male. Alarmed I looked at Jürgen. He calmly got off his bike and grinned at the stern-faced soldier. "Hello. How do you do?"

"Your papers, please." The soldier held out his hand.

Jürgen rummaged through his breast pocket. "Nice day today."

The M.P. glanced at him surprised. "Oh, you speak English?"

"Yes, of course. I learn it in school." He found his paper, gave it to the soldier who studied it, folded it together and handed it back.

I had stayed further back with my bike. The M.P. looked at me and grinned. "Remember your curfew at seven".

Jürgen waved. "Yes. Thank you."

We stopped at one of our favorite places at the *Rhein*, dropped the bikes into the grass, walked out onto a short jetty into the river. The brown water, swollen from the snow melt in the Alps, gurgled and swirled around us. We found a sheltered, warm spot.

"Why did you talk so much with the M.P.?" I asked him annoyed.

"Practicing my English. He was nice."

"Maybe he was," I agreed reluctantly, "but he's also part of the Occupation Force."

For a moment Jürgen looked at me with a baffled expression. Then he shielded his eyes and studied the water. "Wonder how many boats are sunk along here. Will take a while to clean this out if they ever want to get the shipping moving again." He turned to me. "Why did you say that about the Occupation Force?"

With a stick I poked in the crevices of the rock below us, trying to understand my conflicting feelings.

"I don't know." My strong reaction had surprised me too. "I guess—no, of course I'm glad they're here. I'm glad they stopped Hitler and the war. That doesn't mean I like the way they look at us, the way they call us 'Frauleins'. It smacks of the 'conqueror's prerogative'." When Jürgen looked at me with a dubious expression, I said heatedly, "You wouldn't know, they don't look at you that way."

He held up his hands and grinned. "Okay, okay. You still miss the chance to practice your English."

I cupped my face in my hands as I scanned the majestic river. Stately willows in their first spring green dotted the meadows along the banks, so typical for the lower *Rhein* valley. But it was a painful beauty as I thought of the senseless desolation of the last years, a thought that was never far from my mind.

I leaned back against the rocks and closed my eyes. The warmth of the sun behind the flimsy clouds, the gentle breeze, how wonderful to be alive!

My inner conflict, I realized, might never be fully resolved; pain and sorrow over my people's action might remain with me all my life. C. F. Meyer's poem, *Feet in the Fire*, in which he showed forgiveness, of leaving revenge to God, came to my mind again. As nobody could right the wrongs that had been done, I would have to live with what is. But in order to continue to live I could learn to forgive.

With a deep sigh I released a heavy burden, let it slide off my shoulders, float away with the fast current.

After a long while I sat up. "Can you believe the war is really over?" I asked, brushing the rocks below me clean with my hands.

Jürgen thought for a moment. "*Ja*, it hit home when my folks talked the other day about my future, my studies. I realized there is again a future."

As my eyes took in the beauty of the river, peace permeated my whole being. "*Ja*, there is again a future."

Epilogue

Oma Füsser stayed with us beyond her eightieth birthday. After living a few months in an old folks home, as they were called then, she died.

After a long illness Mama died in 1969.

Papa remarried and lived a happy ten additional years until he died in 1980.

Josef died in Jassy in August of 1944. My one possession of his is the slender green volume of the New Testament with his name in it.

Hilde is married, has three children and two grandchildren and lives in the house in which I grew up.

Erika is married, has two children and three grandchildren and lives in the area of *Mönchen Gladbach*.

Jürgen did become my boyfriend for many years until I met the man I married.

Hauptmann Horn visited us a few years later with his wife.

We received a card from a POW camp from F. Kahle, addressed to Erika. But it disappeared before Erika had a chance to answer.

And what happened to me? The twisted path of my life led me in 1957, with a German husband and my daughter of six months, to the United States. It was only when my two daughters, in their twenties, encouraged me to write about my experiences that I utilized the voluminous notes I had about that time. And it was in the reliving of that monumental time that I found healing, that I was able to unearth those buried silent vows that led me to the country of my choice, a choice I never regretted.

Bibliography

2194 Days of War, Cesare Salmaggi and Alfredo Pallavisini, 1977 Arnoldo Mondadori, Milan

Encyclopedia of the Third Reich, Dr. Louis L. Snyder, 1976 McGraw-Hill Inc.

The World at War 1939-1945, John Keegan, 1990 Braken Books, London

Nurnberg Laws, Documents pour servir d l'histoire de la guerre, Vol. IV, Office Francaise d'Edition, Paris 1945

They Thought They Were Free, Milton Mayer, 1955 University of Chicago

Printed in the United States
59727LVS00003B/259-306

9 781928 704881